Cards ! Games

S0-AWR-288

6/22
KK

Powerful Profits:

Winning Strategies for Casino Games

ALSO BY THE AUTHOR

Casino Magazine's Play Smart and Win
(Simon & Schuster/Fireside, 1994)

Casino Games Made Easy (Premier, 1999)

Powerful Profits from Blackjack (Kensington, 2003)

Powerful Profits from Slots (Kensington, 2003)

*Casino GambleTalk: The Language of Gambling and
New Casino Games* (Kensington, 2003)

Powerful Profits from Craps (Kensington, 2003)

Powerful Profits from Video Poker (Kensington 2003)

Powerful Profits from Keno (Kensington, 2004)

Ultimate Internet Gambling (Kensington, 2004)

Powerful Profits from Casino Table Games
(Kensington, 2005)

Powerful Profits from Video Slots (Kensington, 2005)

Powerful Profits:

Winning Strategies for Casino Games

VICTOR H. ROYER

LYLE STUART
Kensington Publishing Corp.
www.kensingtonbooks.com

LYLE STUART BOOKS are published by

Kensington Publishing Corp.
850 Third Avenue
New York, NY 10022

Copyright © 2004 Victor H. Royer

All rights reserved. No part of this book may be reproduced in any form or by any means without the prior written consent of the publisher, excepting brief quotes used in reviews.

All Kensington titles, imprints, and distributed lines are available at special quantity discounts for bulk purchases for sales promotions, premiums, fund-raising, educational, or institutional use. Special book excerpts or customized printings can also be created to fit specific needs. For details, write or phone the office of the Kensington special sales manager: Kensington Publishing Corp., 850 Third Avenue, New York, NY 10022, attn: Special Sales Department; phone 1-800-221-2647.

Lyle Stuart is a trademark of Kensington Publishing Corp.

First printing: April 2004

10 9 8 7 6 5 4 3 2 1

Printed in the United States of America

ISBN 0-8184-0688-7

This book is gratefully dedicated to

Georgina S. Royer

"Veni, vidi, vici"—I came, I saw, I conquered.

—JULIUS CAESAR

In gambling, as in life, there is no shame in failure—there is shame only in not learning from it.

—AN AUSTRALIAN PHILOSOPHER

Remember this each time you go to a casino.

Contents

Preface

This is not a book for the beginner, nor is it a book that lists *all* the various strategies for casino games. Here, I will presume that you already know everything that there is to know about each of these casino games and that you also know all of the "traditional" strategies and how to play them. It is not my purpose to rehash what has already been written about the various basic strategies or other forms of "systems" or strategies for casino games. I have written a series of books about many games in which I explain the basics and the strategies that are used most often to combat house advantages. In these books I also list various methods that will help you play better, last longer with your gaming dollar, have more fun, and profit by exploring and exploiting some of the better principles of play. I have often referred, in those books, to "Advanced Strategies"—those that require much more game acumen, a whole lot more discipline, and a great deal more dedication. These are the strategies and methods that I will show in this book.

Make no mistake about it—these methods and strategies are not for the fainthearted. You will need the proper bankroll, and you will need all your wits about you. If you plan to play casino games with any of these methods and strategies, you'd better be prepared to work at it, not only in the casino, but *before* you ever get there. Your knowledge of the casino games must be absolute; you should already know all the traditional methods, systems, and strategies, why some work to a margin, and why others don't work. Before you read this book you should never have to second-guess yourself about anything to do with casinos, casino games, protocol, strategies, methods, systems, ways of playing, the theory versus the reality, the truths of the games and how they are really played, the means by which casinos combat professional players, the means by which they change the rules on some games to add to their house advantage, and so on. All this you should know before you turn another page. I will not be teaching you any of this here. If you're not sure about something, go back to my other books, wherein you will find the comprehensive coverage of all you need to know before you can take full advantage of what is being offered here.

This book will not teach anything that you should already know. In this book I will talk about *professional strategies as I have developed them,* for those casino games I have chosen to use as examples. This book contains my own personal investigations into methods and means of playing casino games professionally and purely for profit.

Most people go to casinos primarily for entertainment and only secondarily to win money. Although these same people will say that they want to win, the actual winning of money is really not their main priority—having a good time is. This is often exhibited by sighing statements after losses, such as: "Ahh, well . . . maybe next time." There is nothing wrong with that, because these players had a great time and were willing to pay for it. It is wrong to suggest that these players are somehow guilty of a gambling transgression of some kind. Being a "gambler" does not mean you can't have fun gambling. However, making "gambling" a form of "livelihood" is another thing. Even people who claim to be "professional gamblers" often are not. Many times they actually have a lot of money, and gambling has simply become their way of life. This doesn't mean they are losers;

most of the time these people are very good at the games they play. However, they do not always *make* a *living* at it.

There's a big difference between making a living at gambling, as a job, and playing gambling games as a means of lifestyle and life choice. Those who play gambling games as a lifestyle choice usually have a source of income well beyond that which they make gambling. Although these players are very often quite good at the games they play, any serious loss—or a protracted series of losses—may not have as devastating an impact on them as these may actually have on someone who relies on the act of winning for their meal money. These "well-heeled" players, as I like to call them, are semiprofessional players, rather than pure pros. I classify myself as one of these players; I make my living from writing, and from my public appearances and other business interests, and that's where the vast majority of my life's income is generated. I play casino games for profit, except perhaps on occasions when I like to play small-limit live Poker primarily for relaxation and the camaraderie of people whom I know and like. When I play other games—those I play for money—I do this alone, and none of the people who know me are aware of this to any great degree. I have successes and failures, but I do make money. This has become supplementary income to me and not the primary income it once was a decade or so ago. Back then the money I made from gambling was my only source of income. With that I either paid my bills or didn't. And that's where the biggest difference truly lies.

Players who rely solely on income from their gambling profits and have no other source of income—and do not have a vast fortune in stocks, bonds, or investments—are the true professional gamblers. These people's ability to live, pay bills, and support themselves and their families directly depends on whether or not they win. If they lose, they don't get paid. When you go to your job and you hap-

pen to have a bad week—or two—you still get your paycheck. Not so with a true professional gambler—when he
has a bad week, or two, or longer, he not only does not get
paid—it *costs* him money.

It is important that you understand this before you read
the rest of this book. What you are about to read is designed
specifically for the true professional gambler and for the
semiprofessional gambler. Mostly for the semiprofessional
player, because even the best of the true professionals will,
in the twenty-first-century casino environment, need a vast
bankroll behind them for security purposes. There are many
reasons for this, and some of them we will discuss later. The
chief two are, however, the preservation of your security as
a professional player and the preservation of your bankroll.

The security issue has a lot to do with casino surveillance and the use of modern computerized face-recognition
technology. This makes it very hard for a professional gambler, and certainly one who is regularly successful, to hide
his or her identity. Casinos aren't in the business of losing
money and, therefore, they will try to keep out those players who they think know too much, or win too much, or
play too well. This will become a serious issue for you if
you choose to be a true professional. As to the preservation
of your bankroll—that will become a serious issue for you
because of the ways in which casinos change the games or
how they offer them or deal them. Your ability to be a very
skilled financial manager will be paramount. In fact I would
highly recommend that you take some courses in accounting and business management before venturing into the
world of professional gambling. For those of you who may
wish to do this semiprofessionally, and you already have a
secure financial situation, this won't mean as much—but
then you won't always win as much or as often. The mar-
gins of financial success are tiny, and profitability comes cumulatively, and not in single, huge chunks. There aren't any

"Jackpots," per se, to be had here. There is a lot of dedication and discipline, and small increments of financial success.

The methods you are about to discover are accurate, workable, and applicable. They are all my own inventions or modifications of earlier methods. Everything in this book is from me directly, and everything has been calculated, experienced, and played by me. The test figures I show are samples from very protracted data. For example, what I have chosen to identify as my "Blackjack Method" was the result of some nine million hands I played in actual casino situations as well as on computers, over about twenty years. The conclusions I list are those at which I arrived after all these events.

If you want to become a professional or semiprofessional gambler, the most important lesson you will need to learn right now is that *you can't play with the traditional strategies.* Casino managers aren't stupid; they know all about these methods and strategies. I know this because for some ten years I was on the other side of the tables, and I can tell you first hand that casino managers are extremely clever. The chief executive officer, or president, may not have hands-on gambling experience, but many of them do—like Bobby Baldwin, president of MGM Mirage and also a World Champion of Poker (as well as a seriously successful player). Others employ gambling experts who know everything about the games, and I mean *everything.* Nothing will escape them. Therefore, to be a successful gambler—legally, of course—you must be able to outwit them. To do this, you can't play with the kinds of strategies and methods or systems that they all know. For example, counting cards in Blackjack is a perfectly legal means of beating the game, but it is now all but impossible to do this in the real casino. You now need more in your professional bag of tricks. You need not only skills and anonymity, but also methods that will allow you to win, while *looking* like a loser. You want to appear to be a reckless, silly, tourist while *you* actually *know* that you are playing very *skillfully* and *for profit*.

If played well and properly, any player of these methods will look just like any other tourist or loser. In fact, playing these methods well will mean that you will be losing about 60 percent of the time. However, it is the other 40 percent that will account for the profits. The main reason these methods can be so successful is precisely because no single event matters. What *does* matter is the protracted *sequence of events*, each with their cumulatively growing profitability. This is how the casinos make money—they don't win it in huge chunks. They win their billion-dollar profits bit by bit, a tiny slice here and there, often smaller than a tenth of a percent. But add them all together, and you have casinos posting multi-billion-dollar profits each year, year after year. While you can't play exactly like the casinos, you can approximate the means by which casinos extract profits from the games. You can practice the play of these games in the same manner, and take little bit after little bit, all the while knowing that your cumulative effect is highly lucrative. And I don't mean just pennies, nickels, and dimes. This comes to hundreds, and even thousands, of dollars per session block. How much will depend on your skills and the amount of your available capital.

Many of these advanced methods are specifically designed to be simple. Although they do require absolute mastery and knowledge of the game, as well as the ability to memorize sequences, betting amounts, and so on, once learned and practiced they easily become second-nature to you. You will be able to play them so well that you will look precisely like the kind of gregarious loser enjoying the casino experience, that the casinos like so much as a customer. You will look as if you care nothing about losing money, and because you will look like you are losing more and more often, you are likely also to get a lot of comps, free gifts, and invitations. Add it all together, and you will have a wonderful experience, and what's even more important, get it for free and get paid for it. It can be done.

What I am offering you in this book are not "systems"; they are "methods," and there is a difference. In the past few decades, the word "system" has come to mean something "bogus," or something that "assures a win if done that way." Neither description is what applies here. What I have devised are "methods," and this simply means that these are vested in a thorough understanding and application not only of the games, the game rules, the mathematics and statistics, but also the realities of the actual casino games as they are really played. Additionally, these methods are those that I have developed for my own use and have only recently adapted for the general public. I only agreed to this because I no longer play professionally, and because now is the time when anyone can still make them work, before the world of casino gambling becomes completely computerized and dehumanized. Whether they will work for you or not, I don't know. The methods I offer here are skill-based methodologies applicable to the casino games for which they were designed, under the specific guidelines and conditions as stated, wholly reliant on your ability to learn, implement, and manage them under real-world conditions of in-casino play.

I don't know you, and I can't possibly know how skillful you are, what your levels of knowledge may be, how experienced you are in the casino games and casino lifestyle, how emotionally and financially stable you are, and a whole slew of other existential and personality traits I can't possibly know, or anticipate, but all of which will have a direct impact on your ability to make money with these methods. To be successful using these methods will require you to reach a level of expertise, knowledge, ability, skills, physical strength, mental agility, financial stability, emotional levity, good acting, and a great amount of personality, and all of it pleasant, gregarious, and friendly at all times when "on the job." It's hard, believe me. I know. I am pretty certain that only very few people will be able to maintain this level of dedication for more than ten years. It can be done, and if you are young you will have the opportunity to extend the life span of the applicability of these methods. Your success, financially and existentially, from playing these methods will, however, directly depend on you and your skills and abilities. These methods are here as *guidelines*—using them as well as they can work depends on you.

I can't really say that there has been anything "new" in gambling literature for a while. Most of the general literature is just a version of existing strategies, such as card-counting methods for Blackjack, dice manipulations in Craps, or spotting "biased" wheels in Roulette. There's nothing wrong with any of these derivatives on time-honored strategies, and they can—and do—work under favorable circumstances. Many can still be found in several casinos. My other books show such methods, and in them I acknowledge the contributions of my fellow authors, gaming experts, and gambling pioneers in the creation and implementation of these strategies. It is not my intention here to place myself any higher on the plane, or over and above any of these terrific authors or their works. On the contrary—had it not been for their combined body of work, my own revelations would not have been possible. I owe a debt of gratitude to all of them, as does any author of books about casino games.

Nothing made by human beings is ever perfect, and while I am certain that my strategies will work, I am open to comments, criticisms, and suggestions at all times. If anyone finds anything in this book that is wrong, or no longer applicable in the "real world," let me know. Remember, however, that your comments should be about the *method* itself, and *not* about how *you* were able—or unable—to apply it. A failure to win may not have anything to do with the methods and a whole lot more to do with their user. Many people are unable to understand their own limitations, and therefore when faced with failure tend to blame the nail, rather than the skills and abilities of the guy who wielded the hammer. Questioning the result is not the same as questioning the method.

I leave it for you to decide whether or not this book—and these strategies—are helpful, usable, useful, and profitable to you. Only you can make those judgments. Remember that these strategies are not for casual players. If you use these, you must do so exactingly and in full compliance with the sequence requirements. There is no "let's try it for a few times" here. Either you do or you don't. Half measures and half convictions won't work. Unskilled and unknowledgeable play will fail to produce results. Therefore, before you begin to blame the hammer and the nail for your failure, look first at the skills of the carpenter as well as the quality of the wood and the plans of the house. If the foundations are good, the house will stand. If not, it will fall. So will you as a professional—or semiprofessional—gambler. Don't make the mistake of thinking this will be all "fun and games," because at first it will be hard.

Now, if you are brave and ready to enter the world of profits from professional dedication and skill, the oyster and pearl are yours. Open . . . and enjoy.

Powerful Profits:

Winning Strategies for Casino Games

Introduction

Before we begin to describe the strategies themselves, here are a few facts you need to know:

1. This entry in the *Powerful Profits* series, *Winning Strategies for Casino Games*, assumes that you are already familiar with the games themselves.
2. *Winning Strategies for Casino Games* is *not* an introductory book on how to play, and it is *not* designed to teach the game(s).
3. All my Winning Strategies for Casino Games are specifically designed for play by individuals who have mastered the game(s) and are prepared to play and win accordingly.

This book is not meant for novices. If you do not possess the required knowledge of the game(s), I highly recommend that you first acquire the detailed knowledge you will need before playing these strategies. I have anticipated some of these situations and have therefore built several safeguards into some strategies. These safeguards are there to allow for some—but very few—mistakes during each play session.

For example, in the Blackjack Strategy, you *absolutely must know,* at the very least, the standard basic strategy and be able to modify it during play as stated. You should actually know my Modified Basic Strategy (MBS), which I have charted in my book *Powerful Profits from Blackjack.* For Craps, you must know what the bets are, how to make them, and how to proceed with playing the game—and so on for all the rest of *Winning Strategies for Casino Games.* I do not mean to be intimidating with these requirements because most of the strategies themselves are inherently quite simple. However, they cannot be played successfully if you do not know anything about the games and how to play them.

4. To be effective, these Winning Strategies for Casino Games must be played *exactly* as written!

If you do not play them in that specific manner, you cannot expect success. This caution applies to the application of any kind of expertise. You must learn all the details of each strategy and practice before you implement them in a real casino with real money at stake. They are not difficult to learn, but you must be absolutely certain that you know them *perfectly* before venturing to the casino and applying them to your play. Remember that in the real world of casino gambling, there will be many distractions: dealers changing, a pit boss giving you heat, other players playing foolishly, coming in and out of games, cocktail waitresses serving drinks, and so on. Any or all of these—and a number of others—can serve to distract you from your place in your strategy progression(s). If you lose that place you can cause yourself irreparable damage for that sequence.

I have allowed for up to three mistakes per session (in most strategies), but you should know that the first mistake you make will diminish your win expectancy (overall) by about 33 percent; your second mistake within the same session will reduce your win expectancy by about 66 percent, and your third mistake will further erode the efficiency by about 99 percent. Any additional mistakes, and you have defeated the strategy and it will not function as designed. Remember, these strategies have been *carefully crafted* not only to overcome the house edge in the games to which they apply, but also to provide you with an end-result win—regardless of what happens during any individual session.

5. Don't drink alcoholic beverages while gambling! Playing my Winning Strategies for Casino Games requires that you have your wits about you. You are not in the casino for "entertainment," you are there to win money. Remember that, and discipline yourself accordingly.

6. Don't "toke" [meaning to tip] willy-nilly. Occasionally, a small gratuity to a dealer or cocktail server is expected, but don't overdo it, regardless of how much you may be seen to be betting or winning at any particular time. Particularly, don't allow yourself to be "talked into" tokes or gratuities by dealers or other players. Judge when and how much to toke; that way you will be seen as a "stingy" player, but one who does occasionally toke—in other words, a "tourist"—and that's precisely how you want to *appear*. As a rule of thumb, allow yourself about $20 per session for tokes. Casino employees work for tokes only, so it definitely *is* appropriate for you to give them some money, but know how much so that your profit is not diminished.

7. Expect to be viewed as a "silly" or "novice" player, and act accordingly, without being boisterous or obnoxious. *Winning Strategies for Casino Games* is writ-

ten to help you "hide" your identity as a strategy player. Otherwise, you'd be in danger of being escorted out of the casino and perhaps even barred. By "looking as if" you are not a smart gambler, you will prevent these occurrences from affecting and distracting you. Don't be discouraged if other players— or even dealers—try to give you advice on what they may consider to be a better bet, or better play. *They don't know!* People like that may basically have good intentions, but these are misguided, particularly for the purposes of *your* play. Don't let them bother you. Play up to that by reinforcing the "silly player" image if you need to, but by and large keep to yourself as much as possible. Yes, you can be a participant in the general conversations around a gaming table, but always keep in mind that you are *acting* as a novice player or a tourist player, always mindful of the fact that you are involved in a deep sequence of events whose ultimate beneficial outcome has nothing to do with any single event.

8. Take frequent breaks in your casino play. Relax, don't overdo it. If you get tired, rest. A tired player makes mistakes, and you can't afford that. Also, don't play other games while playing any one of the *Winning Strategies for Casino Games* sessions. This could not only distract you from your purposes, but also deplete your bankroll.

9. You are *not* a tourist or a casual gambler, or in the casino for entertainment. You are a strategy player and are in the casino for one purpose, and one purpose only—to win money! Don't ever forget that, or you will not benefit from your play. If you want to be entertained, do it *after* you have completed your strategy play, but don't ever mix.

10. Bankroll—the most important part of any winning

strategy play. You *must* have the required bankroll for each strategy, or you cannot make it work! If you don't have that much money, save up, and play only after you have acquired the necessary stake. Otherwise you will simply be relegated to the other "casino fodder," players who play undercapitalized and thus have to rely on pure luck to win something.

11. Don't be concerned with intermittent losses; they are part of the process. Losses are inevitable, but you are not playing for any one event, any one hand, or any one session. As you will see, Winning Strategies for Casino Games are designed over a sequence of events, each of which appears to be independent of any other, but all of which are part of the same singular event, seen in the "big picture" perspective. Be mindful of this always because it will assist your psychological disposition. Most gamblers fail because they focus on single events; that's why casinos make so much money from them. In your case, *at no time will any singular event ever matter*! They are *not* what they *appear* to be, in *this* practice of strategy play.

Winning Strategies for Casino Games have been carefully designed to perform at optimum levels in actual in-casino gambling on the games to which any such strategy applies. To be successful, each such strategy must be played in accordance with the specific rules and regulations for each individual game, as described in each strategy. You must possess sufficient knowledge of each gambling game in order to be able to apply any of these strategies to your optimum potential. You must be able to play any of these strategies in accordance with the required initial starting bankroll (stake). Suggested bankrolls are listed in each individual strategy. Variations to bankrolls are possible, but you must be able to account correctly for the differences in each bankroll stake, and thereby modify each part of each strategy accordingly. This will become apparent as you learn the strategies. For example, if the starting base unit bet is listed as $10, you can play the strategy at half that rate, but then you must also be able to *decrease* and modify each and every betting and play aspect of the strategy accordingly. This is of paramount importance, particularly in *sequential betting progressions.* Likewise, if you choose to play the strategy at, say, $15 base starting bet requirement, then you must also be able to *increase* and modify each betting and play aspect of the strategy accordingly. And so on.

Each of the strategies has been formatted in equal—or close to equal—increments of bets and progressions. Most casinos will not allow fractional bets, and those that do allow them will immediately begin to look at you strangely, and you will be in danger of being discovered as a "strategy player." Consequently, if you modify the bankroll and betting requirements, do so *carefully* in order to account for equal amounts of bets anywhere in any sequence and under all conditions. This won't be as difficult as it may now sound, but it is important that you do this in whole-chip dollar amounts. (This also applies to fractional differentials, because each such fraction in the betting progression is rounded off to a whole chip unit.)

Don't play with cash money. Always change about one-fifth of your session stake into chips when you first sit down to any of the games, unless your session stake is less than $1,000, in which case always change the entire amount into chips. In some strategies, such as Roulette, you may be required to make larger wagers, so change $2,500 into chips, and have the other $2,500 in your pocket, handy to be used if required. Then, manage your chips, or coin tokens. Always know where you are in your session sequence and overall play sequence. Always have your next bet ready so you don't fumble around for your next bet amount. Be patient, act like a tourist or casual player, and don't be intimidated by anything. Don't drink, and always be in control. Your discipline must be iron clad. For the Slots Strategy, the above applies to coins or tokens used to play gaming machines.

Well, that's it! I do not mean to discourage you, but these requirements—these principles of self-discipline—are of paramount importance if you intend to succeed as a strategy player in the casino. Now it's time for you to open your *Powerful Profits: Winning Strategies for Casino Games* and begin to glimpse your future as a successful casino gambler.

Professional Play

If you want to be a professional gambler, or at least a semi-professional player, are you really, truly, aware of what it will take? Do you really know what you will be getting into? I don't mean just *think* you do—I mean really *know*? What kind of qualifications do you require? There's a lot more to playing casino games professionally, or at least semiprofessionally, than first meets the eye.

Most people come to casinos with at least some knowledge of the games and soon think how great it would be if they could "do this all the time." This is what I call the "infatuation syndrome," and it infects just about everybody who has any kind of liking for casino games and casinos. People are drawn to Las Vegas like moths to a flame, and many burn just as quickly. The infatuation soon wears off as the reality of the games, and their inherently difficult-to-beat odds, hit like the proverbial Mack truck. The smiles quickly fade, and the reason so many pawn shops abound becomes obvious as the hapless wannabe starts leafing through the thick phone book to find one he still doesn't owe money to.

Then there is what I call the "happiness syndrome." This happens when a lucky player hits it big, either by luck or by a combination of skill and luck. As odd as this may sound, this is a very frequent occurrence in gambling towns. Millions of tourists come to town every day, thousands move in every month, and they all play. Just by the simple rules of statistical occurrence, several hundred of them—perhaps thousands—hit big. It is actually a much misunderstood fact that more than 90 percent of all casino visitors actually win. The old story in Las Vegas, told from old-timer to old-timer and to anyone who will listen, goes like this: "It's easy to win money in a casino—it's very hard to go home with it." Therein lies the problem with both the infatuation syndrome and the more lethal happiness syndrome.

The infatuation syndrome usually happens to people who already have a natural predisposition toward casino games, and toward the kind of lifestyle that casinos seem to show and suggest. It's a fascinating world full of bright flashing lights, happy people, lots of money everywhere, and anything you want—for a price. People who call themselves "gamblers" fall easily into this syndrome. The fascination turns to infatuation, and this leads to blindness of the facts, then to self-denial, then to self-doubt, and, finally, to the stark reality that this really ain't what it looked like. The fascination and novelty soon wear off. For some this comes quickly; for others it takes time. Mostly, the more money you have to start with, the longer it will take for the reality to sink in. Sometimes, even these people get lucky. For example, I know a young man who considers himself a professional gambler even though he knows very little about the games or the lifestyle. He can get away with it because he was born rich, and even if he pretends like this for the rest of his life, it won't matter, because he has the money to sustain the fantasy. So be it. He could be happy doing this except for his problem—anger management. Each time he loses, he blames everybody and everything: the cards, the dealers, the other players, the odds, whatever. He will never be happy, no matter how long he persists in this fantasy lifestyle.

Other players aren't that lucky. They will hit the wall of reality sooner, and faster, and with a thick thud. Two jokes about old-time gamblers come to mind: (1) He arrived in town in an $80,000 car, and he left in a $200,000 bus. (2) *Question:* Do you know how to make a small fortune as a professional gambler? *Answer:* Start with a large fortune. Both may be jokes, but they are true and highly appropriate. Even more surprising—both happen all the time. Every day in Las Vegas, where I live, I see dozens of people who could be poster children for these jokes. When I first moved to Las Vegas in the late 1980s—to live here, rather than come to visit every weekend—I rented an apartment. When I arrived at each of the two companies to turn on the power and telephone, I was asked practically the same questions, with the same results. The first thing each asked me was how long I've been in town. After I answered that I only just moved here, both the employees smiled politely and said, "No credit, no checks, cash only, three months' deposit." Now this was news to me. In Los Angeles, where I lived prior to this, I had long-established credit with utilities and a long history of being a paying customer in good standing. I was kind of taken aback by this suspicious attitude, and I asked why. One of the ladies summed up the sentiment from both utilities, and from all subsequent dealings I had with other functionaries in Las Vegas. She said, "Honey, if you last three months, you just might make a resident. If you last six months, you might even have a life. And if you last more than a year, then you get on our real-good-customer list, and we give you your deposit back." I've lived here now fifteen years, and I did get my deposit back, and I did get on the real-good-customer list, even though it wasn't always peaches and cream. However, that story is for another time and another book.

I learned a valuable lesson during those first few weeks. I learned how easily one can move to a gambling town and how equally easily the town can move you out. The point here is that I did learn, I did experience it, I lived it, and I know what I'm talking about. I was the fascination kid, and also the happiness child. I tripped over the rainbow and fell smack face first into the pot of gold. I was already a fairly experienced player, and I just loved being in Las Vegas and all that it represented. I had a great time. I gambled and won. And won, and won, and won a lot. Everything was terrific—until I too hit that wall of harsh reality, with a thud so loud my ears are still ringing. It happened to me too. I fell into the trap of thinking I was better than I was. I fell hard for a while. I went from playing $60,000 and more in a day, to having 11 cents to my name, and all in less than six months. It was then that I took a long hard look at my skills, and knowledge, and the reality of the casino lifestyle. I analyzed all my faults and all my problems as best I could. I decided to investigate how I could have been so good and so bad all at the same time. I started writing it all down, and although I was already writing gambling columns at the time, I began the process that later resulted in several books, and many hundreds more articles and magazine stories. To cut a long story short, I spent the next ten years in the process of learning, relearning, living, and playing. I made a career out of gambling, and in many different ways. I played all the games—I played for small stakes and for big stakes. During that ten-year period I parlayed a lot. I took my $1,600 watch and pawned it for $20. With that $20 I won first $250, then $500, then $1,250, then $4,000, and by the end of that year I had won more than $34,500. A far cry from the early days of heady success, but it was work. I also started a business and worked with casinos, and for casinos. I went all across the country and played in just about every casino there is. I learned how it works from all sides, and I even got a job as a dealer. I learned from the casino floor, to the back rooms, to the board rooms, from the lowliest employee to the highest manager and boss, and all in between. I became very good at the games, and I formed the strategies that I have presented in this book, as well as some that I will never show. Although there is a lot more to this story, let me now finish my personal example by stating that as a man I was also prone to the infatuation and happiness syndromes, no matter how much I already knew at the time. My story is intended to show you two things:

- First, even if you are already a knowledgeable person, perhaps a good player of casino games, you still have to fight the daily battle of not falling victim to the easily acquired infatuation of this casino lifestyle, or become drunk with the happiness of a good win, or a win streak.
- Second, if you do fall into this trap, don't be ashamed. Be ashamed only if you let it defeat you.

If you really, truly, want this life, and you fail, then try again. Learn from your mistakes, and no matter how long it takes, learn, learn some more, practice, and do it again. Find a way. Acquire the knowledge that will work for you. There is no shame in not knowing—there is shame only in failing to learn, given the opportunity. As I have found such opportunities for myself, and learned these casino game strategies, and have made peace with this lifestyle, so I am sharing this with you here. Whatever value you gain from it only you can know. If all you take from this book is just the knowledge that there is more knowledge available, then you will still be far ahead of many thousands of people who either think they know everything, or think they don't have to.

The happiness syndrome is a little different from the infatuation syndrome. The infatuation syndrome usually infects only those people who already have some knowledge about casino games and are perhaps already good players (and perhaps even professional players with a predisposition to gravitating to this casino lifestyle). The happiness syndrome can infect anyone, anywhere, anytime. It can strike without warning and requires no knowledge of casino games, casino lifestyle, or any previous predisposition to gambling—either recreationally or professionally. It strikes as the result of good fortune. For that reason, if not correctly diagnosed immediately, and handled with great care, this syndrome is far more deadly. Because it arrives subtly, and among the fanfare of a great windfall of cash, "happiness" blinds the susceptible player into thinking he or she is "blessed." Some truly are, but these are a rare breed. Mostly the happiness syndrome will infect a regular person who was simply out for a holiday, or a good time.

In my book *Powerful Profits from Slots*, I tell the story of a retired man, the pillar of his community, who never gambled in a casino in his life. Then, after retiring, he and his wife went to a casino resort for a holiday. The man won $250,000 on a slot machine. Then he won another $50,000 on that same machine, and profited a tidy $300,000 in no time. He fell victim to the happiness syndrome in a big way and became a regular casino player who thought this was easy money. He thought he knew everything there was to know, and he refused to learn anything, arguing that he already knew the most essential item—how to win. That man fell hard.

I will tell you another story about the happiness syndrome. A few years back, when the old Sands hotel still stood (on the site where the Venetian now stands in Las

Vegas), there was a cocktail waitress from the Stardust who stopped by there after work for some R&R. She started to play Blackjack. For those of you who don't know, being a pretty cocktail girl can be a good job. Back then they made about $300 per day. Anyway, she started small and was hit with a flood of good fortune. Soon she was betting all spots on the table with black $100 chips, and the wins were piling up. Quickly she grew her stack of chips so that she was playing all the spots on the table with a maximum bet of several thousand dollars. She was hitting, splitting, doubling, and winning on everything. In less than twelve hours of play she had well over $300,000 from her initial $100 buy-in. Everyone was happy for her, particularly the casino employees who knew how hard it was to make any kind of money working in casinos. The waitress's friends and coworkers heard and came by. All told her to stop, go home, buy a house. Even the dealers and pit staff at the Sands told her to stop and go home. Contrary to popular belief, casinos are very responsible when it comes to their customers. Casinos are very glad to see a happy event like this, and recognize the value of a good winner, and a good story. Casino bosses, managers, and CEOs are not the ogres they are sometimes made out to be by people who consider gambling to be a sin, or an addiction. They pleaded with her to stop. They asked her friends and family to convince her to stop. She would not. She kept playing for another twelve hours. Not only did she lose the $300,000 she won, but she lost the $300 she made the previous night serving drinks, then another $1,000 from her checking account, another $2,000 in casino credit she begged for and received, and another $5,000 she borrowed from friends and coworkers. At the end of this twenty-four-hour period, she went back to serving drinks for minimum wage and tips, broke and $7,000 in debt.

Her story is a severe example of what the happiness syndrome can do even to an otherwise knowledgeable person, even someone who was certainly casino wise, if not wise about Blackjack. As a casino cocktail server, she saw it all, and had known what a folly this can be, yet she fell victim to the allure of the happiness of easy-come. Someone in the midst of the happiness of cumulative wins can easily begin to think that it will never end. It always ends. In situations like this, it often ends with a devastating result.

Not all stories of the happiness syndrome are this sad, however. In the interest of balance, I will share another story with you about another casino employee who also played Blackjack after his shift. This was a Blackjack dealer in one of the local off-the-Strip casinos in Las Vegas. It happened a few years ago at a time when this was a "locals' " casino far away from anything, way out on the lonely highway (now in the middle of a development, of course, but at that time a long way from anywhere). This guy was a regular casino employee type, a longtime resident of Las Vegas, already hardened to the realities of the casino lifestyle. (Most casino employees gamble, but most do it responsibly.) This Blackjack dealer got off duty and went to another casino to relax and play a few hands. He couldn't do anything wrong. He kept winning and winning. He started with a $40 buy-in on a $1 table with a $200 maximum. After just a few hands, he was all the way to the maximum $200 bet and soon had all the spots covered with $200 maximum bets (this was a small casino whose tables had a $200 limit, so he couldn't move to a higher limit, even though he was winning). After about six hours of play, he had amassed more than $39,000. Now he did the smart thing: He took $38,000 and put it aside, then played with the $1,000 (plus change) he had left. Soon his luck turned, and he lost the $1,000 (plus change). He quit, took his $38,000, and went home. Why? Because $38,000 was the exact amount he owed on his mortgage. He paid off his house, and he and his family had a better life as a result.

There are many positive stories like this as well as many stories of casino visitors who succumb to the happiness syndrome. I once saw a young man put a $100 chip on a Roulette table and hit for $3,500. He was so happy he couldn't stand it. Later I found out from my friend, the casino host, that the man not only lost it all back, but another $5,000 on top. People like this hit town every day—they also leave town every day. Casinos are not a toy. Casino games are not there to make you rich—they are there to make the *casinos* rich. Donald Trump—the New Jersey casino owner and real estate tycoon—was once asked what it is that he likes most about casinos. He replied, "Owning them." Let this be your first lesson in your quest to become a professional or semi-professional player. This one answer from a hugely successful man will make your life a whole lot easier. Making money by playing casino games is hard. It requires a whole lot of knowledge, skills, abilities, fortitude, mental and emotional strength, a lot of money as your bankroll, and then even more of all of the above. You will need all of this, as well as physical strength, resilience, and health. All are essential.

I now play only semiprofessionally. I play several highly selective games, and only in my special way. The strategies I have shown in this book are all born out of decades of learning, doing, sweating, and then learning, doing, and sweating some more. It was very hard, and it still is. The best advice I can give you is this: No matter what strategy you play, or how much you know about the casino games, or how good you are, gambling is still just that—gambling. This means you can lose. Even if you play a positive expectation game, those "positive expectations" are merely words describing a statistical eventuality that will occur—but just exactly *when* this will occur, no one knows. The "long terms" catchphrase of gambling literature can mean a whole lot of things. Take out your newspaper and look at the graph charts representing the stock market for that week, month, or year. Take a look at the swings. Really high up, then very deeply low, then somewhere in the middle, and so on. Like a roller coaster, sometimes you reach great heights, and other times you fall into deep pits. Getting up there to those dizzying heights of success is like being dragged to the top of the drop on that roller coaster. It's slow and takes a lot of power. Once up there, though, enjoying that height is fleeting. When you reach the top of that roller coaster, you sit on that high, level plane for only a few seconds. Then comes the plunge.

Getting to the top of gambling is a slow, hard process, requiring a lot of power, while the inevitable drop from those heights is 100 times that fast. If you understand the example of the stock market, then you understand that professional winning in gambling is a *process.* It is not a hit-and-run situation, as it may be for a casual player. In fact, the generally accepted advice for casual players is precisely that—hit it, and run. (Let's hope you will run . . . and keep your winnings). As a professional player, once you realize you are about to experience that drop, or start to feel it, your discipline should kick in. Tighten your seat belt, stash your cash, and ride it out, spending as little energy and money as possible until it levels off, and if you still have all your cookies by the time the drop is over, you still have all your winnings. The same applies to the example of the stock market. Just because it falls 300 points in one afternoon doesn't mean that's the time to sell. Long-term investors understand that, and although the catchphrase "long term" applies equally vacuously to stock trading and investments—being just as overused and fallacious as in gambling—institutional investors are those who can truly benefit by the stretch of the statistical equivalency.

A simple principle in number theory as it applies to the analysis of numerical events in randomization tests is the equivalency principle. It simply states that no matter how odd an occurrence, or how nonrandom the randomization model may appear at any given moment, eventually—all matters being balanced—the events equalize. This may take 10 years, 100, 1 billion, or more. There is no limit to the protraction of such events because they are infinite, and the definition of infinity is a non-sequitur truism, and as such is in itself inherently indefinable. Those who stayed in the stock market after the crash of 1929, or bought back into the market after the crash, were in a market that was worth some 600 points. Those who stayed in the market since have seen it climb to 11,000 points a few years ago, and now sits at 9,000 points. Whatever that number may be at the time you happen to be reading this book, the point is that institutional investors can, and do, exploit the very long-term pliability of statistical equivalency. Growth in the stock market is a positive expectation game as long as the population of the world keeps growing, because they are directly interdependent. More people means more products, more needs, more services, more businesses, more money, higher stock prices and values. The "crashes," such as 1929, and those that have happened since, are just those hiccups that institutional investors know will happen, but also will correct. Here's that equivalency principle again, and it will work and continue working regardless of whether we have anything to which to apply it.

Applied to gambling, this simply means that even if you are playing a positive expectation game, or strategy, there will be times when no matter what you do, or how well you do it, you will lose. Sometimes, you will keep on losing and it just won't seem right. Remove yourself and your emotions from the events, and simply realize that they are just happening the same way as the stock market, and the roller coaster. It just will happen, and in fact is happening all the time. Whether you will, or will not, experience such drastic anomalies in the normally placid win-lose situations depends largely on luck—or lack thereof. You might be a person who happens to choose your start in this gambling at a moment, time, and game wherein such a negative streak hits you hard. Or, you may never face such a situation, even though you may face a series of smaller swings. Either is plausible, possible, and happening all the time. Sometimes, you will "luck out" and get a whole lot more than you might be reasonably entitled to expect under the circumstances of the game. Other times you may get a whole lot less, even though you are doing everything correctly. The point of all of this is simply to show you that even a positive expectation is subject to downturns.

Casinos know this; they have a positive expectation on all games. Some of those games make only 0.5 percent for casinos, on average. Other games make them up to 45 percent. Overall, the average casino win expectation is about 20 percent over all of their games combined. Add to this income from other sources, such as hotel rooms, floor space rental, conventions, restaurants, shows, and other facilities, and the casino expects to make between 35 and 45 percent gross proceeds. So, if customers spend $1 billion in the resort over the course of the fiscal year, the casinos can expect a gross "win" of between $340 million and $450 million. The actual figures for the major Las Vegas resorts are closer to $1 billion in gross drop each, with the average among the properties of around one-third of that.

These are the figures on which the casinos base their share income forecasts, and this is how casinos and their shares and bonds are valued for investment and return. This also determines the cost of the money they may borrow for expansions, debt reductions, and so on. Nevertheless, even though casinos are fully cognizant of these "positive expectations," they also know that just because they are "positive" expectations doesn't necessarily mean that in this quarter, or in this year, they will actually make exactly this amount. Some years, or quarters, they may make a lot more, and others a lot less. Just because the "game"—in this instance the game of owning the casino—is a positive expectation game, doesn't mean that it will always pay off that expected percentage—like clockwork. All this means is that the general expectation is positive to that percentage, and therefore over the course of the "long run"—however that may be applied to this game—the profits should come close to these percentages. In the world of business and finance, these percentages often come very close to these forecast expectations. In the world of gambling, however, positive expectations are often grossly misunderstood by the players. The major reasons for this misunderstanding are twofold:

- First, the players do not understand the principles of long-term equivalency or how this directly affects the game they are playing.
- Second, players are human and they get far too emotionally involved and attached to the game and its results.

The first problem can be overcome by education and the realization that positive expectations are still nothing more than "expectations" and, therefore, are not a guaranteed result in just this moment or sequence. The information in this book should help you understand that perfectly. The second of these two problems can be overcome with discipline. With this you have to help yourself; I can't help you. I can help guide you into the arena of self-discipline as it applies to gambling, but the rest can only be done by you, for you. Becoming emotionally attached to the game, the results, the events, the strategies, the play, the environment, the fun, the excitement, the fascination, the happiness, the despair, the anger and resignation, the wins, the losses, and everything else this embodies, is to become a victim of your professional life, and not its driver. Being a victim is easy.

It's like sitting in a car with no brakes at the top of a hill with a 3,000-foot rocky precipice at the end of the road, getting in, pushing the car off the ledge, and then sitting there lamenting your bad luck as you plummet to certain doom. Who was the cause? Well, you were! Nobody forced you into that car, nobody asked you to drive to the top of the hill, and certainly nobody forced you to push off while inside the car. In fact, nobody even forced you to leave your house. *You* made that choice. So, if you gamble like that, the ruin you will inevitably face is *your* doing, and yours alone. Nobody is asking you to do this, nobody is forcing you, and you always have the right, freedom, and opportunity to quit at any time. *You* are in control; these are *your* decisions. Face them, and don't lie to yourself. Being able to discipline yourself with absolute honesty is the hardest thing you will ever do—if, that is, you do it truly honestly. If you do, you will discover things about yourself you won't believe. In addition, this will help you separate yourself—and your emotions— from what is essentially nothing more than a sequence of numerical events. Actually, just events, because "numerics" is merely what we ascribe to them to assist us with explaining them.

Once you are able to gamble this way, to understand the reality of "expectations," and to understand and be able to overcome personal discipline issues and separate yourself from emotional attachment to events, you will be free to gamble for profit. When you win, you will understand the win and how it was achieved, and it won't mean either fascination, infatuation, or happiness beyond appreciation for a job well done. When you lose, you will understand it for the inevitable fact it was, and move on without any further emotional disturbance. Analysis of the losses will help you improve your skills if they were the result of some deficiency in your approach to the game. If this was not the cause, however, and you are truly perfect in everything you have done, it was simply that statistical occurrence that will inevitably happen, so you file it and move on. It's very easy, once you achieve this level of calm. This will also mean that doing this will most definitely not be fun; therefore, I again remind you that playing casino games with these methods is *not* intended to be fun, it *is* intended to be *work*. Though work can often be fun, in the casinos fun can easily result in a lack of discipline. Pick your games from which to make profits, and pick others from which to gain fun. Personally, I have several games I play for profit, and when I do it's hard work. To balance this, I like to play live poker, which I play for fun. Although I know the game, and its theory and playing principles, most of the time I enjoy it simply for the camaraderie of the players and the enjoyment of the game itself. Wins that come, do come. Losses that come, I limit. Fun comes almost all the time. When it doesn't, I go home. When I play poker for profit, I play differently, and usually in a different casino. That's just me. You can do whatever works for you.

Casinos are an institution. Like the institutional investors, they are an entity, and not a person. Their win expectations are always positive, and they will continue to make their profits for as long as such entities exist. They have no "personal investiture" in the games, or events. They simply offer them, and there they exist. We, as players, however, are human beings, with a finite existence, and with an even more finite exposure to the games we will play. During these short events, we will experience wins and losses far in excess of whatever equivalence proportions there may be in the overall statistical infinity. We will either win a lot more than we statistically should, or lose a lot more than the games' program, or in-built house edge, should dictate. This is where these strategies and methods, as I have developed them, come into focus most profoundly. They are created to take advantage of the games in these very finite and short-term slices of our exposure, while at the same time applying the principles of sequential event exploitation and the cumulative growth aspects of both the stock market and roller coaster examples I used earlier. These strategies are designed to allow you to play as much as humanly possible as an institution, as the casino, without emotion and attachment. They are designed to help you climb up the ladder to the top and gain as much money in this process as possible, while also severely limiting and curtailing your bets when you hit that roller coaster fall into the pit, so that when it levels out at the bottom again you will still have the majority of your wins with you, and have not lost it on the way down, as most casual players will always do. Again, when the climb resumes, these strategies and methods are designed for you to start the next climb with more, to bet more in the positive situations, and to bet a whole lot less in the negative situations. I make no claims about success, because that is up to you. All I can do for you is offer you the framework upon which to build your own success. These strategies require skills, abilities, and intelligence, as well as common sense, and a whole lot of the other attributes I describe throughout this book. Your climb to success, and your fall from grace, can be as fast and as profitable, or as devastating, as you make them.

Although the strategies in this book buck the "normal" explanations of the "establishment" among gambling literature, it is precisely this flexibility that allows them to be so applicable and so workable. Casinos can only defend against strategies that are all part of what has become the "normal standard" of gambling advice. Learn this, do that, and so on, and you will gain a 0.02 percent advantage over the house. This is all fine and useful for the casual players. Casinos know that these casual players account for 99 percent of all their players, so they use rules changes and game alterations to combat a growing awareness among these players, and consequently no such strategies can ever be used professionally for continued success. The methods and strategies in this book take the approach that is used by the institutions themselves and apply the principles as I have stated them here throughout. They are odd, they seem strange, they look wrong, but they make money. There is no defense against them, because the casino won't even know that you are playing this way, if you are clever enough and don't make it obvious, or say it. As long as casinos offer these games in these forms, these methods cannot be defended against by the casinos. Their only choice will be either to stop offering the games entirely, in which case they will have to stop doing business and casinos will cease to exist, or alter the rules and paybacks so severely that nobody will play there anymore, which will also result in their going out of business. So, for the very small percentage of players who will now be able to use these strategies and methods to make money from the casinos, this will be a great and profitable time. Casinos will still make money, despite the few hundred millions of dollars or so you, and readers like you, will now be able to make from them. There are fat times ahead for those who can do this right.

I do caution you, however, that doing this "right" isn't easy. I have said this before, and I will keep on repeating it because it is very important: Professional gambling, or at least semiprofessional gambling—is extremely hard to do well and profitably in both the short term and long run. Many try, but only a few succeed. So, to help you succeed better, the next chapter offers what I call my "Keys to Winning." These universal principles of gambling, personal skills and discipline, selection of games, and general guidelines will make you a better player no matter what game you choose.

Keys to Winning

There's a "Keys to Winning" chapter in most of my books, and for a very good reason. Winning is not only the result of blind luck. Although sudden fortune happens to some people, including those who know little or nothing about casino games or gambling, the *sustained* kind of luck seems to favor those players who have mastered these keys. Being lucky every now and then isn't hard—even the blind squirrel will find an acorn once in a while. When a professional player wins, what others often perceive as the strike of luck is very often the result of a prolonged series of events.

The other night I was playing one of the games I play for profit, and I was cashing out just under $5,000 when an acquaintance happened to walk by and marveled at my "good luck." I agreed, and we had a nice conversation about how lucky I get. He was also aware that I had "cashed in" several times before on these games and wondered how I could be so lucky so often. Again I smiled and we continued our discussion. He is a nice man, and we have run across each other in the casinos for several years. I don't know him very well, but I do know him well enough to understand that his play is primarily for recreation and not professional, so, I would have hated to tell him that this "good fortune" was the result of a sixteen-hour investment in time and effort, a $2,500 bankroll for that session, and a whole lot of prior research, knowledge, and experience on these games. I would have hated to tell him that I spent sixteen years studying this game and have developed a method to exploit it. He would not have understood or would have required too lengthy an explanation. Though I enjoy sharing my knowledge and experience, when I play for profit that's what I'm there for, not for chitchat or to educate or inform others. For that I write these books.

Being a professional player, or at least playing semiprofessionally, means that the casino is your workplace. It is your office, your factory, your plant, your job. You don't want distractions, and you certainly don't want unwanted and unsolicited interference, no matter how good natured or well intentioned it may be. This applies to other players, and particularly to casino employees. Many times other players or casino employees seem to think that just because you are there for long hours you are lonely and in desperate need of being talked to. They hover around and pester you, and when you ignore them they get offended. One day I was playing a game, and winning a small amount, when a person whom I consider a friend sat next to me and began to question me about video poker. He kept on and on and on, pestering me with repeated questions. It soon became obvious this person just couldn't understand the subject, no matter how carefully I tried to explain it, so I finally told him to read my book. That didn't stop the pestering, and I wound up having a losing session because of this; I left with a small loss instead of the profit I worked for. Again, since he was a friend, I didn't want to be blunt, and since this was a small game in which I played really more for enjoyment, I didn't mind that much. The point is this: When you play, don't take friends and family with you, or make friends at the game or the casino. Keep to yourself and to your game, and concentrate on what you are doing. As soon as you see yourself being disturbed or distracted, stop it. If you can't stop it, end the session and leave. It is better to do this than to prolong the experience and perhaps lose a friend as well as money. This is part of the reality of the casino lifestyle and of the professional player. You will encounter this frequently as you start playing more and more, and start spending more hours at casinos where other players and employees begin to know you. Frequency of such visits will bring familiarity, and with that will arrive other persons' apparent needs to talk to you and interfere with you. Sometimes, if you happen to care for that person—as was the case in my example—it will be better to simply leave and stop your work than to risk losing a friendship. After all, they mean well—they simply don't know, or are unable to understand, how you play and why you play the way you do. In these circumstances, such misperceptions can become distracting and often annoying, but at the same time they are one of your keys to success: When these things happen, it is obvious that everyone else thinks you are there just like them— playing for relaxation and entertainment. This also means you have successfully hidden yourself from prying eyes and have succeeded in being viewed as just another of the casual and losing players. I will discuss this later in the chapter on hiding your identity as a professional player.

This is just one of the Keys to Winning, but it is really the final step in a long process. Before you get to that point, you will require a lot more learning and practice. This means not just the games, but learning about yourself and practicing on yourself what you learn. I don't expect you to be perfect. None of us are. We all fail sometimes. The more often you do something, the greater the likelihood that you will screw it up at one time or another. When and if you do, don't be ashamed of it. Face up to it and accept it; don't hide it or analyze it. Understand it and learn from it. Being able to learn from our mistakes is one of the primary reasons why we are the dominant species on this planet. From time immemorial we have had this ability, and that is what has set us apart. Don't discard it now just because you may feel like a fool for having been so stupid. I've got news for you—pros screw up just like ordinary people. Except when they do it, it's usually a lot bigger and a lot more visible. Be aware of this, and if such happens to you, accept it, deal with it, and move on. People who respect you always have and always will, and probably more so now that they have witnessed you deal so forthrightly with your own failings. It is empowering and encouraging. Those who don't respect you probably never will, so why worry about trying to impress them? People who don't know you may make smartass cracks that could hurt you, but why give them the satisfaction of a reaction? Swallow it and remind yourself that a professional gambler must have thick skin. It'll pass, believe me. True friends will remain so even if you fail. If they don't, they weren't your friends and won't be. In the end, all of this centers only on you—you must decide whether a failure was so hard that it ends your ambitions in this pursuit, or if it was merely a learning bump along the way to greater glory.

If you choose to end your career as a professional gambler, or a semiprofessional player, don't be ashamed of that either. It is a profession that only the very gifted can do successfully. Enjoy it, talk about it, make it a part of your life, and if you fail, learn from it, understand it for what it was, and move on. If the failure was incidental, recognize it for the small bump it really was, and don't let it influence your career as a player. If the failure was more dramatic, such a failure is a window of opportunity into the rest of your life.

What you do with such an opportunity directly decides your eventual success as a player and will directly affect your decision. None of this will be easy, but all of it is very possible and achievable.

At the beginning, however, there are the more mundane things to do and learn. My Keys to Winning include aspects of play and life that are essential ingredients in your success as a gambler. If you choose to be a professional gambler, a semiprofessional, or just a casual player, the following Keys to Winning will serve you well: *knowledge, patience, bankroll, selection, discipline,* and *win goal.* And that's why I have called them the "Keys to Winning." Put all those together, and *apply* them correctly, and you *become* lucky. At least that's what people will say when they watch you win and wonder how you do it, or how come you can do it so often.

Many people—mostly those who look down upon strategy or method players—will say that strategy plays are a waste of money and that you can only win if you're lucky. To them I say, yes, I'm lucky, but those of us who play the *smart* way *know* that our luck is derived from the proper application of knowledge. For example, when you go shopping and you see one store advertise peanut butter for $1.25 and another store advertise the very same product for $0.89, you go to the store where the price is better for the same product, right? *That's applying your knowledge to your financial benefit.* Those who buy the more pricey item either don't care about money or are losers without knowing it. So, if you are in a casino and see some slots with a sign that says, "Up to 94.7 percent payback," and the casino next door has the same slots with a sign that says, "98 percent payback," where would *you* play? If you're a smart slot player who wants to win, you'd go to the one that says "98 percent payback," because you know that advertising which says "up to" doesn't mean that all the machines pay that much, plus you also know that 98 percent is better than

94.7 percent. Put those two together, and you have *made a knowledgeable decision.* This applies equally well to any choice of game, not just slots.

This is pretty much common sense, but many people lose sight of the commonsense principles of everyday life as soon as they visit a casino. Suddenly they become blinded and forget to make their "shopping" choices work for them. As a result, many will lose and wonder why, and even more will wonder why they haven't had the kind of good play and profits as those people for whom wins seem to come so easily. It comes down to the first of the keys: knowledge. To be a winner, and to win more often than most people, you must apply your powers of *knowledge,* and choice, and combine this with the other keys.

How do you acquire this knowledge? You've already started. By reading this book and learning what is shown here, you are on your way toward becoming an *informed* player, and therefore a *better* player, whose luck is *calculated* and not merely a blind act of good fortune. There is a lot more to being a winner than many people imagine. Therein lies the greatest problem with most players. They don't learn from their own past experiences, or the experiences of others they have witnessed, known, or heard about. All they can see, or remember, is that one time they were really *this* lucky, but not all the other times when they were *not* lucky. Most of all, they never realize that mere blind luck is like that blind squirrel finding an acorn once in a while. Once in a while blind luck happens, but there are long "whiles" in between such happenings, and they may never happen to you again. Such people not only fail to learn from experience; they don't even realize that learning is necessary. Even the most rudimentary information, such as that offered by most major casino resorts in the hotel rooms, is more knowledge than most novices have. Unfortunately, many such people ignore even that information.

This example of the really "green" novice—and blind luck—may be extreme to some extent, but it serves to illustrate a wider problem among players who want to be better than they are. Even players who have been to casinos several times, and are now familiar with the games, how they work, and how to play them, and may possess some of that rudimentary knowledge from the in-room pamphlets, or booklets, or merely from information obtained through conversations with other players—even these people do not necessarily behave, or play, in a more profitable manner. Just because you have been to a casino and have played before doesn't mean you already know all you should know. Maybe you have won. Maybe you have lost. Perhaps you have won and lost, and are about even. What if you only lost a little. Does that make you feel comfortable about your casino expertise? Being "comfortable" is an important concept. Many people feel "uncomfortable" at the beginning, either because they are among those very "green" novices or have only recently become familiar with casinos. As with most things we do, there is a "learning curve." This simply means the time it takes most of us to learn at least the very basics of whatever it is we are planning to do, or are doing. Once that is achieved, there is another concept commonly known as the "comfort factor." This is the point we reach, eventually, after having done whatever we have contemplated through the learning curve process. We reach the comfort factor when we have had direct experiences with that particular situation and have found that we liked it, that it was good, that it was profitable, or at least that it didn't really hurt that much.

We usually "like" something because it does something pleasing for us, such as being entertained by playing casino games. We think something is "good" when the entertaining experience we like so much also proves rewarding in some way. This leads us to the part that we call "profitable," and although this normally means that we made some money, with casino games this could be as simple as having received a win of any kind—even a small win that, in reality, meant an overall loss. But just the act of getting it, with the other factors combined, often results in our *perception* that this was "profitable," in which case we usually think of "profit" as something in addition to mere money: the casino experience, for example, or the camaraderie among players, or the fact that we were there with a loved one and shared a happy time, which had little to do with the act of profiting from this particular game or event. Maybe we reached the comfort factor after having lost money, but we got some play for it, and therefore the other factors in this human equation were satisfied. We thought of this as the "payment" for that series of experiences; even though we lost money, we still feel okay about it because it "didn't hurt that much." For most people, the loss of money is a "hurtful" experience. However, many people will become more resistant to that feeling after having played for a while. They quickly find out that the loss of money is an integral part of the playing experience. No one will win all the time. Losing is just as much a part of playing as is winning. And losing happens a lot more often than winning.

Once we all start to realize these human factors, we have come to the comfort zone, that point in our psychological approach to gambling where we are no longer in wonderment about the games and no longer in fear about the loss of our money. As a player, when you reach this point of familiarity with the game and the comfort level regarding the experience, the money, the game, the winning, and the casino environment, you have developed what can be described as "casino familiarity," or perhaps "gaming resilience." Either means largely the same thing—you are no longer a novice, and the act of playing casino games no longer scares you. Now you have a decision to make, and a very important one. You can continue being happy with what you know, continue to play with this minimal familiarity, and "hope for the best." This will relegate you to join the vast majority of casino players who have reached this point of familiarity with the games, and continue to try for the stroke of blind luck. These are the players who feed billions of dollars into the casino's coffers, and these are the people who are very largely responsible for the cumulative huge losses suffered by casino players every year. (If you really think about it, the numbers are staggering. In Nevada alone, casinos "win" over $9 billion each year. Nine times one thousand millions—of dollars!)

How easily the "comfort factor" translates into huge financial losses! As a consequence, if you continue to be happy about all that you already know, or think you know about playing casino games, you will be part of this great mass who lose each time they play, even if they sometimes win something. So, the second decision you must make for yourself is whether you want to "graduate" from merely the comfort level and reach a point of "expertise." This means that you should try to become a professional gambler, or at least try to play like one. It *is* possible to win, you know. And no, you don't have to trust blind luck, and you don't have to stumble around in the dark like that poor blind squirrel still looking for that acorn. I am well aware that the "learning curve" can be difficult to overcome, while the "comfort factor" is easily reached. Therefore, I seek to simplify the information and make it as clear as I can with as much impact as I can impart to it. By investing your time in reading this book, you show that you have the desire to improve yourself as a player and reach a level of expertise. This is the second of the two choices I described, and you have made it right here. It's not easy. Simplicity belies complexity. Casino games are serious gambling games that can, and will, take your money if you don't know what to do and how to do it to the best level the game allows. To learn this takes time, and the willingness not just to learn it, but also to apply it, and apply it correctly. To help you do this, along with all the other information in this book, I repeat the Keys to Winning, given earlier. These are, in order of importance:

- Knowledge
- Patience
- Bankroll
- Selection
- Discipline
- Win Goal

Oh, how simple it seems when we just look at these words. Sure, you say. *No problem.* I can do that. Can you? Really? Be honest, now. I can tell you from direct personal experience that keeping yourself diligently to these principles is extremely hard to do. If, that is, you want to do this always, all the time, each time. To be a successful professional player, and win most of the time, you *must* adhere to these principles. If you go to a casino and leave just one of these principles at home, or take only a portion with you, or slip and lose one or more, or a part of one, you're sunk. You're the *Titanic* on a collision course with the iceberg, and there's no stopping the final result, or the consequences. And that's no joke. Believe me. I know. I don't expect you to be perfect at all times. Just *most of the time.*

I don't expect you to become superhuman and suddenly be able to practice these principles with perfect ability. That simply won't happen. Any "system" or advice you may read that says "Do this and you will win" is fundamentally flawed, because no human being can be perfect at all times. We are frail creatures—mentally, physically, and, most important, emotionally. We get upset. We get angry. We get mad that we have done everything perfectly, and still we lost. It happens. That's also part of life, and certainly part of the gaming experience. Even when you take all these principles with you, and do everything perfectly, there will be times when you will lose. Statistical anomalies infect every aspect of gambling. All the games, including the methods and strategies in this book, are prone to such fluctuations. My point here is to let you in on the "secret," which will allow you to overcome these problems, these feelings, and these moments of anger. That's why knowing these principles, as I have outlined them, is so important. Not because you will become "perfect" as a professional gambler, but because *you will become more secure in your gaming,* more steady in your approach, more confident in your end result, and more conscious of your expectations. And these are the real secrets to your success at gambling. So, in more detail, I now address each of those principles individually.

KNOWLEDGE

This should be relatively easy. Knowledge is the "learning curve," the decision to improve yourself, and probably the reason you bought this book. Knowledge means to learn as much as is possible, with as definite a direction toward your end goal as possible. Knowledge means to know not only that the casino games exist, or what they look like and how to play them, but also how to play them *well.* Playing well also means incorporating into your knowledge all the other principles of these Keys to Winning. And it also means not stopping here. Knowledge is growth in understanding and in continual improvement. For casino play, this means everything I have written here, from page one to the last page. All of this is the knowledge that is necessary to achieve more than just blind luck. Learning it will have a direct and positive impact on your play, and on your life, and specifically on how you approach the casino games the next time you visit a casino.

PATIENCE

I am often surprised at how easily people get upset. They get upset when they don't win. They get upset when they do win, but they don't think it's enough. They get upset if they don't hit the jackpot. When they hit a secondary jackpot, they get upset that they didn't hit the top jackpot. And when they hit the top jackpot, unless it's something in the millions, they get upset as to why they couldn't hit it sooner. Are you this kind of player? Does this fit your playing profile? If it does, then you aren't patient. Playing casino games for profit can be a very prolonged experience, one which requires the utmost patience. Wins will happen, and although sometimes you may be lucky and get that good win right away, most of the time it will not come that easy. You will have to work for it for a while. This may require you to do several sessions, and perhaps even visit several casinos. Maybe it could mean that you will have to make several trips before you achieve that desired win goal. Setting achievable win goals is part of the art of patience.

Patience is not a skill or science; it is art. Skills can be learned. Science can be learned. But you must be born with the ability to be patient. You cannot *learn* to be that way. Fortunately, almost all human beings are born with that ability. The vast majority of us are born with the ability to learn languages, to deal with our environment through our senses, and to find out how to survive. These are all inherent abilities. We also have the ability to be patient. Unfortunately, the pace of our modern world rarely rewards patience, at least visibly. Although most achievements we see publicly are the result of hard work and a lot of patience, when we are made aware of these achievements they have already happened. To us, they seem to have happened overnight. The old story among actors who finally gain star status goes something like "After thirty years of acting, suddenly I'm an overnight success." This is true for many other disciplines, especially gambling. As a professional or semiprofessional player, one of the aspects of patience you will face constantly is the fact that you will be totally anonymous. The greatest mark of success for a gambler is that nobody knows about him. If you do this correctly, none of your friends will ever know. Perhaps only your spouse will know. Be that as it may, if you become a successful gambler, neither your friends, acquaintances, family, nor the casinos, will ever know (unless you brag about it; then there are other aspects of self-discipline you will have to deal with, as shown below).

Patience also means that you must be patient about your lifestyle and your successes. You can't be a braggart, because that will cost you your success. To others you must continue to be that anonymous tourist who keeps going to the casinos and feeding them with his money. This is the hardest part of patience and discipline. By all means, enjoy and flaunt the great events, such as when you hit what appears to be a lucky break, streak, long shot, or jackpot. Reinforce the belief that you were really lucky, and that every now and then you get lucky. After all, you worked for that luck, you deserve it. But then be patient, and go back to being anonymous.

Success in playing is not merely a once-in-a-lifetime blind luck event. You can be successful as a player each time you play (or at least most of the time), but only if you develop your art of patience. Notice I said *develop* rather than acquire. Like the ability to draw, you must practice and learn, learn from doing, and learn from mistakes. It won't be easy, but then nothing worthwhile is. Developing patience means that you will curb your natural reactions—the emotional bursts of exuberance when you win, anger when you lose. The first trick to developing the art of patience is to realize that great and glorious wins *will* happen and that equally great and horrendous *losses* will also happen. Second, develop your ability to curb your reactions to those extremes. Be happy when you win, but don't start expecting to win every time. Remember that the money you *don't* lose back today will spend very nicely tomorrow when you have a cooler head and a clearer perspective. Curb your reaction when you lose, too. Don't start to question yourself beyond reason. If you feel you have forgotten some part of your knowledge, look it up. See if you were correct, and if not, learn from the experience. When you realize that you did everything correctly and still suffered that great and horrendous loss, curb your instinct to blame everything and everybody, and try not to destroy yourself or the solid foundations of your playing abilities. Remember that pendulum of overall probability simply swung against you. It will swing back. That's the reality, and it will always happen like that. It may take what you consider a long time. The phrase "a long time" means something entirely different to us than it does to the universal event statistics. What you may consider "a long time" may in reality only be a tiny fraction of a microsecond in the overall scope of universal time.

It's all relative. If you play for two hours and you don't reach your win goal, was that losing streak "a long time"? Well, for you, perhaps. But the universe doesn't revolve around your particular perception of reality or length of time. Patience, therefore, is the art of being able to react to each situation *without overreacting to it.* You will have to work this out yourself, because no person is identical to any other, and no two people deal with the same set of circumstances in exactly the same way. Therefore, no specific advice is possible. However, a plausible *guideline* to achieving patience *is* possible, and that's what this section of this chapter is all about. By realizing that patience is a requirement for profit, you will become far more at ease with the process. This will relax you under a variety of circumstances and situations, which will in turn allow you to take a far more rational and less emotional approach to playing casino games.

BANKROLL

All the Keys to Winning are important, but Bankroll is perhaps the foremost. The reason is quite simple: Without money, you can't gamble. Gambling is all about money—losing it and winning it. You can't start without it. Even credit is money, and so is a credit line at the casino. It doesn't matter how you acquire your money, but whatever money you bring with you, send to the casino cage, or get in credit at the casino constitutes your bankroll. This is the money you have designated as your gambling stake. It should not be money you need for rent, mortgage, food, clothing, or health care. It should be accumulated "spare" money, something you can afford to lose without having a devastating impact on you and your family. Any gambling bankroll should be made up of money that you have designated as *expendable*. This doesn't mean that it should be treated as already lost, and hence treated recklessly; after all, it's still your money, and it still spends the same. Many people make the classic mistake of setting aside their gambling money with the conviction that it's already gone, dead, done, lost, and therefore it means nothing. Wrong! This is a defeatist attitude and definitely not a professional approach. Thinking like this will result in two inevitable occurrences. First, you have already convinced yourself that you are a loser, that you will lose, and therefore this money is already lost, so you will gamble recklessly, without thought or regard to the value of the money. As a result, you will play badly, you will make mistakes in the strategies you choose, and you *will* lose, thus reinforcing your conviction that "Ah, well, it was already lost. I knew it." You will be happy in your loss, therefore, because you convinced yourself that it was inevitable.

Second, you will not play knowledgeably and certainly not in concert with these Keys to Winning, or with the strategies so carefully crafted to avoid these occurrences. So, again, you will lose. When you do, this becomes yet another reinforcement of your initial starting attitude. "So," you now say to yourself, and quite possibly to anyone who will listen, "it was only gambling money. I knew I was gonna lose it, so what? It was my 'mad' money, anyway. Ah, well. Maybe next time." You have now thoroughly convinced yourself that you are a loser and justified your initial defeatist attitude by making sure that you lost. If this is how you think, throw this book away. The loser attitude has no place in life, and certainly none in gambling. Your bankroll is your lifeline; it is essential and should be valued, protected, and handled with care. In addition, it must be sufficient to carry the weight of your action.

Many people go to casinos to play, often with the conviction that they are—or can be—professional players. They bring a bankroll far less than what is required to start any kind of play on even the lowest-of-the-low games. Not only that, these people take that meager bankroll and go for the big, expensive bets. They start with the $25 and $100 games, or even higher. That's like going to the top of a bungee jump, unhooking yourself from the bungee cord tying a short shoelace to the tower instead, then smiling at the people around you as you jump off the tower to your inevitable doom. As silly as this sounds, so many people are guilty of this that it is unfathomable how this can continue. These people do this again and again. It becomes a self-defeating cycle for them, and they wonder why they "never seem to have enough" to win—another catchphrase of the perennial loser. Don't be like that. If you go to the casino to play, take enough money with you so that your starting bankroll is at least sufficient to support your action, the strategy you choose, or your expected action. Like the bungee cord, don't jump off if your action is designed for $2,000 and all you have is a $200 lifeline. The amount that should be in your bankroll must be determined by several factors.

First, it depends on what this money means to you at that time. If this money is truly unencumbered, you will feel a lot better about making it a true bankroll. If this money is not completely unencumbered, such as when a portion of it could be used for something else, but that something else is not one of the essentials to survival, you may not handle the bankroll as well or it may not be big enough. As a general rule, any gambling bankroll should always be made up only of entirely unencumbered money, no part of which is needed, or could be even considered as being needed, for something else. Unencumbered money is free and not scared. Encumbered money will always be scared money, and in gambling, scared money will fly away quickly. Playing with scared money means you are afraid to lose it. This doesn't mean that you have adopted the defeatist attitude discussed earlier. It simply means that you have allocated at least some part of your bankroll either as an inadequate amount, or being encumbered upon something else—perhaps borrowed from a credit card, which means you will have to pay it back, and probably have to do so at great stress to you, or your family. This is a very bad way to start your bankroll. Always start your bankroll with free money, which will become a solid gambling stake, not something you'll be frightened to lose.

Second, the amount of your bankroll should be determined by the kinds of games and strategies you intend to play. To use slots as an example, if you want to play $5 Reel Slots, your bankroll should reflect that action. If you want to play higher limits than that, your bankroll should be equally higher. If you plan to play $1 Reel Slots, or the Nickel Video Slots that require you to play $2.25 per spin (forty-five coins), your bankroll should adjust to that. Whatever your intended action, your bankroll should be adequate to withstand fluctuations, not only in your fortunes as you play, but also in your decisions concerning the *kinds* of games you will play. For example, you may have decided to play $1 Reel Slots on this trip and allocated your bankroll for that action, perhaps based on the $1 Reel Slots Strategy shown in this book. When you get to the casino, however, you discover that the kinds of machines you wanted to play are either occupied, unavailable, or no longer there. Now what? Your bankroll should have a "slush" factor, allowing it to withstand the necessity for such on-the-spot decisions. What if you saw another kind of machine, or game, perhaps something you have read about, and decided to play that instead? Your bankroll should be adaptable to such deviations from your initial starting strategy.

So, how do you arrive at the bankroll figure? Hard to say. It's individual to each player, and to you. You know yourself as well as your circumstances. All I can do is offer you *guidelines* with the hope that you will learn enough in this book to adapt this guideline to your specific situation. Each of the strategy methods you will read here has its own section on the recommended amount of bankroll necessary to play each strategy to its optimum potential, based on the minimum stake requirements. You can play each strategy at higher levels by simply increasing the value of each unit, being careful to accurately prorate the remainder of the wagering recommendations as they apply to each such method. However, you should not play these strategies at lower stakes.

If you play at stakes lower than those shown, you won't make nearly as much money, and may quite likely be forced to play on games or with rules that are not to your advantage. You should, therefore, stick to at least the minimum unit value amounts as shown and recommended in each strategy, using them in accordance with the stated rules and wagering differentials.

SELECTION

This is the part where "skill" in gambling comes into the picture. Many people believe that winning depends purely on luck. Though it is correct that some games are passive games—such as slots or Roulette—and, therefore, you cannot control the outcome of the event, it is not correct to say that playing such games involves no skills. I don't mean merely the skills of being able to play the game. I am referring to skills such as game selection, game detail, size of the wager, payout hierarchy, play methodology, size of bankroll, play duration, time when to play, and where to play. There is a lot more to being a winning player than just showing up in the casino, putting your money down, and hoping for the best.

Each of these skills is part of the "learning curve," and "comfort zone," which all of us have to reach. By acquiring these skills, you can become not only more knowledgeable, but also more comfortable. You will find that you are no longer a victim of the mere chance of luckily selecting just the right game at the right time, but in reality do so for the right reasons. You will now actually be able to approach your casino visit with the ability to specifically look for the kinds of games you know are among the better options, and do so with a solid plan of attack. Not only will this result in more confidence and comfort for you when you play, but also it will directly translate to regular profits. Although you won't win every time, or perhaps achieve your win goal every time you play, you will now be able to realize that this is a part of the overall approach to the game. You will no longer be a victim to such emotional swings as deep disappointment when you don't win or reckless exuberance when you do. Although curbing these emotional reactions is part of Patience, as discussed previously, and also Discipline, discussed later, the selection skills will contribute to your overall keys to winning in a way in which the casino games will no longer hold the "secret," but will divulge it to you, because you now know what to look for and how to do it to your best advantage.

Now let's take a look at some of the selection skills in more detail. Remember that even though each is important, the sum of the whole is far more crucial to your winning success than any single part. Often, you will have to make adjustments, even while you are playing, because in the real world not all of these skills will apply all the time—neither will all of the advice I am offering here, nor the guidelines.

Game Selection

This very important skill can be acquired through the Knowledge part of these Keys to Winning. Notice that while Patience was an "art," these are "skills". Game selection includes several items: What kind of game or machine? Reel Slots, Video Slots, Video Poker, other kinds of Slots? In which denomination? What kind of game? Blackjack? Roulette? Craps? At what limits? Which strategy will best apply to which game under which conditions and rules?

As with all these skills, the answers to these questions are all part of the overall picture. Your success in gambling depends on all of these abilities. Such answers will be supplied by yourself. The kind of machine or game and denomination may be determined by your bankroll, interest, or win goal. Other factors will influence how you approach the other skills among the skill of game selection. Generally, you should select a machine or game that is easy to play and understand. This is the simplest and best advice to get you started. From this point on, your skills will dictate further advancements in your play.

For the Slots Strategy: Machine Selection. This is also part of game selection because often machines and their games can be one and the same. However, many machines may have more than one game, such as multigame Video Slots. Other times, even simple single-game Reel Slots may have different games inside the cabinets. These games may look the same as the ones you have decided to select, but may not be. The easiest example is among Reel Slots that offer standard pays with the use of double symbols. There are many such games. Often, these games also have similar-looking symbols, but if you look closely you will notice that these are only "wild" symbols, and not the "double-up" symbols. This is also found quite frequently among similar-looking machines that may have the double symbols, but on one machine they also substitute for all the other symbols, as well as double the pay, while on the other machine they may only double *that* pay, but not act as "substitutes" for other symbols. Even though these machines look absolutely identical, there is a profound difference. You will find Reel Slots like this everywhere. This is also true of Video Poker games, where two identical looking machines can have extremely different pay and play programs (For more information, refer to my books *Powerful Profits from Video Poker,* and *Powerful Profits from Slots.*)

A host of such subtle differences exists among many of

these games. It is consequently even more important that your machine selection also includes comparisons. This will require a little legwork on your part, and some skills in observation. Among Reel Slots, this will be easier and faster, because you will mostly not have to look much beyond the belly glass of the game to find out what kind of symbols it has and what they do. Among the Video Slots, you will have to do more investigating. You will need to read the help and pay screens, learn the payoff and bonuses structure—and the amounts—then compare these with other machines of their kind, and especially to other machines that look the same. You can usually save yourself some time by first looking at the top Jackpot amounts, which should give you an indication about the differences in the machine's pay and bonus structure. There will be no substitute for your diligence and your ability to apply the skills and knowledge you have acquired. Your success as a slot player will, therefore, directly depend on your abilities to do these things.

Brand Names. This is closely tied in with the previous item. Machine and game selections are often influenced by the *manufacturer* of the game and machine. It's the same principle as shopping at the market or discount store. For example, you may plan on buying a certain brand of peanut butter. But you see a generic, or store brand, instead and buy that. It looks the same. It spreads the same. But it doesn't quite taste the same. What's the difference? Well, the price. You probably saved a few cents by buying that store brand. If you read the label on both jars of peanut butter, the list of ingredients may actually be the same. They may both say "contains whole crushed peanuts," but the product you bought for those few cents less just doesn't seem right. Most often the reason for this is—as far as peanut butter is concerned—that the *quality* of the peanuts is different. Like anything that grows, there are levels of quality. These levels of quality extend not just to the original peanut, but also to where it was grown, the soil conditions, and how often it was necessary to "medicate" the plant by spraying it with pesticides or growth additives. Then, how well was it roasted, ground, and prepared? How long has it been since it was bottled and shipped? And so on. All this influences the final "taste" of the product. The brand-name product may have consistency in quality, and hence taste, but the generic or store products may vary widely in quality and taste, because they may use ingredients from a wide variety of sources, regions, and quality. This doesn't mean that such generic products are always bad; many are just as good as, if not better than, their counterparts.

Among Slot Machines, this is similarly so. There are some very well-established "brand names" among manufacturers of Slot Machines. I consider IGT and Action Gaming (as well as Anchor Games) as the best Slot Machine "brands" and therefore the standard by which you can judge any Slot Machine or Video Poker Machine, its performance, its pay program, and its potential for your profitable play. One of the "secrets" of successful Slot play is the acquisition of knowledge regarding Slot Machine manufacturers, and familiarity with their products. Begin your machine and game selection by first identifying the brand names of the machines and games. Once you have done that, you will gain the standard by which to compare the other games available on the casino floor. Some machines and many games will look the same, or be very similar to the "brand name," but may not play or pay quite as well. By simply being able to recognize the brand name of the machine or game, you will be well on the way to making intelligent and informed decisions.

Size of the Wagers

This is part of your Bankroll discipline and will depend largely on which strategy you decide to play and with which game. These are very fluid concepts, because most of the actual details depend on your own personal circumstances. I cannot anticipate how you personally may approach this subject, but I can offer you some suggestions and guidelines. Once you have identified the details of what this game offers and how it plays and pays in accordance with whatever the house rules may be (or the pay programs if it is a machine), your next step is to decide how much you will invest. This is part of your bankroll decisions, but in this case we assume you have already settled on your bankroll for this method, and are now simply deciding how much to invest, and how many coins, or lines, you will play.

For the Reel Slots, this should be easy. Look for a two-coin machine with simple double-up symbols that also substitute for the other symbols. For other Reel Slot Machines, *you* must judge the kind of play that you will give them. If it's a straight "doubler" machine, you may wish to play only one coin. If it's a "buy-a-pay" machine, you should *always* play maximum coins, and so on, for whatever the required decision may be, based on your skills of applying the knowledge you have acquired.

Among Video Slots, this selection principle is more complicated. First, you must learn the details. Once you have done this, and now understand exactly what this machine is, and how it plays and pays, then you can decide how many coins you intend to play. Your first decision should be regarding the number of available paylines. If the machine has five lines, the absolute minimum must be five coins. If it has nine lines, then this is nine coins. And so on. This should be automatic for any such Video Reel Slot

Machine. *None* of these should be played with any fewer than the minimum one coin *per payline.* At least. Without this absolutely minimum action, you will be a loser no matter what you have learned, and if you even thought about playing such Video Reel Slots for any less than this absolute minimum, then you have not learned very much yet. But you will. You will learn this two ways. One is the easy way: follow this advice from the information gained here. The other is to play this way and realize that you have won, but didn't get paid because you didn't play at least that minimum of one coin per payline. Once you do this, you won't ever forget it. It is essential for any kind of play—and particularly any strategy play using these methods—that whenever you play any of these multiline Video Slots, you play *at the very least* the minimum one coin *per payline* to activate *all* the paylines. However, your decisions do not end there. In addition, you should determine whether you should play the *maximum* coins or not. This will depend on the other information about the machine and the game. All of this information becomes necessary when you make a decision that will cost you money. Some of these machines should *never be played for less than the maximum coins allowed.* This is because on these machines, you "buy a pay," and therefore if you play any less than the maximum bet, you will not get the best bonuses, the best pays, the Jackpots, and will not get the best payback percentage of which such a machine is capable by its play program. On other machines, which may look similar, or actually look the same, the best way to play them may be by the mere one coin per payline, because these machines do not offer the "extras" for maximum coin play. You have to find this out for yourself, then judge your wager selections accordingly. As a simple guideline, follow the Slots Strategy rules regardless of whether it is a reel machine or a video reel machine. This will help you overcome any decisions or questions, and will generally be a lot better for your success.

Size of Bankroll

This is a very important part of your playing discipline. Each strategy in this book has its own section about Bankroll, and the selection criteria as these apply to each strategy. Please refer to each of these as they appear in later chapters.

Play Duration

Similarly to the Bankroll selection, the duration of your play on that particular machine or game should be governed by the amount of money that you have allocated to this session and your ability to physically be able to sustain the play effort. This should first and foremost be determined by the *method* you are playing as listed for that particular game. However, there are some additional principles that apply universally. For example, no matter which strategy or method you are playing, or where you may be in its progression, if you get bored, stop. Being bored means you have lost interest in this game, and if you keep playing you will waste your money and your time, because you will not play the game—or the strategy—correctly and will easily lose sight of your win goals. It's a trap. Be aware of it. This applies particularly to Slots. Playing Slots, especially Reel Slots, can often get boring, notably when you play for several hours at a time. If your attention span is short, and you tire easily, or become upset, or gain any kind of a negative emotion, plan your play duration in short bursts. How short? Well, that depends on you. You will need to choose according to your own particular situation—personally, financially, psychologically, and emotionally. This doesn't mean you need to cancel any individual session you may be playing for whatever strategy you are employing, regardless of the game. If you feel tired and bored—simply stop, interrupt the sequence, but keep a note of where you are. Then rest, regain your composure, and resume the game at that point and continue the strategy. Although this is not the ideal situation, it is better to do this than to continue if you are mentally or physically drained. You may also choose to simply take the win (or loss) at whatever point you may be in the process of that method, and end there even though the method itself dictates otherwise. Only you can make these important decisions and will have to make them if you suffer any such fatigue or boredom. Though these are individual variations on the strategy principles and rules, none of these rules are such that they cannot be modified. Since by the time you go to play any of these strategies you will already have mastered them, and the games to which they apply, it shouldn't be hard to make these decisions. Just remember this simple rule modification at all times: If you are tired, bored, or somehow not functioning at your best, stop playing—the money you save today means that you won't have to win it back tomorrow. This will make your next session a lot easier to handle if you find yourself in these circumstances. Making good profits from gambling doesn't just mean winning—it also means saving losses.

Time When You Play

This will be affected by your general lifestyle. Most people get up in the morning to go to work at 9:00 A.M., come home after 5:00 P.M., then have dinner, and so on, and go to bed.

This dictates the kind of lifestyle they lead. Coming to a casino, most people entirely forget this, and start to act as if there were no need to sleep, rest, or do anything other than indulge in total abandonment. That is okay. There's nothing better than to become that free. For a while, that is, and without losing your head and your money while doing it. Unfortunately, many people get so wrapped up in this sudden freedom that they forget their rational mind. That is bad. If you want to have this "mad time," it is perfectly okay to do so. Just be aware that it will cost you money and may cost you your well-made plans as well. Once you interrupt your routine, you will become trapped in paradise and can easily lose sight of even the most basic human reason. If this happens to you, you are lost, at least for the duration of this trip. But fear not. It can be overcome. When you plan your trip to the casino, regardless of whether you happen to live next door or have to plan a vacation to fly or drive there, you will become enthusiastically enthralled in the experience. Plan for it, and that way you will be able to allocate time, resources, energy, and bankroll to these experiences. You will then realize that's part of your casino plan and will have a great time enjoying it. Then, when you tire yourself out, remind yourself that it's time to get rest and regain your composure and reason, because now it will be time to go and play to win. Playing to win requires a clear head and a rested body. This becomes even more important when applying any of these strategies and methods in an actual casino situation.

Such dedication—with a clear mind and rested body— will also require you to make some adjustments to your "normal" lifestyle and life's schedule. Playing to win may require you to play at "odd" hours, because that's when the pickin's are good. For example, most people tend to crowd around the games at dinner time and just after. Bad time.

Everyone plays then, and the selections are few and far between. If possible, play either very late at night, such as after midnight, or very early in the morning, such as from about 5:00 A.M. The best time to play is usually from about 3:00 A.M. until about 9:00 A.M. This is the time in between the end of the rush from the night before, and prior to the rush from the "normal" morning risers, who play before and after breakfast. There are very good reasons for this kind of play. First, there will be fewer players. You will have better choices among the games and therefore be able to make better selections. You will also get better service from the employees, because there are fewer people for them to look after. Second—if your play is on Slots—the machines you will select are quite likely to have been given a lot of play the night before and therefore more primed for your skilled selections and play. In fact, if you want to do this and can handle it physically, stay up for some hours during the busy times the night before, and watch the machines you think you will want to play. Don't play, just watch. See which machines get the heaviest play and what, if anything, they have paid out. This kind of prior research can serve you well when you rise early the next morning and go hit the machines before the day crowd hustles in. Of course, you may want to go to bed early so you *can* get up early. Fine. You can still get the information you want by asking the employees. They may not know for sure, because they have just come on duty after the swing shift leaves at 2:00 A.M., but I can assure you that if there was any kind of a significant win on the previous shift, these people in that same area will have heard about it. Although this is nothing more than simple empirical research, and is only useful as a guideline, and just one more piece in the overall informational supply, it provides a good gauge by which to modify your game selections. As a general rule, try to play whenever other people are not playing. Stay away from crowds and times when machines and tables are crowded. That's not the time to play. That's the time to watch and learn and remember.

There are, however, some games to which this may not apply. The Craps strategies, for example, are better played during busy times so that you can get your bets in and exploit the game while the dealers and pit staff are too busy to pay too much attention to you. This can also apply to Blackjack, under some circumstances. Playing with the Blackjack Strategy as shown in this book also means that you are timing your number of hands; therefore, the faster you can get through the sessions the better. At busy times this will mean an extra hour, perhaps an hour and a half. During less busy times you can accomplish this in half that time. The same applies to the Roulette Strategy. At busy times the spins will be few and far between as the dealers take care of the multitude of other players. This will not only mean that you will have to spend several hours per session, but it will also make it more difficult for you to place your bets. These are some of the details, and nuances, of play that you will have to determine for yourself. Generally, Craps, Pai Gow Poker, and Let It Ride are perhaps the only games that should be played during busy times, while all the other strategies should be played during the off-hours. Of course, these decisions are part of your overall game and time selection skills, and by the time you get to them you should be well skilled in how you approach each and every decision and method. Again, these are only guidelines, because each casino—and each game within each casino—will be a little different every time you play or come in. Your overall profits will be enhanced by your ability to select the right game at the right time, along with the appropriate method and wagering strategy. You can acquire these skills only after becoming thoroughly experienced not only in the games and their methods, but also with the casino environment and this playing lifestyle. Each reader of this book will have a different "rhythm" to their play, as such applies to their own lifestyle and personality. You may be best equipped to play as I recommend, while another reader may be better off playing precisely at the times I suggest avoiding. Each of you will be able to make that decision for yourself as it best fits.

Casinos: Where to Play and What Kinds of Games to Play There

Which casinos to play in? Well, if you live near one, or two, and that's it, then your choices are simple, provided these are the casinos you want to visit. Generally—in the United States—the best casinos are in Las Vegas, Nevada. Games in the state of Nevada are usually much better than any other state, while those in Las Vegas are the best of all anywhere. On the East Coast of the United States, games in Connecticut are better than in Atlantic City. If you want to know which casinos in the Midwest offer the better games, I refer you to the *Midwest Gaming and Travel* magazine, published in Waseca, Minnesota. You can look it up on the Web under the same name. Overall, nothing can beat the games in Las Vegas; they are the best, and with the best variety as well as the most of the newest games and machines.

DISCIPLINE

Of all the Keys to Winning, this one sounds the simplest, but it is the hardest of all. We all understand the value of discipline, especially when it comes to our money. This is accentuated when we talk about the casino environment.

Everything in the casino is designed to separate us from any sense of reality. The casinos are a wondrous land, where everything seems possible—as long as you have money. Money is the lifeblood of all of this excitement. Without it, you are nothing more than dead wood, and you will be flushed out in a hurry. Having discipline as part of your winning objectives saves you from the inglorious fate of being washed clean, hung out to dry, and tossed away.

Having discipline as part of your tricks of the trade when you go gambling simply means to make the commitment to play wisely, with reason, and with goals in mind. If you want to have your "mad time," budget for it, realize it, recognize it, and place it as part of your overall game plan. Even that will then become part of your discipline.

Making a commitment to self-discipline when going to the casino is very easy. *Keeping to it* once you get there is extremely hard. So hard, in fact, that the vast majority of all people who arrive at the casino completely convinced they will not allow this experience to get the better of them, do just that. And fast, often as soon as they walk through the door. Suddenly, they see the excitement, the games, the flashing lights, the sounds of money and chips—the entire atmosphere captures them. In the door they go, and out the door go their well-meaning and carefully conceived plans, their sense of discipline, and all their other senses as well. It happens to just about everyone, even hardened veterans of the casino lifestyle. All of us are human beings, and we are not perfect. We have failures, and lack of discipline is the greatest failure of all. We see it everywhere around us. For example, schools no longer teach discipline. Rowdy and disruptive students are no longer punished. They are "counseled" instead. We are producing a society where adults have no idea of what discipline is. When they are faced with it, as when they enter the workforce, or the armed services, they are in complete shock. No wonder, then, that most people who go to casinos can't understand what "discipline" really is and how it applies to their gaming success or financial failure.

To offer the easiest guideline, discipline in gambling simply means to remain conscious of the value of your money, and of your desired goals and objectives. It means, mostly, to not allow yourself to be drawn into the very comfortable, but very financially deadly, sense of "why not, it's only money" syndrome. Once you have experienced the casino lifestyle a few times, you will often hear many people say things like that. These people are trapped in the losses that they have incurred and are now trying to rationalize it for themselves. They don't actually expect anyone else to listen to them, or to really understand what expressions such as this really mean. They have just resigned themselves to the loss of all their money, and to the "I no longer care" attitude. That's the danger sign. Once you stop caring about the value of the money you are using to play— or are winning—then you have lost the discipline which comes with realizing that this money isn't just coins, tokens, or gaming chips. This money actually *spends*. Therefore, discipline really means just to remember this, and play accordingly. Such a perspective is important in any kind of gambling, but particularly so if you plan to play professionally. A loss of discipline to any significant extent will defeat the best of any strategy and method of play. Without discipline and dedication, no matter how good you may be in your strategy play, you will eventually lose. This is, perhaps, the most important lesson you must learn—even before you get to the strategies themselves.

However, being disciplined in your approach to your gambling definitely does *not* mean that you must be, or should be, a miser. Playing too carefully is also a prescription for disaster. I have already mentioned that "scared" money flies away quickly. Don't play that way. To win, you must play aggressively and with a sufficient bankroll to justify your level of action. All of this is covered in the other Keys to Winning, and in the rules and methods of each strategy. Discipline is the glue that holds it all together—but if ever the glue stops holding, it all falls apart.

WIN GOALS

What is a win goal? In simplest terms, a win goal is the realistic expectation of a certain win amount based on the potential of available wins relative to the bankroll allowed, session stake allocated, expertise at the game, strategy used, plus time at the game. This simple formula will equal your end-result profitability in winning situations, and end-result saving of money—which would otherwise have been lost—in negative situations.

For example, most gamblers will say that a 2 percent win goal over and above the session stake is a very great achievement. The casino, for example, has a win goal of around 2 percent for most Blackjack games, around an average of 5 percent for Slots, and about 20 percent over all the games they offer. Some games make them more money because people play them badly. Although basic Blackjack, for example, can be played to less than 0.5 percent casino advantage, most players will play the game so badly that the casinos actually yield anywhere from 2 percent to 6 percent, and often even more, on a game which can actually yield a *player* advantage—if played properly and with skill.

For Slots, the average expectation is around 5 percent to perhaps 8 percent, depending on the casino, where it is located, and what the competition is like. In Las Vegas, the casinos strive for approximately 5 percent as their *average* win goal for all of their Slots combined. Sometimes more, sometimes less, but overall around this figure. The reality is, however, that the Slots will pay the casino much more. Overall, the casinos will get about 80 percent of all their revenue from Slots, and their average win goal expectation over all their machines turns out to be around 12 percent, and sometimes more. The reason is, primarily, that slot players play badly. They choose machines that don't offer the best value or which offer low payoffs and low payback programs, and they generally play like silly children—amazed at everything regardless of the price.

The difference between the casino and the player is that the casino can easily have a much lower win goal, because their doors are open 24/7/365. Their games make money all the time, without ever needing a rest or a break. Human players can't play like that. Though the casino can easily offer a game from which it can reasonably expect only less than 1 percent profit, it will get this all the time, always, over the short term as well as the long haul. You, the player, can't play like that. Therefore, whenever gamblers say to me that they expect a 2 percent return and consider this as good, I politely tell them that's great, and quietly chuckle. These "gamblers" are trying to play like the casino, trying to beat the casino at their own game of survival, trying to "outlast" the overall game percentages. This will result in nothing more than the gambler's eventual ruin and a whole lot of frustration in between.

Gamblers in general must have win goals not only commensurate with their bankroll, session stakes, and so on, but also with the realization that their exposure to the game will only be a very short slice of the game's overall event-reality. Therefore, such win goals cannot—and should not—be measured in percentages relative to the way that the casinos figure their own odds and win goals. Rather, these win goals should be measured in terms of what the game *can yield,* especially if played correctly, and if selected in accordance with the various selection criteria required. It is also important at this point to introduce a derivative of the win goal criterion, called the win expectation. The win goal is what you have set as your desired objective, realistically based on the various principles already amply demonstrated. The win *expectation,* however, is based within the reality of the game itself and, most specifically, in that very short-term slice of that one specific game's event experience.

For example, if you are playing the Slots Strategy on a $1 Reel Slot Machine that takes two coins as maximum, with a session bankroll of $100, and whose top jackpot is $2,500, with a secondary jackpot of $800, your win *goal* should be the top jackpot and/or the secondary jackpot. Otherwise, why play it? However, based on the event-occurrence of that specific very short-term slice of your exposure to this machine and game, your win *expectation* should be twenty coins, or $20. This is a 20 percent improvement over and above your starting session stake. Where else can you get such a big return on your investment that quickly? And what if you don't hit the Jackpots, and only make a $5 profit, falling far short of the win expectation as well as the win goal. Have you lost anything? You still made money. And that's the most important part of both your win goals and your win expectations. *Be glad you got what you got.* Remember that here— in this example—you are playing a slot machine, which means you are playing a game with an in-built house edge, and therefore *a game with a negative expectation.* This means the game will always make money for the casino in the end. If you hit it for *any* kind of a win, then you have caught the game at the right time and made money *in spite* of the fact that it's a negative-expectation game. If your stock rose by $5 per share, you'd be ecstatic, right? Well, why complain if your session at this slot machine resulted in only a $5 win? Any win means you have beaten the game. Be glad you did. Put it away, and set yourself up for the next session.

To continue with this example, what if you lost instead of winning? What if this machine was just a real dog, and no matter how well you have selected it, and played it, you just picked the bad one at a bad time. It will happen. In fact, overall, you will pick a winning machine (or game), or have a winning session, only about 40 percent of the time (the actual percentage is 41 percent of the time, based on my analysis—see Blackjack Strategy for details). However, if you do it correctly, your *overall wins* will more than compensate for your losing sessions, and you will still wind up a winner in the end. So, this machine was a bad one, and your end-of-session result was a loss of $75. More than two-thirds of your session stake. This is about as bad as it can get. You suffered a 75 percent loss of your session bankroll—but the point is, you still have $25, or 25 percent, of your session stake left. It all adds up. Put it away, mark it as your session result, and move on to the next session. In the next session, you may have a $75 win. So, the sessions combined, you are even and have accumulated Slot club points and comps besides. What about the next session? There you may make that $5. So, now you are ahead by 5 percent, along with the accumulation of all your Slot club points, comps and freebies, and have done so despite the fact that your first session was such a devastating loss. The point is that throughout your casino visit no playing session is ever independent of your other sessions. All your playing sessions are *combined* to reveal the profits over the entire block of all sessions brought together. Whatever results you have achieved at that point determine your average per session win expectation percentage and your win goal achievement levels. This information can be used by you to more accurately reflect how well you played; it can then be used to modify your goals and expectations for future sessions. But you must take *everything* into account, even the value of all the additions you have earned, such as your comps and freebies and club points. All of this combines to affect your goals, expectations, and final relative results.

This now brings us to the final item in this chapter, the overall win goals and overall win expectation. This is set by you based on bankroll, skill, and other abilities, as stated here in this book, as well as whatever other information and skills you may have acquired. If you have understood what I have attempted to illustrate, your total win goal for your casino visit should be directly relative to your bankroll and comfort level at the games, as well as your other gaming and playing skills, including selection skills. As a guide, your overall win *goal* should be to double your bankroll. Your win *expectation* should be to come home with 20 percent over and above your bring-in bankroll. If you achieve anything close to this, then you have just beaten the casino, and you have done what only less than 1 percent of all casino players are able to do. You have become a good, knowledgeable, and responsible player. Congratulations!

Practicing these playing principles, even though your general approach to gambling may not be as your primary source of income, is very different from the perception held by most people. The "allure" of the professional gambler is a myth. I call this the "James Bond" syndrome, which is a significant misperception among the general public about what the life of a professional gambler is really like. This was not always so, but has become part of the mind-set of most people over the past fifty years, certainly from the time of the first Bond film in the early 1960s. The suave, sophisticated, perfectly manicured and made up, well-dressed gentleman with the martini (shaken, not stirred) and an endless supply of money and blondes (not necessarily in that order) are all entertaining to watch, but have no bearing on reality. Many high rollers actually do try to appear like this, aspire to this, or attempt to put across this sort of persona, but usually not professional gamblers. They are very wealthy people who like to pretend and can afford to buy this illusion with the millions they lose at the tables. That's why the casinos love them, want them, and seek them out. If these players were consistently beating the casinos out of the tens of millions of dollars they instead lose, the casinos would be in trouble and would most likely bar such players from their casinos, instead of sending their private jets out to retrieve them.

The reality of the professional gambler is a lot different from this "image," popularized in TV and film, and by some of the more visible wealthy high rollers, known as "whales" in casino parlance. The true professional gambler, and certainly the semiprofessional player, who enjoys success lives in a world that is filled with the complete *lack* of the so-called trappings of success. These are players whose actual survival directly depends on their ability to win money. Most of these players play for what could be considered small stakes. Perhaps $4,000, $5,000, or $8,000 per month, maybe more. These people pay their bills, feed their families, and invest for their retirement directly from the wins they make from the casino games they play. They mostly make an average income, depending on the level of action they can give. Some make about $45,000 per year, some more, some very much more. A few even in the millions. However, the majority of such players—those who are true pros—are found in the medium-income category. They could easily be employed in a variety of jobs, any of which would probably pay them a comparable salary or wage. They choose, instead, to make their living at gambling. The main attraction is the relative freedom that this lifestyle can embody. There's no set time to go to work, for example. When you don't feel like working that day, or week, or month, you don't have to. You can leave at any time and come back later, or not. You don't have to do the same thing or be at the same place every day. You don't have a boss, or a "hierarchy" at work to worry about, and nobody is lording over you looking for an excuse to get you fired, or stab you in the back, or use you as a climbing stone to their clamber up the ladder. These are all powerfully meaningful reasons why this lifestyle can be so attractive.

There is, of course, also the downside. You have no steady paycheck, no retirement insurance, no health insurance, no employer contributions to your IRA, no job security, and no benefits. All of this you have to handle for yourself from your winnings. You also have the responsibility to properly catalog your action and file and pay your correctly itemized taxes. This often means you will have to employ a good CPA to make sure you have the proper tax forms filed correctly. Although you will have the possibility for several tax breaks, credits, and refunds, you will nevertheless be scrutinized carefully, and all your action should be well documented and reported. Among all of these requirements, add this one as your number one priority: Do not cheat the government! Report everything as best as you are able, and be honest. If you wind up owing taxes, make arrangements to pay them off. Trying to save a few dollars by underreporting, or not reporting your income, will bite you. Maybe not now, or in a year, but at some point. If you want to be a pro— or play like one—make these arrangements before you ever start, and then maintain your records. If you have a regular job, your employer does most of this for you—that's how you get your withholdings already made for you, and how you get the W-2 forms already nicely completed. As a gambler, you don't get this because now you are responsible. You see, it's not all just great clothes, great dames, and dry martinis (shaken or stirred).

The reality of the professional gambler embodies not

only all of the required knowledge, skills, and art of the game, but also a lot of tedium, both in life as well as "on the job." There's nothing in the world as tiring as having to sit at a gambling game day after day, week after week, and perhaps month after month, and not be winning, all the while seeing your precious life's bankroll slipping away. That's the greatest danger faced by any professional gambler, and it is usually called the "Gambler's Ruin." Simply put, this means that long losing streak, that inevitable situation where he will lose no matter how good he is at the game and the strategy or method he is using. It will happen, and sometimes it happens to the hapless professional, and if it does it is a test of courage and endurance few can handle well, or live through. To be properly prepared for this also means that you will have to come to terms with the reality of the gambling world and forget all of the theories and hype. The reality is a simple fact: The games are mostly set against you, and to win you will have to not only overcome this, but swing it positively in your favor and then also do this to a point where it will actually result in a meaningful income. This is extremely hard to do, and even harder to do consistently. It can be done, but it is far from glamorous.

Finally, there's the loneliness. You will constantly be in a casino that is crowded with people having a great time. You will be facing the influence of free drinks, free food, free promotions, and so on and on. You will have to carefully select which of these are to your advantage, and which are not. Most of these fun things are not to your advantage. They are there to influence the gregarious masses who come to enjoy themselves and freely spend their money. That's what the casinos want, that's what they're in business for, and that's what they count on. You, on the other hand, are there for everything *other* than this—although you *can* have a good time at your job (which this is), you are there to win money. To do this you need to be able to concentrate and avoid these distractions. You need to *appear* as just another customer happily losing money, yet all the while knowing that you are not. You will need to reinforce the image of the loser, especially if you become known as a regular, and a regular player, in one or more casinos. Finally, you will need to be anonymous. Even if you make friends among other players, or friends outside of the casino, or with the casino employees, at no time can you ever tell them what you are really doing. Even if they try to "teach" you how to play better—according to what they think they know—you have to be polite, listen, not be distracted, and go on with your own play without trying to teach them the truth. No matter who, no matter how or when, your success is directly related to your anonymity. The most successful professional gamblers—the true pros and not those fanciful gamblers who play *at* being pros because they can afford it—are measured by the lack of knowledge about them. The best gamblers are people you never heard of. When Ken Uston and his Blackjack teams were hitting the Nevada and Atlantic City casinos for millions of dollars in the 1970s, no one knew about them. That's what made them successful. To this date you mostly won't know even who his team players were. You may know about Uston himself, because you may have read the books. But that was long after the teams had made their money, and neither Uston nor his team players were playing professionally anymore. The point is that while you are doing it, no one should know who you are and what you do and how you do it. If you choose to write about it later—as I am doing—that's perfectly okay. You have decided to show yourself, and to make the rest of your life into a different career, such as Uston did, and others like him, when they became gambling-book authors instead of pure gamblers and professional players as they used to be. This, too, is lonely, and hard.

If you're prone to being a "sociable" player, or person,

think hard before you commit to the life of the professional gambler. You may not be cut out for it simply because of your personality. You must enjoy being alone, spending long hours by yourself, and even longer years. To truly become good, you will require practice. Even if you learn all of these Keys to Winning, and then learn the strategies, having first mastered the games themselves, even then you can't just walk in and hit it big. This is a *process,* and *not* a once-in-a-lifetime score. It will take time, and it will take a lot of learning, adapting, and practicing. It took me ten years of learning and playing before I was able to do this success-fully, and even then I could only maintain that level of ded-ication for a relatively short time. I started somewhat late in life, and that also had an impact. Professional gambling is a young person's game—the older you get the harder it will be to maintain the physical requirements and the mental sharp-ness. Young players giggle at this because they feel invinci-ble. After they hit forty-five, they suddenly realize it's not as easy as it once seemed. The point is that being a professional involves a lot of areas of personal lifestyle, discipline, and abilities well beyond merely the casino games themselves, or the strategies you choose to use. We all have our strengths and weaknesses. Knowing which are which, and how far to push them, will eventually determine whether you are a successful player, or if perhaps you are good but should look for a different line of work as your main source of in-come. There is nothing to be ashamed of—the shame would exist only in trying to deny the reality of what, and who, you really are. Once you know, the rest becomes a lot easier.

Of Men and Math

Many professional gamblers enjoy a high profile. These players have reached a certain status in their profession and have become known through their accomplishments and the media reports of their wins. Most are professional poker players, such as those who win the World Series of Poker, the World Poker Championships, or, more recently, are featured on the television program "World Poker Tour." Such players generally become household names, at least in the poker community and the gambling community at large. As their names become well known, they often parlay this notoriety into other businesses, such as sponsorships, endorsements, or their own poker-related books, websites, or businesses. This is good press for the gambling industry, which was viewed as some kind of a "sin" until just a few years ago.

There is a big difference between players who become known because they win big and those who become known because of their work as gamblers. Players who win big may not be professional gamblers, even though they sometimes like to be known that way. Such players can be your Aunt

Millie who wins the Wheel of Fortune progressive Jackpot on her favorite 25-cent Slot Machine, and because she plays there every day the local press dubs her the "Queen of the Professional Gamblers." Just because she plays that machine every day doesn't make her a professional gambler—it simply makes her a frequent casino player—the very kind that the casinos like to attract in large numbers. Although there are professional Slot teams—groups of players bankrolled by a specific individual or syndicate, who then play all the progressive machines in a particular location until one of them hits the Jackpot—players like Aunt Millie aren't really professional gamblers and neither are the Slot teams.

What defines a true professional gambler is more akin to a combination of factors, such as skill, reliance on winning as a sole means of income, general anonymity, ability to blend in, be seen, be known, but yet remain unknown for his accomplishments, and perhaps avoiding the spotlight. Many of the great Poker players of the world are described as "professional" gamblers, although in recent times that meaning has been somewhat altered from its original perspective. Back in the glory days of legalized gambling in Nevada, around the time that the Flamingo was built in 1948 and 1949, there were quite a few "gamblers" who later became part of gambling folklore. There are many books about these "old timers," so I will just mention three: Benny Binion, Johnny Moss, and Nick "the Greek" Dandalos. Benny Binion came from Texas to Las Vegas and opened the Binion's Horseshoe Casino in downtown Las Vegas, where it still stands. To this day, it is the home of the World Series of Poker, perhaps the world's best-known gambling tournament. Sometime around 1949, Nick the Greek asked Benny to put on a Poker showdown between himself and Johnny Moss to find out who was the best gambler in the world. Benny agreed on the condition that the match be played in public view. So, for the next five months Nick the Greek and Johnny Moss played

Poker in the window of Binion's Horseshoe Casino, while crowds of interested onlookers gathered to watch. Johnny Moss eventually beat Nick the Greek and walked away with the $2 million, or so, in money won.

That game was the basis for what later became the World Series of Poker. Some twenty-one years later, in 1970, a half-dozen or so of the world's best Poker players gathered at Binion's Horseshoe Casino in Las Vegas for what was then dubbed the "World Series of Poker," the name now synonymous with high-stakes professional Poker and gambling tournaments, and with professional gamblers. Johnny Moss again won the title, as he did the next year. He was perhaps the best ever all-around pure Poker player in recent history. And so the legend was born, and still today that very same series attracts worldwide attendance and publicity. The winners achieve almost mythical stardom in the world of tournament Poker, and gambling in general. Books about them, the games, and the various gamblers abound—which help to dispel the lingering myths about the corrupt nature of gambling. With over 8,000 entrants into each World Series of Poker, the total prize money is more than $20 million, with the first prize for the championship event topping $2 million plus. This is truly high-stakes action by any standard. You can often hear or read about these players betting $200,000 or more per hand during such tournaments. It sounds "risky," but what you may not realize is that these players are not playing with their own money. This is not the kind of "money" that pays utility bills and buys dinners and clothes. This is "tournament money," and a wager of $200,000 is not a wager with "real money," but one with "tournament chips."

Yes, it is correct that all participants in such gambling tournaments must buy in with real money, and even though such amounts may seem large, they are nothing like the amounts that these players will be wagering during the tournament. The buy-in into the World Series of Poker Championship event is $10,000 in cash, and all entrants start with $10,000 worth of tournament chips. So, in a way, they are playing with real money—up to a point. You see, the majority of the entries are from either sponsors, backers of players, or from participants who have won their way into the championship through what are called "satellites." A satellite entry costs about $125. Several of the recent world champions won their way into this tournament by spending only this amount of "real" cash. Even if you are among the few who actually pay the $10,000 to get into the tournament, eventually you will be wagering amounts much larger than this. If you win and have all the chips, you won't get to "cash them in," because their combined total value is more than the prize for the winner. You're still only playing with $10,000 in your "real cash," and all the rest is just play money. It therefore becomes a lot easier to risk a wager of $200,000, or more, per hand, because your objective is to win the tournament—or at least get into the money—rather than to win that pot right then and there and walk away with the real cash winnings. This is the major difference between tournament play and ring games. Tournament players are often very good at winning tournaments, and many of them make several hundred thousand dollars each year as their income. In that sense, they are professional gamblers. However, these same players are often very bad at the ring games, where the objective is to make the profit from each pot won, and not from outlasting everybody else until you are the only one left. In ring games, players who go broke can buy back in, and then can beat you, regardless of how much you won from them until that point. This doesn't happen in the major tournaments, because they are all freeze-out, with no rebuys. For this reason, many professional Poker players cannot really be called professional *gamblers,* because they play for a finish with a pot of gold at the end, not for sustained profits from day-to-day wins. The late, and great, Poker champion Stu Unger was a terrific gambler—at many games and not just Poker. He won the World Series of Poker three times. When he died—sadly very young—he was broke and living in a cheap motel in Las Vegas. Why? Well, he was a *gambler,* and he would wager on everything and anything, at any time. But even he was *not* a *professional* gambler, because he couldn't sustain the wins. One story about his exploits illustrates the point. Shortly after winning the World Series of Poker the second time, with a record $1 million in prize money, Stuey (as he was affectionately known) lost $900,000 of it the very next day in a ring game.

His story serves to illustrate the wider chasm of difference between tournament Poker players and real-world professional gamblers. Although many of the great players are absolutely marvelous at playing in Poker tournaments, they can be hopelessly outclassed in ring games, or in other forms of gambling that require winning to be immediate, compact, and consistent. It is this "immediacy" that separates the successful ring players from the tournament pros. Even though the tournament pros get most of the attention, and can win big prizes, the real professional gamblers are those who play in the ring games, day in and day out, and actually make a living by winning a little each day, just like a salary. Mostly you won't ever hear about them, and that's the point—a professional gambler wants to be anonymous, for many reasons. Although successful tournament players gain notoriety and publicity, they can't translate this into steady and regular casino wins, so the casinos don't mind them because they mostly lose when they play anything other than tournaments, and also because their names bring other gamblers into their casinos. In 1949, when Johnny Moss won that $2 million from Nick the Greek Dandalos, it was Nick's money he won, not "tournament" chips. These players cut their teeth, so to speak, on real gambling games, and Poker was just one of the games they could beat for consistent profits. Now, in the twenty-first century, these two fields have become significantly polarized. Those who are highly successful tournament players are often very bad gamblers and terrible ring game players. Conversely, those who are very good ring game players are very often lousy tournament players. Although it is true that there are several well-known players who can successfully play in both, they are the exception rather than the rule. Most of the time—since the world of gambling has become so specialized—those who are good at ring games stay there, and those who are good at tournaments play only those, and little else, unless it's for recreation, charity, or media events. Yet even these are not the kinds of players who may be considered truly all-round professional gamblers.

This "specialization" in gambling has become necessary largely because of the way the casinos altered many of the rules of playing, such as the alterations to Blackjack games, making it much harder to win than it was in the days of Moss, the Greek, and even as recently as Uston and his Blackjack card-counting teams. Those who go after the really big money fast are now mostly relegated to the various gambling tournaments, because that's where the biggest money can be won the fastest, with the least up-front financial risk. For someone who makes, say, $300,000 per year in income, buying into a tournament for $10,000, $5,000, or $2,500 seems a small price. Since there are only about a dozen or so of these tournaments per year, such players can be expected to invest around $150,000 or so of their own money buying into these events, playing one such tournament per month. In a year, all they have to do is finish in the top twenty most of the time to make twice their money back in prize money, but often they make many times more. Several such well-known Poker tournament players make around $500,000 per year—and never win a tournament (or actually get crowned as the winner—many times the final few players make "deals," and because of that the top money winner may not actually turn out to be the winner of the tournament).

There are tournaments for Blackjack players, for Slot players, and for players of other casino games, but they are not very popular, and certainly not nearly as profitable as the Poker tournaments. The reason for this is the skill factor, and the clear mathematical definabilty of the game of Poker. Most traditional Poker games are played with a fifty-two-card deck. This makes it quite easy to calculate the relative potential holding of an opponent by keeping track of cards as they are dealt and by extrapolating the percentages of relative holdings by odds of occurrence. Many Poker books break this down to a pure science. Also, Poker is the only casino game where the casino doesn't participate directly—they merely facilitate the game. All the action is between the players. The casino takes a "rake," a percentage of each ring game pot, for example, as its "fee" for facilitating the game; other than that the action is all between the players. Other casino games are called "house banked games," because your action is directly against the casino. In such games the casinos can alter the rules, pay off at less than true odds, and thus assure themselves of a mathematical win all the time, on each such game where this results in a player negative expectation. Even though such a negative player expectation may be low—such as a mere 0.02 percent in Craps with 100 times odds, or 0.5 percent in Blackjack with Basic Strategy—it still makes money for the casino, regardless of what the players do. Not so in live Poker, because there the players play against each other; the casino—the house—can't change the rules or alter the game or the payoffs. That's why the casinos charge the "rake," and why live Poker is the only game that can consistently be played for profit. This is also why many professional gamblers play this game almost exclusively and why it is this game that has attracted worldwide attention as the premier tournament game. Of course, this also means that the kind of professional gambling that was possible in the 1940s, '50s, '60s, and even into the '70s and '80s is now all but impossible. It is because of this difficulty in beating the traditional casino games that most professional players have turned to either live Poker ring games or the Poker tournaments. These are perhaps the only two remaining and relatively "safe" vestiges of professional gambling.

All of the "accepted" and "traditional" strategies for beating casino games have been rendered virtually useless by the casino's relentless meddling with the rules of the games, such as changing the Blackjack payoffs from 3:2 to 6:5 and having machines shuffle games. Casinos keep trying these gimmicks, and they always bite them in the butt in the end. In the mid to late 1960s and early '70s, casinos tried to change the rules of Blackjack so severely that they nearly killed the game. Then in the 1980s the Slots took over, and casinos ripped out table games by the hundreds because they thought Slots would "work for free" all the time; they turned casinos into arcades. Now, they are trying to change the rules of Blackjack again and alter the dealing and shuffling procedures, which will result in the game losing its popularity even further. Many casinos are getting rid of their table games altogether because of the labor costs, taxes, and table costs, but removing all table games would turn the casinos into video arcades, limiting the appeal of the casino experience.

Though in the 1960s and '70s the changes to games like Blackjack were made largely to combat the perceived advantages by skilled card counters, these days such changes are motivated purely by corporate greed. Most of the largest casinos are owned and operated by publicly traded corporations, and because of this they seem to think that exploiting the customers results in more casino profits. Although this will succeed in the short term—because most casino players don't understand they are being exploited—eventually the casinos will suffer a backlash like the one they did in the late 1970s and early '80s and will have to liberalize their games again. It is a disgrace in the gaming industry that many casinos have changed Blackjack payoffs from 3:2 to 6:5. If you find a casino that pays Blackjack as 6:5, tell the pit boss you are leaving because of this and will not play there again until they change it back. Also, avoid all Blackjack games using shuffling machines.

Many "traditional" methods, and systems, for beating the casino games have been developed over the years. Some were hugely successful for a time, such as Thorp's 10-count, and the later Hi-Lo count (which I called the PM Count in my Blackjack book), but none of these can be played any longer to anything like their theoretical potential. This has placed even "good" casino games into the realm of the negative expectation games. Although even today the expert card counter can still find a few Blackjack games where absolutely perfect card counting can still yield an overall profit, these are very rare, and very few players can actually do this. It is simply no longer true that "established" strategies can work as well as they once could, and as their theory allows. Many people—writers, commentators, and players—still claim that the mathematical realities of casino games cannot be overcome. I agree—if we are speaking in universal terms within the infinity model. As long as we consider this in the universal sense, where there is an infinite sequence of occurrences, the mathematics—as understood within the mathematical model—and percentages and odds will equate to these math models. But that doesn't mean a hoot to you if you go to play and don't win the $0.05573 cents you "mathematically" should, or lose $10,000 when you should have "mathematically" lost only $2.

In relying on these infinity models of statistical expectations, as derived from the probability models, every "traditionally accepted" gambling strategy is already fundamentally flawed. It simply cannot, and will not, work as designed, because the design is based on a protracted series of events that you will never be able to actually do. When you are playing with any of these "established" strategies, the best you can do is either hit the game for a lot more than its statistics indicate you should win, or for a lot less. There simply isn't any median. You will either win a lot more than you should, or lose a lot more than you should. Casinos can, and do, rely on these math models, because they are an *entity*—and as such they can, and do, exploit the infinity model of event frequencies within the statistical probabilities. Players, on the other hand, are human beings and cannot play the same game the same way—we are not an entity. Even if we profit in the short term, we will not—and cannot—profit in the long run. Therefore, using strategies based upon the same kind of mathematical data, the same kind of perspective, and the same kind of approach can only result in the entity's win and the human being's eventual defeat.

In the strategies and methods as I am showing in this book, reality means only one thing—money won. Who cares how? In these cases, I don't care whether the "reality of the universe" is, or is not, mathematically sound as professed by the statisticians, or whether it is ethereal or indefinable. In these strategies and methods, all I care about is the money. I am prepared to assume that money exists, that it is what it appears to be, that it is a desirable thing to have, and that it can be won from casino games. Accepting these assumptions allows me to prepare a series of circumstances that exploit the inevitability of wins in the short term and maximize the financial yield from them. That is all. I slice up my universe in to ten sessions making one block, ten blocks making one event, and so on. I don't care about the billions and billions of events that will, eventually, prove that my "theory" will "cost" 0.00112345876 percent—or whatever—in edge on the games. All I care about is the fact that I will take home an average profit of $1,600 each time I play a ten-session block of Blackjack. The universe, the math, and the stats be damned—it doesn't mean a hoot for your dollar today, this moment, this minute, this session, this block, this casino day.

Casino workdays are just that, and the action with these strategies is designed to make money winners more often than money losers.

Being the Unknown

Perhaps the greatest advantage of playing casino games with the strategies in this book is the simple fact of hiding your expertise. Casino executives and their employees are not fools. For every system player who walks in the casino hoping to score big, there are several employees who know that system better than the wannabe gambler. For every card counter who thinks he knows Blackjack better than the casino pit boss, or the gaming surveillance supervisor, there are pit bosses, dealers, and eye-in-the-sky surveillance experts who know it better than he does and could probably do it a thousand times better than he can (and most of them did before becoming casino-employed experts). In fact, many of the key gaming employees of casinos—those whose job is to watch out for various cheats, system players, or card counters—are either former players themselves, former card counters, cheats, or mechanics (really good card dealers). Though cheating and counting cards are two entirely different things—cheating *is* an illegal activity while card counting most definitely is *not*—casinos don't like either and tend to lump both together even though they absolutely do not belong in the same classification. Card counters, and skilled players, are just that—people skilled in winning *legally*. Card cheats, mechanics, thieves, and other manipulators of games and equipment are there to *steal*, and *not* to win legitimately.

The expert players, card counters, system players, experts, and strategy players are all intelligent people who have mastered the game and are now able to exploit the game's weaknesses for profits, perfectly within the casino's own rules of the game, without the use of anything other than their minds and abilities. No professional gambler, and no casino expert, will condone cheating of any kind, or any illegal activity. Expert players pride themselves on their expertise and their ability to win legitimately.

It is extraordinarily unfair, but sadly a fact, that casinos classify expert players among the dregs of the cheats. This is like telling the latest Nobel Prize winner that he's a bum because his field is number theory and casinos don't like him because he could win too much. This is such a gross error and misconception on the part of the casinos that it is truly a shame. Casinos are missing incredible marketing opportunities by taking advantage of any wins that such players may gain. The main reason for this is, of course, the corporate culture. If you have read my Blackjack book, you know what I mean in the chapter on "How They Think vs. How We Think." If you haven't read it, please do. It will give you an insight into the mind-set of the corporate gaming executive and will allow you to better understand why they look at professional gamblers as a threat. There are some private casino owners who won't object if you want to play well at their properties. One such man is George Maloof, owner of the Palms Hotel and Casino in Las Vegas. George, who (along with his family) also owns the Sacramento Kings professional basketball team, is a high-rolling gambler himself, and he knows the value of a good game. At his property, he welcomes good players. He knows that even great players won't win all the time, and the value they generate as their exploits become known means a lot more profit than the loss they may incur for the casino when they win. At a recent party, my friend and fellow gaming author Frank Scoblete—an accomplished Blackjack player—asked George point blank what would happen if he spotted a card counter at his casino. George said nothing would happen. That's the difference between the corporate casino and one whose owner is not only a player himself, but who also recognizes the value of skilled players. While at some Strip casinos you will only get paid 6:5 for your blackjacks, and get tossed out if they even think you are some kind of a good player, at George's Palms Casino you are welcome. Similarly so for some of the other smaller casinos, those who recognize that gamblers come there to gamble, and if they can't get the good value games, they'll go elsewhere.

Unfortunately, situations and casinos like this are very rare. In most casinos, you will have to hide your identity as a strategy player. If you are successful, you will be able to play continuously and in anonymity. If you are not successful, you may be asked to leave and perhaps barred permanently from that casino. That is the greatest danger faced by professional gamblers. Although casino surveillance technologies were installed to combat cheating, this same technology is also being used to target intelligent players, professional players, card counters, system players, and strategy players. The original purpose of surveillance was to catch cheats— people who would mark cards in Blackjack or switch dice at the Craps game, and so on. Later this was used to track card counters and to keep an eye out for known troublemakers, such as drunken players who caused a ruckus, barred players, or mob figures. Now this has been further extended to include anyone who the casino thinks is playing intelligently and winning too much. Even if you happen to get lucky, and if anyone at the casino even suspects that you may be playing intelligently, they can, and will, stop you and ask you to leave. More and more frequently casino surveillance technology is being used to simply stop players from winning.

This technology is now so advanced that it can scan your face and match you to a national database of people who have been to any casino. For example, if you walk into a casino in New Jersey, regardless of whether you play, win, or lose, your face is immediately captured by a surveillance camera and your features added to a national database of people who have been to a casino. Let's say that a year later you walk into a casino in Las Vegas, and play and win. The surveillance cameras automatically capture your face, the face-recognition software picks up on the key features, and the computers immediately scan the database for a match. In seconds up pops your picture from a year ago, when you walked into that casino in New Jersey. Your entire gaming profile is displayed. If you are listed there as a winner, or a suspected professional player, you will be instantly scrutinized, and if you continue to win you will be marked and asked to leave. This kind of technology has become so sophisticated that even if you were to alter your appearance, the computers can see through the disguise. They simply match the identifying features of your face that you can't hide or alter, such as the distance between your eyes, the distance between your cheekbones, your ears, your eyebrow ridges, and so on, all of which are exclusively yours and cannot be hidden. They will always reveal your true identity in the same manner as DNA and fingerprints.

Therefore, strategy players and professional gamblers have had to make adjustments and alterations to the way they gamble. The first alteration that such professionals had to make was to move down in limits and limit their wagering spread. Previously, card counters, for example, could make minimum bets of $10 and then move in a bet of $200, or more, when the count was distinctly in their favor, then go back to the minimum when it wasn't, and so on. This was a spread of twenty times the minimum unit and is extreme even by those standards. Most of the time card counters like to use no more than a four-times spread—for example, using $25 as the base wagering unit, then increasing it to four for a total of $100 in favorable situations and never more than that. Their incremental increases are likewise more measured, such as going from $25 to $35, and then to $50, and then to $60, and then to $25, and so on, never more than four times the base unit wager in spread. That way they hide their identity as a card counter, because anything larger than this would immediately become a red flag, if not to the dealer, or the pit boss, then certainly to the ever-watchful "eye in the sky." If you're betting $25 a hand, and occasionally make a $30, $40, or $50 wager, and then suddenly you jump to $250—which is a ten-times spread— you will set off bells and alarms everywhere, particularly if you happen to be wagering $2,500 per spot and suddenly jump to $25,000. That's how professional card counters used to be able to bet, but the casinos have learned this and are now watchful and vigilant for any signs of it, regardless of how small a wager. Reasonably, though, most casinos won't bother you if you are wagering less than $25 per base wager unit. If you are on a $5 table, for example, and you suddenly break open and jump to $50, you may get a quick look or two, but won't attract much attention. Even if you were to jump from the $5 minimum suddenly to the $500 table maximum—a huge spread that in reality no smart gambler would ever attempt—even then you would most likely be looked upon as a fool or wannabe, and most of the time all you'd get would be some smiling smirks behind the counter as the pit staff shares a chuckle about the wannabe card counter.

For these reasons, the real professionals who used to play in the $100 and $1,000 games have now either disappeared, gone broke, been barred, or moved to the small stakes—the $10, $25, and $50 games. They have also substantially lowered their win goals and expectations. While the famed Craps player Eric Karras was able to wager millions of dollars per roll—he won over $48 million—he wasn't really a strategy player, as was later affirmed by the fact that he lost it all. His kind of action the casino doesn't mind—and neither do they mind the "whales" who play several hundred thousand dollars per hand, such as the Baccarat players. These players are all losers because of the games they play and how they play them, regardless of how much they may win in one trip or another. One of the most famous stories of such players is the one of Mr. Wong from Hong Kong, who in the 1980s was well known worldwide as a high-stakes Baccarat player. On one trip he won $68 million in South Africa, then lost it all; won $46 million in Australia, then another $26 million in Las Vegas; then moved on to Atlantic city where he lost it all and locked himself up in his suite at the Trump Plaza demanding an extra $6 million in credit, which the casino refused to give him since he was already $26 million in the hole. The Donald himself later approved that credit, much to his chagrin, because Mr. Wong proceeded to win back not only that $6 million in credit, but also the $26 million he lost, then another $16 million on top of it, at which point he left. He returned to Australia, where he lost it all plus another $48 million. A few months later he was found dead in Hong Kong, having taken a swan dive from the top of a very tall building. It turned out that Mr. Wong had been embezzling millions from some people who didn't like it very much.

These are the stories that form the folklore of gambling. Whether true in total or only partially doesn't much matter. They are entertaining to know, and they tell well among gamblers and casino players alike. The truth remains, however, that anyone who aspires to be a professional gambler, a semiprofessional, or at the very least a knowledgeable and successful strategy player, must be aware of the odds against him, not just among the games themselves, but also in the way casinos try to recognize and combat intelligent players and frequent winners. Therefore, to be able to achieve consistent wins, and be able to hide your identity as a strategy player, you need more than just the same kind of strategies that everyone else also knows. This is the primary reason why I developed the strategies in this book; they are the first attempt in a long time to create something new. Not very much "new" has been done in the kinds of strategies that can be successfully employed in casino games. What has been done are either various versions of the traditional and established strategies or the propagation of the many "get rich quick" systems being sold in various forms. I would like to make it clear that I differentiate between these methods, and such "systems." Most of the "systems" that you may read about, or buy from direct mail and such, offer a guarantee—if you don't win, then do this and so on. Well, I don't offer any guarantees, for two reasons:

- One, these are *methods,* not systems. They are vested in many years of research, experience, and analysis. I make them as simple as they can be, and as workable as possible in the real world of today's casino.
- Two, the actual success of these methods depends on those playing them, on their abilities and their skills.

Primarily because of the second item, there cannot be any guarantee offered. I can't possibly anticipate how you may or may not be able to play. I have no means of knowing where you will play and if that casino will even offer games that can fit the parameters that these methods imply. There are literally hundreds of individual variables, and as carefully as I can structure these methods, in their ultimate incarnation they all rely on the player's ability to learn and implement them. So, expect to win, but rely on your knowledge and skill, and use these methods as well as you can.

I have crafted these methods to be their own disguise. When you master them to a point where you can play them without thinking, you will start to enjoy both the wins and the experience. Furthermore, I designed these methods specifically to appear to be precisely the kind of silly plays that casual and novice gamblers would make. These strategies are not designed to be variations on existing traditional strategies, although some do use several of the established principles, such as tiered wagering. However, while casinos are on the lookout for card counters, players who will play the Blackjack Strategy as shown in this book will never even be suspected of being intelligent players, and certainly not card counters. The same applies to the Roulette and Craps strategies, and to a lesser extent to the Slot Strategy. Slots are slightly different, because casinos don't expect anyone to be able to beat the machines by means of a strategy, so they don't pay nearly as much attention to them as they do to the table games and table game players.

Each of these strategies is designed to make you a winner in the *overall sequence,* regardless of any individual event result, and regardless of any session result. So, you may be losing and losing and losing, and the dealers will commiserate with you, the casinos will give you comps and freebies and rooms and food and so on, and all the while you are quietly smiling because you know that you are actually winning, even though it simply doesn't look that way. And that's precisely the beauty of these methods—they make you and your play look just like the foolish gambling that most casual and tourist players do, but all the time they are working silently and relentlessly to the end-result profit. If you do it correctly, that's what you will end up with—a profit. And it simply doesn't matter what happens along the way, what happens on this hand, this roll, this spin, this pull, or whatever the case may be. Neither does it matter if this session was a profit or a total loss. It all works out in the end, and it is *not* a long process. The longest any one block of sessions can last is about eight hours or so, give or take some time depending on the game, the speed of the events, you, other players, and so on. If you must extend the sessions in your block to several days, that's okay too. It will even work if you continue the session next month, or next year, as long as you keep your position at the time you stop as absolutely accurate, and resume without having compromised the preceding results or the current position within the method. You will now be able to play as much as you can handle, make good money, and no one will ever know you are a pro. If you do it right, that's exactly where you want to be—anonymous, but with profits in your pocket.

And so now it is time for the hard part—the nitty-gritty of it all. Here are the methods, each in its own chapter. Study carefully. You must know not only what the words mean, but also what they mean as a *whole.* You will need to study well, because once you hit the casino there won't be any room for mistakes, and no room for second-guessing. Be prepared. They aren't easy to learn, or easy to use, at least at first. Eventually, they will become very easy, but the first time you read them they will seem hard. Don't be discouraged—it only appears hard because it is so new. Think on it some more, then read again. Practice at home. Then practice for small stakes at small casinos (if you think you must) to get the feel of it. Then learn some more and correct your mistakes. Only then go and do it for real, and make sure you have the resources required.

Strategies for Roulette

INTRODUCTION

Early in the twentieth century, a man broke the bank at Monte Carlo, playing Roulette. There was even a song about this man, widely popular at that time: "The Man Who Broke the Bank in Monte Carlo." His exploits became legendary, as he did this for three years straight. At the time, and particularly in the European gambling establishments, Roulette was extremely popular as a gambling game, patronized to a very large extent by the gentry and the titled elite of European society. The fact that this man—let's call him Mr. R, for "Mr. Roulette"—was actually a commoner had little to do with the extraordinary popularity he achieved.

The way they played Roulette at Monte Carlo in those days, and still do to some extent, was at a large table with the wheel in the middle and two table layouts either side of the wheel. Betting was always fast and furious, as was the excitement. When a successful gambler won more money than the table had available, a ceremonial "black shroud" was placed over the wheel and table, signifying that the "bank was broke." This was called "breaking the bank," and the term

89

stuck, now being common jargon in many languages for a variety of related occurrences. The game was then closed for a short time, more money was brought to the table, which was then opened again, and the game continued.

Mr. R would come once each year at holiday time and play Roulette, breaking the bank on many occasions, which netted him more than 100,000 francs (French currency) each time. Over his three-year reign as the undisputed champion gambler, he won almost 2 million francs, a figure of huge proportions for the times. He was widely rumored to have developed the one and only "system" to beat the wheel, and his continued success fueled his notoriety. However, on his fourth and subsequent annual visits, he lost everything he won, and then some. His "magic" was gone. Later in life, he admitted that he really didn't have any system and that he just got extremely lucky. Such a consistent lucky streak is very uncommon in any gambling game, or even in life, but it is mathematically possible. Mr. R's exploits were just that one gigantic aberration in mathematical probabilities, one which has not happened since. The folklore surrounding Mr. R, and other similar exploits by numerous other gamblers with gambling games, have fueled a preponderance of "systems," particularly for Roulette.

The most widely used system for Roulette has been the Martingale and its derivative, the Super-Martingale. These two "systems" are still utilized by casual gamblers who think they will beat the wheel, not aware of the major flaws in either. The Martingale simply calls for a gambler to double the last bet on each losing occasion. For example, starting with $5, the next bet will be $10, the next $20, the next $40, and so on. The Super-Martingale calls for the bet to be twice the amount of the previous bet plus the original bet amount, in effect a three-time wager. For example, starting with $5, the next bet will be $15, the next $45, the next $135, and so on. The major problems with both these "systems" are the enormity of the required bankroll, the huge size of some of the bets, and the house limit. In Roulette, and especially in Roulette, a sequence of consecutive losses can be extraordinarily long. Streaks of thirty-two deep, and longer, losers on even the "even-money" bets are reasonably common, although by no means frequent in such extremes. And if you are playing these "systems" straight-up, your sequence of potential losses can be astronomically higher. Therefore, you will wind up in a no-win situation.

First and foremost among the flaws in these "systems" is the house limit. Modern casinos, and in fact all the casinos in the world, today and in the past, institute house limits precisely to combat the possibility of an open-ended Martingale-style progressive system. Regardless of what limits the house game may have, whether $500 or $5,000, the fact is that with any of these "systems" you will quickly run up against the house limit. That means you cannot make the next bet in the progression, thus assuring you of being a loser no matter what you do. Even if there wasn't a house limit, the situation would be foreboding. In many instances, it wouldn't be uncommon for a $5 starting bet to become a $5,000 or $50,000 bet somewhere along the progression, and all to win just the $5 initial amount. Excruciatingly suspect and dangerous. Casinos who detect that you are a "Martingale-type" player will love you! They will send limousines for you because they know that no matter what happens, you *will* be a loser.

There are two basic kinds of Roulette. There is American Roulette, which uses the two house numbers: "0" and "00," and there is European Roulette, which has only one house number: the single "0." The differences in overall house edge and player's odds are profound. European Roulette holds only about 2.7 percent for the house, while American Roulette holds a steady 5.26 percent for the house. This is because the odds are derived from the available number bets (thirty-eight total straight-up on American Roulette) and the fact that the biggest payoff possible is only 35:1 (straight-up) on any one number (definitely not true odds, but that's why casinos pay that way, to make their cut). Factor those into each other, and you'll get the average of a steady 5.26 percent. It is better, therefore, to play European Roulette wherever possible, because the house edge is so much lower. Many U.S. casinos now offer European Roulette on some tables, but the betting limits are usually very high. This is done to overcome the lower house edge. Casinos know that they are giving up almost 50 percent of their edge on European Roulette, and therefore they will demand higher action to compensate for these "better" odds, even though a house edge of 2.7 percent is still high and tough to beat.

The Strategy for Roulette, which follows, is based on American Roulette, because that's the game most widely available in American and Canadian casinos today. It can be played equally well on a European Roulette game, and the winning percentages inherent in it will increase slightly due to the overall better player's game; however, not significantly so as to prevent you from playing this strategy even exclusively on the American wheel. All further discussions, therefore, will refer to American Roulette, even when only the word "Roulette" is used. To see what the American Roulette Wheel looks like, please see Figure 1.

What makes Roulette traditionally a tough game to beat is the steady house edge. The rounded average of this house edge, 5.26 percent, remains constant on each and every spin, because neither the wheel, nor the numbers, "remember" any previous event or events. It is only the human players, and their psychological makeup, who "think" that they are detecting some kinds of "patterns" in the events. Not so, since the spins of the wheel have no such thing inherent in them, each spin being a new event, which begins at the beginning of that one spin and ends at the end of that one spin. Nothing else counts. Yes, there are deviations

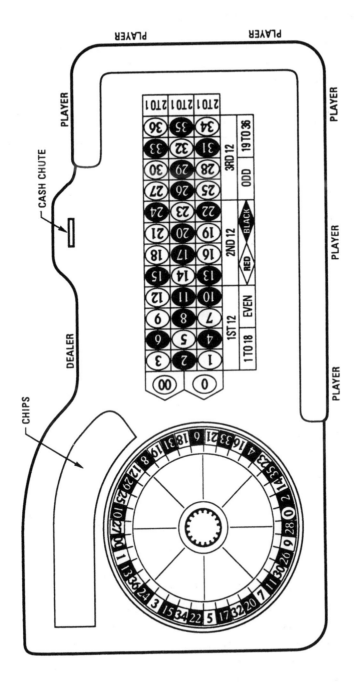

Figure 1. The complete layout for American Roulette as it appears in the casino.

from the overall mathematical probabilities, but these are also accounted for in the mathematics of probability. And don't be fooled by the "even-money" bets, such as Black & Red, because they are *not* even money. In reality, they are only a 47.35 percent bet, and not 50-50. Therefore, in order to have any kind of a successful strategy for Roulette, you, the player, must educate yourself *out* of the common mistakes made by most players.

- First, forget the thought that the past is in some way indicative of the future. Just because the ball landed on Red, say, thirteen times in a row, does *not* mean that it will do so the next time, and so on for any such sequences of what *appears* to you to be a pattern of events. It is not; it is only an illusion, and casinos, and the game, win money from you, and players like you, because of these psychological nuances of perception.
- Second, forget the nonsense espoused by the purveyors of single-progression systems for Roulette. They are all bogus. You cannot defeat the wheel by progressions alone, nor by even-money bets.
- Third, don't listen to what casinos tell you, or how dealers, or other players, may tell you to bet, regardless of whether it appears that the player giving you such advice may be winning at that particular moment. It's all bull, and pure luck.
- Fourth, don't believe all the hogwash about "biased" wheels, and so on. Yes, the wheel is a mechanical device and it can "warp," become "out of balance," and so on, but that's largely a folklore theory and not true practical advice. The fact is that all casino wheels are balanced on a regular basis, climate control is very steady, and the protective shielding and accompanying security of the wheel all prevent any exploitation

of such situations. And even if you did spot an unbalanced or a biased wheel, your wins are still not assured, and you may still lose more overall than you win.

- Fifth, don't believe the "stories" of dealers who can "shoot the ball wherever they want it." Yes, it is possible, and there are dealers who can theoretically put the ball consistently in one area of the wheel by the way they spin the wheel and shoot the ball, but that's all in test cases under laboratory conditions and all but impossible in actual casino situations. If this were not so, dealers would be in constant collusion with friends who'd play the wheel accordingly and win so much money that the casinos would stop dealing Roulette and the dealers and their friends would be arrested immediately for fraud.

- Sixth, modern Roulette wheels have had their "pockets" altered. Roulette wheel pockets used to be fairly deep, with tall sides, and this allowed the ball to more firmly come to a stop when it hit within the pocket itself. But this was being exploited by some systems similar to those described above; therefore, modern Roulette wheels—particularly in America— are now being manufactured with very shallow pockets whose sides are considerably shorter. This further "randomizes" each spin result, since the ball can no longer be firmly "trapped" inside any specific pocket. This is not cheating, it is simply a further assurance— for the casinos—of a more statistically correct randomness of each spin and its result.

For these reasons, and others like them, Roulette is thought to be unbeatable. The fact that its popularity in American casinos is so low testifies to the defeats suffered by players. In fact, Roulette, as played commonly, is a really bad bet. Slot Machines pay better, and Roulette is, for all intents and purposes, just a bad Slot Machine since you, as the player, have no control of what happens. Modern Slot Machines are much better for your overall winning percentages, because most of them only hold 2 percent for the house, and some can be played to over 100 percent payback.

So—what is a Roulette player to do?

Play Roulette as a smart "worker." That's the basis of the Strategy for Roulette.

If you wish to play Roulette for entertainment, you're a loser even before you start playing. To beat this game will require you to approach the game as a professional and to treat your playing as a job. You have to play mechanically, automatically, and without any emotion. Just like the game itself and just the same way that the casinos deal the game: like a machine, everything always the same.

In the Roulette Strategy, which follows, you will learn how to defeat the wheel, provided you do it precisely, constantly, like a machine, without emotion, and without mistakes. You will need the required bankroll (listed below) and you will need patience, because the game is inherently extremely slow. You will also need resiliency in order not to become flustered by the casino distractions and other players. You will need dexterity in order to make your bets quickly and accurately. You will need sharp mental skills in order to keep track of what bets you have made, which bets you are about to make depending on the outcome of each event, where you are in your sequence, and how to deal with the outcome of each event and sequence. Finally, you will need pinpoint accuracy at all times.

These are essential elements, because if you fail in any one of them while playing, you will defeat the benefits of the strategy you are playing. As I said, it will be a job. It won't be a lot of fun along the way, but it will be fun once you start to add up your winnings. Also, your winnings will be incremental, so don't expect to become a millionaire in one session. The sequences are designed to "hide" your identity as a strategy player and to accumulate profitability over numerous sessions. Now, be prepared to do some learning.

Of the four strategies I have developed for Roulette, the first one being presented is the easiest to play and the payoffs are very good relative to the investment required. This strategy, like all of my strategies, is predicated on the player's complete knowledge of the game and odds and payoffs on all bets. It has been designed to combat the house edge and provide an end-of-sequence profit for the player. It can be adapted into variations, including multiplayer partnerships. In all cases, accurate play with no mistakes is essential. Otherwise, your results won't meet expectations. I will assume that you know the game and do not require explanations of what the bets are or how to make them. If you don't know the game, or think you don't know it well enough, I highly recommend that you first learn all you can. Finally, you should be aware that although the board is sequential, the wheel is not. Numbers on the board run from 1 through 36 plus the "0" and "00," while the numbers on the wheel are non-sequentially arranged as virtually diametrical opposites, with very few exceptions. The number 1 is directly opposite the number 2, and so on, as it is on the wheel, while on the board these numbers are sequentially displayed one next to the other. This is important.

ROULETTE STRATEGY #1: QUADS

This is playing the board, rather than playing the wheel. There are twenty-two possible quads on the board, plus the basket. Stay away from the basket bet. A winner on a quad pays 8:1. The Quad Strategy is based on playing several quads in cross-bets, combined with straight-up bets plus splits. Straight-up bets pay 35:1 and splits pay 17:1.

Rules

1. Bet eight (8) consecutive quads, with cross-bets. Here is an example, but you can play *any* such groups of quads, as long as they are consecutive and you cross-bet each group:

   Example:

   [1, 2, 4, 5] + [2, 3, 5, 6] + [4, 5, 7, 8] + [5, 6, 8, 9] + [7, 8, 10, 11] + [8, 9, 11, 12] + [10, 11, 13, 14] + [11, 12, 14, 15]

2. Bet your key numbers.

Your "key" numbers in the above example are: 5, 8, and 11. If you play different quads, your key numbers will be different. They can actually be called your "key wheel" numbers, because a hit on any one of them will give you multiple winners for all surrounding bets as well. Here, I will also refer to them as the "inside" numbers, because they are the "core" of this multibet wheel. But don't confuse these terms with the more commonly understood uses of these expressions, because here I am using them specifically and only as they apply to this method, and nothing else. This means you will have three bets, one chip unit on each of the three "key" numbers.

3. Bet splits on your key numbers. This means—in *this example*—that you will have ten split bets covering the following numbers:

[5 + 2] [5 + 6] [5 + 4] [5 + 8] [8 + 7] [8 + 9] [8 + 11]
[11 + 10] [11 + 12] and [11 + 14]

4. On your outside numbers, bet these straight-up. In the above example, these numbers will be:

1, 2, 3, 4, 6, 7, 9, 10, 12, 13, 14, and 15

These are the "outside frame" of the previous example. Again, remember that these numbers are here used only as an example. You can select any numbers you wish, as long as they can form this table pattern of interlaced quads with core-3 wheel, and a 12-number outside frame.

5. Each time you have a LOSS, increase the total bets by the next amount called for in the betting progression.

6. Each time you have a WIN, decrease the amount of the next bet back over all wagers to the betting minimum unit you have chosen.

To see what this looks like—as per my example—refer to Figure 2 on page 100.

Analysis

You have now covered fifteen of the thirty-eight numbers, and done so with cross-cross-cross bets. If you hit any one of your inside key numbers (5, 8, or 11), you will be paid 35:1 for that one number, plus four times your split bets at 17:1, plus you will hit four of your quads each paid at 8:1, plus you will retain your original bets on each of these winners. That one bet and hit on any of the "keys" breaks down as follows:

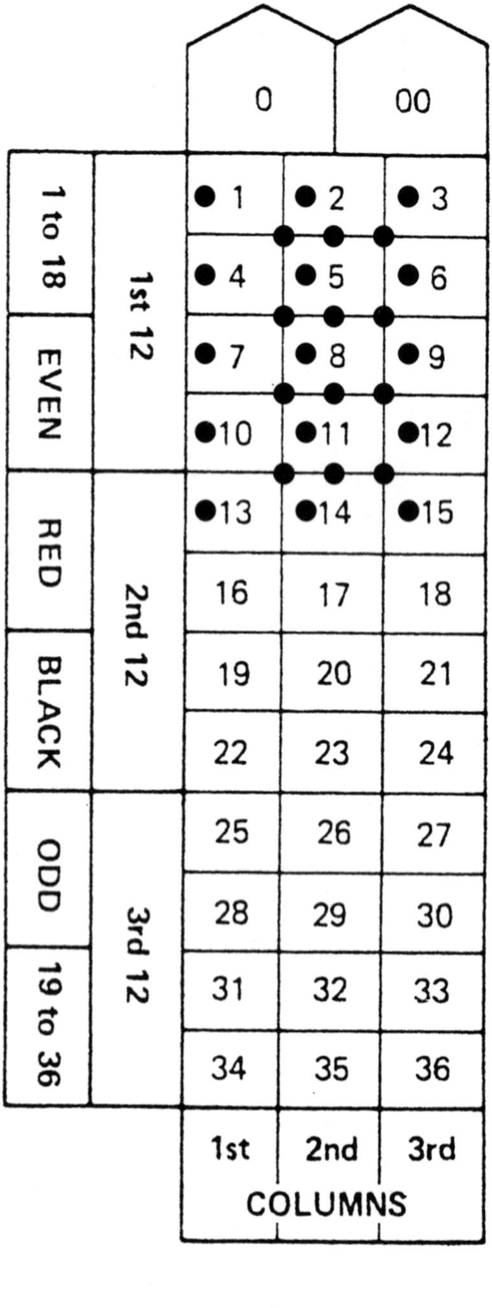

Figure 2. Roulette Strategy #1: Quads

Investment:	3 + 8 + 10 + 12	=	33 (chip units)
Gross payback:	35 + 68 + 32 + 4 + 4 + 1	=	144 (chip units)
Net profits:	Gross minus investment: 144-33	=	111 (chip units)

So, in this event, you won $111 clear (assuming your chip unit = $1—if your chip units equal $5, it is that much higher, and so on). Prorated payoffs apply to all other circumstances, including those without any hits on your inside numbers. You can calculate these for yourself. That's it. Now apply your betting progression, as follows.

Betting Progressions

Having bet fifteen numbers in this way, you have covered slightly more than one-third of the available thirty-eight numbers. This means that you will win a little more than 33 percent of the time, but lose otherwise. However, prorated for the progression, your losses will equal only 33 chip units, while your gross will be at the low-end 41 chip units, for a gross profit of 11 chip units, with an average gross profit per win of about 65 chip units. Since your losses will average to a little less than 66 percent of the time, and your profits when you hit will average higher-per-capita than cumulative losses, you will always have a positive outcome.

But—in order to overcome the inevitable "cold" streaks, you will need to employ a betting progression. This is *not* the "Martingale" style progression, but a derivative of my tiered wagering and fractional differential, as I outlined in my book *Powerful Profits from Blackjack*.

Since your losses are about two-thirds of the time (statistically somewhat lower), increase your bets by the nearest highest (or lowest, as appropriate) equivalent of two-thirds increments. If you're betting $1 as chip-units, you can't put down 66.66 cents, so go up by $1. The next sequential loser, take your $2 bet ($1 + $1 on the previous scenario) and increase this by two-thirds, which will again be $1 (and not the $1.3333). So, your bet is now $3 (1 + 1 + 1 so far). Your next increase will be two-thirds of that, which is $2, so the next bet will be $5. Now if you lose again, the next increase is two-thirds of that, which is $3.3333, but since you can't bet in odd amounts, your next wager will go up by $3, and so the next bet in the sequence will be $8, and so on. Continue this *in whole dollar amounts* for *five consecutive losses,* and then continue two-thirds incremental increases to the nearest highest dollar amount for the next five consecutive losses, then continue with two-thirds nearest highest dollar amount increases for the next five consecutive losses, and so on. Statistically, you will hit a winner a little more than once in each three spins, on average, so your progression will not reach the table maximum nor wipe out your bankroll.

To make this easier to understand, look at the following progression bet reference chart. It is based on a starting unit chip value of $1. However, this can be played for any chip unit value, as long as the table amounts and limits allow. For example, if your chip unit value is $5, then everything in this chart is multiplied by the factor of 5. If your chip unit value is $2, then everything in this chart is multiplied by the factor of 2. If your chip value is 50 cents, then everything in this chart is less by half. And so on, for whatever chip unit value you decide to select as your own.

First Series of Five Events

CHIP UNITS	$ VALUE	CORRECT TWO-THIRDS	ACTUAL INCREASE	NEXT BET
1	$1	0.6666	1	$2
2	$2	1.3333	1	$3
3	$3	2.0000	2	$5
5	$5	3.3333	3	$8
7	$8	5.3333	5	$13

Now that the first series of five losing events happened, and we are still in a losing progression, the next series will start with the last wagered amount, which was $13 on each stipulated bet. The next series of five additional consecutive wagers will come out as follows:

Second Series of Five Events

CHIP UNITS	$ VALUE	CORRECT TWO-THIRDS	ACTUAL INCREASE	NEXT BET
13	$13	8.6666	9	$22
22	$22	14.6666	15	$37
37	$37	24.6666	25	$62
62	$62	41.3333	41	$103
103	$103	68.6666	69	$172

This is the end of the second series of five events. Overall, this was—so far—a losing streak of ten consecutive events. This means that during these ten spins—using our betting example as shown earlier—not a single number out of the fifteen we have covered has hit. In our example we have covered the first fifteen numbers (1 through 15) with our bets. This means that there are twenty-three other numbers (including the 0 and 00) that must be hit in order for us to lose. Therefore, in this protracted series of consecutive losses, those other twenty-three numbers would have to be hit equally sequentially. Both are quite possible and are not statistically unlikely. Although there is a general statistical parity in accordance with expected probability of events, this doesn't mean that it will always be so. Losing streaks of ten deep, such as in this example, do happen, and happen frequently. Even longer losing streaks are possible; however, this method accounts for even those incredible anomalies. Since you don't have to be concerned about running up against the table limits (in the majority of situations), all you have to be concerned about is the size of your bankroll. I recommend at least $1,500, but you should have immediate handy access to about $5,000 (such as on deposit at the cage, or casino credit, so you can draw a marker at the table immediately), with a total accessible bankroll of at least $10,000.

Most casinos will have betting limits at Roulette with a $2,500 maximum inside spread, and a $5,000 maximum outside. In our method, we are covering a total of thirty-three wagers on each spin. These are the 3 keys + 8 quads + the 10 Splits + the 12 number frame = 33 total wagers. Each round, therefore, we must multiply each chip unit by 33 times, to account for the total wagers. So, to continue with the above example, now modified to include only the actual wagers as shown, the above progression of bets will result in the following real expenditure:

First Series of Five Events

TOTAL UNITS	$ VALUE	ACTUAL INCREASE	NEXT BET	CUMULATIVE LOSS
33	$33	33	$66	$33
66	$66	33	$99	$99
99	$99	66	$165	$165
165	$165	99	$264	$264
264	$264	165	$429	$429

As you can see, when we suffer a consecutive losing streak of merely five events, our total cumulative loss to this point is $429, even though our last wager was only at $8 per wager. However, $8 per wager x 33 total wagers = a total board wager of $264. Upon the loss of this, the method calls for the next series of five wagers to begin the next progression of the previous wager, which is $13 on each number = $429 total spread.

Second Series of Five Events

TOTAL UNITS	$ VALUE	ACTUAL INCREASE	NEXT BET	CUMULATIVE LOSS
429	$429	297	$726	$693
726	$726	495	$1,221	$1,155
1,221	$1,221	825	$2,046	$1,947
2,046	$2,046	1,353	$3,399	$3,267
3,399	$3,399	2,277	$5,676	$5,445

Once we reach the ten consecutive losing streak mark we will encounter trouble. The tenth wager will require a spread of $3,399 and this will be over the standard $2,500 inside betting limit spread. It is in this situation that this method, at these wager levels, has its greatest problem. If a statistical anomaly of these many consecutive losses does occur, we will not be able to make the tenth wager in the correct proportion to the required progression. Of course, if we are playing 50-cent chip units, this will not be a problem just yet, because at half the total wager amounts we will not run up to this level until a sequence of the eighteenth consecutive loss. Many tables that offer the 50-cent chip unit values may also offer lower betting spreads, so it is important first, and always, to check out the table limits, and table, you are about to play. Generally, I would recommend that you look for the "high limit" Roulette tables, where the minimum inside betting spread is $25. Since even at $1 chip unit value you are spreading $33 total inside, you will be able to play this method quite successfully at these tables, because most of these games have much higher total wager limits. For example, the "high limit" salons, and games in most Las Vegas casinos—among those that offer these types of games—will have $5,000 inside and $10,000 outside betting limits, with a $25 minimum inside wager spread. This means that in the previous scenario, on these games, you will be able to continue with the progression, even if this series of consecutive losses does actually happen this way.

While it is statistically assured that, at some point, a streak of this many losses in a row—or more—will happen, the actual odds of this happening to you while you are playing are quite low. The exact number depends on the variables of the circumstances, but if you calculate your average exposure to the game for the total hours you will be playing with this method, multiplied by the total number of days and years in your lifetime that you will play this, and arrive at the number of events that you will face in a lifetime, and factor this into the overall probability of occurrence of a consecutive losing streak of ten-deep with a 15-in-38 odds of a win, you will find out that such situations will not happen nearly as often as it may appear when considering an arbitrary opinion based on, for example, a casual reading of the above example. Yes, it is quite possible to suffer a ten-deep losing streak when considering a wager on a single number, or wagers on either/or situations, such as black-and-red, or odd-and-even. I have seen what would have been losing streaks of many more than that in a row, which of course means that the other side of that wager had that many winning events in a row. However, in this method it is important to remember that we are not looking at single numbers, we are looking at a cover of fifteen out of a possible thirty-eight on American Roulette, or out of a possible thirty-seven on European Roulette (which is even better). Therefore, all our calculations have to take this into account. If this is done, at least as reasonably as humanly possible, you will soon discover that the average losing streak you will encounter is about three events deep, while the longest average losing streaks will be about five events deep. The rest of the time you will win more regularly, such as one win, followed by one loss, followed by one win, followed by one loss, and so on, with several two-of-the-same events in a row, and then back to the norm.

Actually, based on statistics, you should have a winning event slightly more than 34 percent of the time, based on the number spread among all possible events. This means a win about one time out of three. This means that, on average, you will have two losses in a row, followed by a win. So, since you will always increase your wagers after a loss, and go back to the starting point after any win, you will, on average, always be assured of three times the win amount relative to the loss, giving you an overall profitability ratio of 3:1, less the expenditure in the spread, resulting in an average win expectancy of about 65 chip units (or 68, depending on the sequence and bets).

Of course, win amounts will vary, as will the profitability of each event. However, you must remember that the session is composed of numerous events and that no single event is the key determining factor. If we continue with the number spread as shown earlier, and we hit only numbers in our frame of twelve, which are the outside numbers for our method, we will at best get paid only 35:1 for that number, plus 8:1 for it being part of the one quad. For example, there are four numbers in this method that are what I call "orphans," meaning they are not cross-bet on all possibilities, but are the "corner" numbers of the frame. Continuing to use our spread example as shown earlier, these would be the numbers 1, 3, 14, and 15. If any one of those hits, then you will be paid only for the number hit at 35:1, and only on the extra 8:1 for the number being part of only one quad. This is the worst you can do for any win. Any other number in the spread that hits will always have more ways as winners. For example, numbers 2, 4, 7, 10, 6, 9, 12, and 14 are all interconnected and part of at least two quads and one split. There is yet another refinement possible to this method, and that is to streamline the tiered wagering and modify the fractional differential to make it easier to handle in the real world of the casino, with all those distractions and—most likely—interferences from other players making their bets, and so on.

Since we now know how to bet, and how to select the number spread, and we have learned the various correct wager amounts and their whole dollar incremental increase equivalents as they apply to the wagering progression, we can now add a further refinement by making it a little simpler. Of course, by making it a little simpler we are actually modifying the proper fractional differential. This means that we can be either aggressive or regressive. By being aggressive, we will make our refinement higher in whole-dollar increments than would be called for by the standard wagering progression, as shown earlier. By being regressive, we will make our refinement lower than called for in the standard wagering progression, as shown previously. What this means is that if we want to hit the game for bigger wins faster, we can be aggressive, but we also increase our risk of exposure to that statistically inevitable occurrence of a protracted series of consecutive losses, which will eventually happen. By aggressively refining our wagering progression and increasing the fractional differential, we will be more at risk at hitting the table limits faster and shortening the possible sequences of average loss events versus average hit frequency. Doing this means we will win more a lot faster, but significantly increase the likelihood of an inevitable ceiling. Though the method always accounts for such situations, aggressive modification to this method, in tiered wagering, makes it statistically more plausible that our financial requirements will run up against the casinos' table ceiling before we can realize our next sequence. This also means we will require a much higher bankroll. This method is recommended for those players who have large bankrolls and who can play in casinos and at tables where the ceiling limits are at $25,000 and higher, such as the private gaming salons where the inside spread can be $25,000 and any outside wager up to $50,000. We are, of course, only concerned with the inside spread for this method, but these are the indicators to look for to determine the viability of the table as that applies to this method, and, more specifically, to this aggressive wagering modification.

Aggressive Table of Wagers

EVENT NUMBER	UNIT BET	INCREASE	NEXT WAGER	TOTAL
1	1	2	3	$33
2	3	2	5	$132
3	5	10	15	$297
4	15	10	25	$1,122
5	25	5	30	$2,112
6	30	20	50	$3,762
7	50	5	55	$5,577
8	55	5	60	$7,557
9	60	15	75	$10,032
10	75	25	100	$13,332

As you can see, this is a very aggressive progression, taking the fractional differential into the "X-Zone," or what has become popularly known as the X-Treme. This table was prepared for a sequence of ten consecutive losses. It can be safely played on most "high roller" Roulette tables, whose table maximums are in the $10,000 to $25,000 inside bet spread range, with a minimum of a $25 inside starting wager spread. This wagering method can also be safely played on most tables with a $5,000 inside spread requirement, which would allow this to continue to the seventh level. Realistically, if you are at such a table, and are betting like this, and you would want to make that $5,577 event number eight bet spread, chances are the pit boss will let you. It is also quite likely that he would let you make the next two series of bets as well, seeing that you have lost a whole lot of money by then. However, do remember that this negative losing streak is likewise X-Treme. Although it will happen, sometime, this doesn't mean it will happen for you each time you play. As stated earlier, your average will be about three events, of which two will be losers and one a winner. So, most of the time you will be wagering in the one- to five-events range, with an average outlay of about $739, for a total event-five cumulative wager risk factor of $2,112.

You also have to take into account that the previous chart shows consecutive *losses*. This is important to note when you consider the bankroll. Most of the time you will have a smattering of winning events along with some losing events. Each time you have a losing event, increase your wager by the next correct amount, as called for either by this aggressive method or the earlier more balanced increases. Most of the time you will hit a winner once in about three events, with the greatest sequence of losses of about five consecutively. Since each time you lose you increase your bet, when you do hit a winner you make up for the losses. Also, you immediately decrease your wagers all the way back to the starting base unit amount. In the examples used here, that is $1 per chip unit value, and a starting spread of $33 (33 chip units). While sometime you will hit the orphans, where your payoff will be less, there will be enough times where you will hit the side walls of the frame for the double-quad and one-split, and a few times when you will hit the "keys," each of which will give you a four-quad and four-splits. Viewing each single number, or each single bet—merely by itself—is not the correct position. All these bets are interconnected and work together. Therefore, while some hits will pay less, and some intermediate, there will be those occasions when you will hit the medium as well as the "keys," and this will make substantial profits. Of course, we can—and should—also consider that there will be times when all the winners will be only on the orphans. If this is so, you can count on only about an 11-chip unit win, on average. This will mean that your overall profits will be smaller. With a protracted series of X-Treme cumulative losses, you may even find yourself in a situation of a session loss. There may be several such session losses, and if this happens you have hit into a very unlikely—albeit statistically possible and expected—protracted series of statistical anomalies, that X-Treme, where you will be suffering the session losses in a significantly extended sequence. It is at that time that your total abilities, and bankroll, will determine whether or not you will overcome this. The point is that such a protracted series of losing events is not only extremely unlikely, but that the converse will also happen, whereby all your events are always winners, or winners more of the time, as well as more frequent hits on your high-value wagers.

To sustain this method will require that you learn not to consider any individual event as the determining factor in what you perceive as either success or failure, and also learn to understand that individual events, or sessions, have absolutely nothing to do with the overall profitability of this strategy. This method is based on sessions being in cumulative blocks, ten sessions per block, then ten blocks per group, then ten groups for series, and so on. While you may have seven session losses, and only three session wins, the block itself will be a winner. Or, if you have a block loss, this will be one out of the ten blocks, and so on. This method is designed to work within the 98 percent time frame that statistical events will fluctuate merely within a few percentage points of either one extreme or the other, negative or positive. As stated earlier, your events are likely to fluctuate between one and five as the most frequently occurring situational reality. The remainder of the extreme fluctuations, both positive and negative, are confined to the 2 percent time frame when everything will happen totally in the widest of all swings, like all winners consecutively, or all losers. Earlier, I showed you one such extreme, which was the protracted series of ten consecutive losses, and how this will affect your bankroll, total capital expenditure, and betting requirements, as well as the effects this could have on table limits. The majority of the time, when applying this method, that will not happen. When it does, the good news is that it may not happen while you are playing, or not while you are playing with this method. And if it does happen to you, by that time you will have accumulated enough wins to overcome that series of losses, even if you did suffer an actual financial loss—and that in itself is even more remote because this method allows for it, cumulatively, overall, in all sessions, blocks, and series.

Even though this method may not appeal to some players, perhaps due to the financial requirements, it can still be played regressively. While I am not showing the regressive chart here, because it is a much easier calculation to do for yourself, it isn't hard to progress your bets with less aggressiveness and start at lower per-unit chip values. For example, most casinos that show their table limits as a minimum of $5 really mean that they require a minimum of a $5 total inside *spread*. This means you can easily ask for, and receive, 25-cent chips and still play this method. All the figures, including those for the aggressive progression, can be applied and used. All you have to do is divide everything by 4, because everything will now be worth one-fourth of the values shown in my charts. You can also progress your bets regressively, meaning you will add the next unit value at the lower increments. For example, if the correct next increase is 1.6666 units, and the recommended fractional differential is two units, you can instead choose to increase by only one unit—effectively *regressing* the next highest value and factoring it as the next lowest incremental value instead. It all depends on you, your abilities, and—most of all—on your bankroll (also on resiliency and determination, qualities of the professional—more on this later). The best thing about this method is that it is adaptable to you and your situation and circumstances. All you need to do is learn it, understand it, and adapt it to fit you.

Bankroll

Playing at $1 chip units, you will need a minimum of $2,500. I recommend $10,000 as your total stake. You don't have to spend it, and in fact you won't. But there are those statistical anomalies where you will hit a long losing streak, and as a result you will require the larger bankroll to sustain your game.

Quit *only* when you have had a hit on your inside numbers! This will assure you of your end-result profit. As an alternative, quit if you have doubled your starting bankroll, if you have made a minimum of one-third clear profit, or—in those very rare occasions—if you have lost your entire stake and cannot make the next bet. If you are in the "middling" situation, where you are neither winning nor losing any significant amounts, quit after 100 total events—about two to three hours, depending on the speed of the game. But when you know you are about to quit, or want to quit, or are ready to go, never do so until you have hit the last winning event, which is not an orphan. You should always end your sessions on the hit of a winner on at least one of the eleven numbers that are your quads, "keys," and splits (your orphans are the other four numbers of the fifteen-number total spread). This will assure you of a good win. However, if things are not going well, quit after any one winning event, but try not to quit on losing events, unless it is one of those X-Treme anomalies we discussed earlier. Usually, 100 spins should be enough per session, with ten such sessions in a block.

If you can afford it, take a bankroll ten times the suggested limit, and divide this into ten sessions, each an individual occurrence. Then combine your sessions together, and in the end you will have a large profit without the individual session amounts being a single factor. You can adapt this principle from the Blackjack Strategy session wagers, as I outlined in my book *Powerful Profits from Blackjack*.

And that's the story for Roulette Strategy #1.

ROULETTE STRATEGY #2: DOZENS AND COLUMNS

Of the four Roulette methods in this book, the fourth is the most successful, but also the hardest to play and maintain. For this reason, it is listed last. That one will require hard work and extremely good game acumen, but it is by far the most profitable. Nevertheless, it is so difficult to manage that I caution you in playing it, because you will first need to practice. Do not be discouraged—once you have learned it and mastered it, it won't be nearly as difficult as it may now sound. Don't expect miracles, though, and don't expect luck to follow you if you don't have the abilities, skills, and game knowledge required. There is no shame in admitting that you are not cut out to play like this. Few people are. All I hope to accomplish in this book is to show more people how these methods can be employed, and how they can be exploited to make serious money—and that requires serious dedication.

Roulette Dozens and Columns

In Roulette Strategy #1, we discussed playing the board as opposed to playing the wheel. (We will get to playing the wheel a little later.) This method is also playing the board. It is called playing the "Dozens," or playing the "Columns," because that's precisely what you will be doing. On the Roulette table layout, six clearly designated betting areas, on the Outside, form the basis for this method. You should select one, or the other but not both.

There are three "Dozens," each containing twelve numbers:

- First 12
- Second 12
- Third 12

There are also three "Columns," each also containing twelve numbers in a row:

- First Column
- Second Column
- Third Column (see Figure 3, page 116)

Either of these pay 2:1 for a winner. This method, therefore, is based on playing either the dozens *or* the columns.

Dozens are easier to play if you are sitting at the long end of the table. Columns are easier to play if you are sitting at the bottom of the table (the narrow side, directly opposite the wheel).

The playing principles are the same and work equally well for either play, because the payoffs are the same, and the number of "numbers" is likewise exactly the same. There are twelve numbers in each of the three Dozens, and

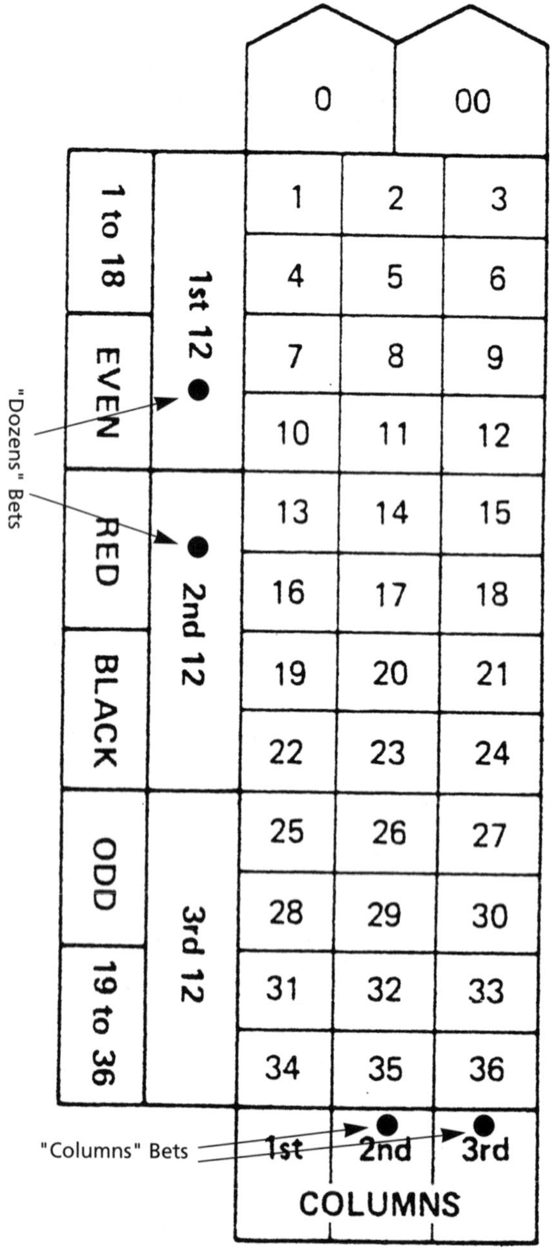

Figure 3. Roulette Strategy #2: Dozens and Columns

in each of the three Columns. The 0 and 00 house numbers do not figure in either of these bets. Therefore, if the 0 and 00 show up, all your bets lose. Otherwise, you have a 2-in-3 chance to win, on either method. This is probably the easiest strategy to use. Here's how it works:

Rules

Bet 1 chip unit on each of the first 12 and second 12—or, if you are playing Columns, or the first and second Column. It can be the first and third column, or the second and third Column, or the first and third Dozen, or the second and third Dozen, because it doesn't matter which—as long as you have two bets going on two of the three betting possibilities. This way you will have bets at 2:1 payoff riding on two-thirds of the available numbers on the wheel (other than the 0 and 00 house numbers, and for that reason the single 0 European Roulette is a better bet for this simple strategy). You have two bets going. You have two out of three chances to win (barring the 0 and 00 from consideration, because that doesn't affect this method). For the sake of simplicity, all examples will be for bets on the first and second Dozens.

So, you have bets on the first and second Dozen. This means that a losing event can happen only if the ball hits any one of the twelve numbers in the third Dozen, or the house numbers 0 and 00. Therefore, you have twenty-four numbers covered with your bets on the first and second Dozens, and fourteen numbers that can be a loser. This is odds of 24:14 that you will gain a 2:1 winner.

Of course, when you do hit a winner, that also means that one of your other Dozens bets lost. So, your winner will pay you at 2:1, for a gross of 3 chips (your original bet plus the 2 chips you won), but you will lose that 1 chip bet on the other of your two Dozens bets that did not win. Therefore, you wagered a total of 2 chip units, and you ended up with 3 chip units. This gives you a profit of 1 chip unit each time this hits.

If you hit a winner on either of your Dozens each spin, you would always make that 1 chip unit profit. However, the real world doesn't work quite that way, so there will be times when you will lose both your bets. Furthermore, it is statistically possible—and eventually inevitable—that you can face a protracted series of losses if the ball keeps landing an inordinate number of consecutive times in the Dozen (or column) you happen not to have covered, and/or including the house numbers of 0 and 00. For this to happen it would require that the statistical probability of the ball landing so consistently among the fourteen numbers you do not have covered had reached a point of an unusual anomaly. This can, and will, happen, but not nearly as much, nor for as long, as to cause you financial harm.

This particular simple method isn't a miracle, and, indeed, no methods anywhere in this book dispute the inevitability of recurrent or incalcitrant statistics. All we are trying to achieve here is a method of playing the game under real-world casino conditions that results in a financial benefit to us during the time we are playing, with as much of an extended exposure to the game as possible. It is important always to bear in mind the inevitability of statistical occurrences, and resultant anomalies, but it would be imprudent to consider all our methods as victimized by them. As I have stated earlier, these methods are designed with these events in mind, fully conscious of the fact that all are parts of protracted series of events, sessions, and blocks. No single events, nor any single session, nor any single block are defining factors in the end-result profitability of these methods. It is, however, important to try and remember this if you happen to sit down at the Roulette table—or any of the other games listed in this book—and suddenly find yourself exposed to a protracted series of losing events, with seemingly no upturn in sight. It will happen. When it does, you should be smart enough to recognize it for what it is (one of the statistically inevitable occurrences), take your session loss within the limitations of these methods' inherent stop factors, and move on to the next session.

Playing the Dozens (or Columns) will mean that you will have a slightly less than two-thirds chance to hit a winner each spin. Slightly less than the perfect two-thirds because of the possibility of the occurrence of the house numbers 0 and 00. Under perfect conditions, you should hit a winner twenty-four times out of thirty-eight and lose fourteen times out of thirty-eight. This means, on average, that you will lose about 36.85 percent of the time, meaning you will win at the average rate of about 63.15 percent. Even by the pure statistics, this is quite a good win rate. The trouble is that you won't win very much, since you can bank on only 2:1 for each hit, with the loss of the other wager unit on the dozen (or column) that did not hit, for a profit of only 1 chip unit for each win (relative to the number of chip units in play, of course). The second problem arises when you hit a series of losers in a row or experience more occurrences of losing events than you should, statistically speaking. Each of these situations, especially if they are anomalistically frequent, can dig quite a hole in your playing bankroll. We do, however, have this covered, and the solution is in the tiered wagering and fractional differential principles I discussed earlier.

Since the average hit frequency of this method is higher than most—at a win rate of around 63.15 percent—we need to get more aggressive in the wagering. You may also notice that as the win rate increases, more aggressive wagering becomes necessary. Also interesting to note is the fact that as the win rate rises, the total amounts of the net win decrease.

This is the simplest principle in casino wagering: the easiest it is to hit, the less it will pay, and vice versa. What we are always trying to achieve is the best possible parity of events versus their profit potential, while always structuring our wagering in ways that assure us of the end-result profitability. In the case of Roulette Strategy #2, the small incremental wins and the frequent rate of wins demand that we take a very aggressive approach to our wagers, particularly initially. With an expected win rate of 63.15 percent, we expect to make our 1 chip unit profit in about two times out of each three spins (a little less, to be statistically appropriate, but for the sake of the example, this is close enough).

So, if we started with merely a $5 chip unit—which is the minimum outside bet on most of the tables where we want to play—we would at best get $10 in profit, on average each three spins. We also want to play on tables where the house table limits for outside bets are high, such as casinos that offer Roulette games with a $5,000 outside bet or higher. Actually, we should try to seek out tables with $10,000 to $25,000 outside betting limits. This will provide us with a better game, and better range spread, if we really want to get aggressive. Of course the minimum total bet requirements will most likely go higher as the table limits increase, probably requiring at least a minimum total outside bet of $25. Let us therefore allow that in this example we are playing at the table that has a $10,000 outside betting limit, with a minimum bet requirement of $25 for outside bets. We should start at the very minimum with a $15 per Dozen (or Columns) bet, giving us a total outside spread of $30. Naturally, if the house rules are that each bet must be at least $25, we would place two such bets for a total of $50, and so on, but you can easily adapt that for yourself once you have mastered this method and have found out what limits are at the Roulette table you are considering for this play. A little investigation before sitting down will give you this information, and you can then modify your wagering strategy accordingly and get your betting methods established and learned before you sit down to play.

Continuing with our example, let us consider that we are allowed to make the two $15 bets, for the total starting chip value of $30 for both bets. With a bet of $15 on each of the first two Dozens (or Columns), we will gross $45 for each hit—the 2:1 win at $30 plus the $15 bet that remains on the table. Since this also means that we lost the other bet, we have to deduct the loss from the gross. So, when we started this first bet, we put $30 on the table, and now we have $45 in front of us—the $30 which is the 2:1 win, plus the $15 that stays on the bet that won. Since we don't have to make the bet that won again—that amount is still there—we deduct the $15 we lost for the other wager that didn't hit, and this leaves us with a $15 profit. Betting this way, therefore, means that each time we hit, we win $15—assuming, of course, that we always make the same wagers, which we won't, because if we did we would lose in the end, especially when we hit streaks of losses in a row. To overcome this, we need to increase our wagers, and do so more aggressively. Since we know that we should win about two of every three spins, a series of losses provides us with the opportunity to increase our wagers aggressively, knowing not only that we will hit very soon (statistically we expect this to happen about 63.15 percent of the time), but that when we do we must not only make a profit, but also overcome the accumulated losses we have incurred in the losing streak. Additionally, since we also have a loss limit (based around our session bankroll), we will never run up against a catastrophic loss in those situations where the serious statistical anomaly of consecutive losses hits us squarely as we sit down. Also keep in mind that since we do expect a frequent hit ratio, we are going to get really aggressive in the early stages of consecutive losses and taper it off a little when we begin to experience the protracted series of losing events, contrary to the expected probability. While this means that on some occasions we can actually lose in this series even when we do hit the required winner, the point is that no single event, session, or block is ever the considered result. Only the end sequence is the determining factor, and this can be as little as ten sessions in just one block or as many blocks as you can afford. The point is that even in such an anomalous losing streak we either recover so that we make a profit, recover so that we make less of a session loss than otherwise, or—in that rarest of all cases—lose only our *session* bankroll, but *not* our *entire* bankroll.

That is very important to remember, not only for this particular method, but for all the strategies in this book. If done properly, playing these strategies will mean that you will always have the best of everything when the winning is happening, making many times more money in those situations than without the implementation of these strategies, while losing very much less in proportion to those situations when the anomalous losing streaks occur so severely as to impact your session. Furthermore, each of these strategies has in-built loss limits, meaning that you can never lose more than you have allocated to that session or block. Losing less and less often is just as important as winning, perhaps more important. The old joke among professional gamblers goes like this: *It's easy to win—but it's hard to go home with it.* Point well made. While the majority of people win, an equally large majority of them will eventually lose because they don't keep the wins. Using these strategies forces you to keep more of your wins and face fewer losses. Keeping the lid on runaway losses and therefore eliminating anything that could even be considered as "chasing the money" means that these strategies have inherent value far beyond just the winning potential. They stop you from losing, and stop you from wasting your wins—in addition to maximizing your wins.

The following chart shows the wagering method for exploiting this strategy. I will use the $5 value as 1 chip unit, which means that the minimum will be a requirement of 3 chip units per wager, for a total initial outlay of 6 chip units ($30 total). I will apply the dollar values where appropriate to try to make this as clear as possible. Please do remember, however, that the chip value can be anything you decide. For example, instead of $5, you can easily make your chip value $10, and this means that instead of $30 per bet (at the $5 chip unit value) you will now have a $30 bet for each wager, for a total initial outlay of $60. Or, you can make your chip unit value $25, which means that the starting chip unit value for each wager will be $75 (3 chips per wager), for a total initial starting value outlay of $150. And so on. Whatever you decide, you can adapt this wagering differential in appropriate fractions by extrapolating based on the initial $5 chip unit value as I show here. It should be easy, if you understand the principle. If not, just remember that when I list my example for a $5 chip unit value, and you want to use $10 as the same value, everything in my examples will have to be doubled. If you want to use $25 as your chip value, everything in my charts will have to be multiplied by the factor of 5. And so on. I hope it's clear now. Remember that you have to continually consider whether the event was a "win" or a "loss," and therefore what the next wager should be, for how much, and what the total win or loss is up to that point:

Aggressive Table of Wagers

EVENT NUMBER	UNIT BET	INCREASE	NEXT WAGER	TOTAL
1	6	6	12	$30
2	12	8	20	$90
3	20	10	30	$190
4	30	10	40	$340
5	40	20	60	$540
6	60	30	90	$840
7	90	60	150	$1,290
8	150	80	230	$2,040
9	230	100	330	$3,190
10	330	120	450	$4,840

You will notice that this is a streak of ten losers in a row. This means that the ball would have to hit in those fourteen numbers we do not have covered ten times in a row. While this is not unusual, it would be a distinct statistical anomaly. Also notice that by the tenth event, our total exposure to the game was $4,840. The next wager called for—the eleventh—would be at the 450 chip unit rate, or $2,250 total, which would be a wager of $1,125 on each of the two covered Dozens (or Columns)—and all increases still in manageable whole unit values, easily accounted for in the real-world usage of chips of $25, $100, and $500 values. We can readily extend this chart, but I will leave that for you to do yourself. Simply apply the fractional incremental differential to additional increases in total wager value, and you can continue to use this wagering table for as many events as your bankroll will handle. Based on the above, if we make the eleventh wager, our total financial exposure up to that point will be $4,840. This is very small compared with the overall bankroll you should have available for this or any other method. The staple requirement should be that you have access to at least 1,000 times your minimum wager, which in this case is a $5 chip unit, and, therefore, your bankroll for this session should be $5,000. You should actually have 1,000 times the combined chip unit value, which in my example was $15 (3 chips) per wager, and therefore you should have a total of $15,000 available overall, per session. More, if you are playing at higher stakes. To make the calculations of the actual money value a little easier, here is the previous chart broken down by the actual dollar amounts:

Aggressive Table of Wagers: By Dollar Value

EVENT NUMBER	UNIT BET	INCREASE	NEXT WAGER	TOTAL
1	$30	$30	$60	$30
2	$60	$40	$100	$90
3	$100	$50	$150	$190
4	$150	$50	$200	$340
5	$200	$50	$300	$540
6	$300	$150	$450	$840
7	$450	$300	$750	$1,290
8	$750	$400	$1,150	$2,040
9	$1,150	$500	$1,650	$3,190
10	$1,650	$600	$2,250	$4,840

Don't forget to divide each total wager by two, because these are two wagers, one on each of the two Dozens (or Columns). For example, in event 4, the *next* total wager called for is $200, which means a bet of $100 on *each* of the *two* wagers. Also note that the total expenditure doesn't change, because here we are not changing anything—we are merely extrapolating the chip units into actual dollar amounts. Again, you can continue the table well beyond these ten events, for as long as your bankroll allows, and for as long as you don't run up against the table limit for outside bets. In these examples, I have used the $5 chip unit as base value, on a table with a minimum outside bet of $25, and a limit of $10,000. Whatever the limits are at the tables you consider playing, you will have to adapt these betting requirements accordingly, either higher or lower as the situations dictate, of course always mindful of your session bankroll.

How much this wins depends on when in the order of events the winning situations happen. The inevitable fact is that a winning session will always happen—we just can't forecast exactly when. Based on the expected probability of events, we should hit a winner twice in every three spins. But, as you will no doubt find out (if you haven't already), gambling games in the time of our exposure to the playing session don't always conform to laboratory statistics. Therefore, you are quite likely to run up against streaks on consecutive wins and losses roughly around the middle of the above scale of ten events in a row. As long as these are winning events in a row, simply stick to the base amount and cheerfully collect your 3 chip units profit each time ($15 in our example). If this continues unabated, you are happy because your session is always a winner.

Of course there will be—and should be—some losses along the way. Each time a loss happens, follow the betting scale shown. When you get your win, go back to the beginning. When you have consecutive losses, go up the betting scale for as many in a row as allowed for by your session bankroll and table betting limits. If you ever run into one of those long losing streaks and you can't make the next bet, stop the session. You can always start another session later. Most of the time you will have an experience with this method that will result in your wagering being roughly around the middle of the scale. You will have a few winners in a row, followed by a few losers, then a winner, then some losers, then some winners, and so on. In losing streaks, you will most likely never end up at the tenth or eleventh schedule of wagers, or higher. In my twenty years in the casinos, I have seen a streak of fifteen consecutive losers on the Dozens only once. I have seen plenty of five, six, seven, and eight losers in a row, followed by the win. I have seen only a handful of nine, ten, and eleven consecutive losers on these bets. It does happen, and it will, but it's awfully rare—so much so that it will affect your overall session losses only less than about 1 to 3 percent of the time, often much less. In the reality of your exposure to the game, with this method, you are much more likely to experience the win-loss scenario I showed earlier, with wins and losses scattered in consecutive events of around three, four, or five in a row. This will put your wagers square in the middle of the scale and allow you to make nice profits regularly so that even when you do hit one of those losing sessions, you will still have a profit in the end because no single session, or even blocks, will ever defeat you. Here's how the wins break down: The following chart shows what your gross will be when you hit a winner after the numbered event, along with what your total exposure had been so far, providing you with the net profit as shown. Again, these are based on my values in these examples. If your chip unit values are different, you will need to prorate these figures to match:

Aggressive Table of Wages: Win Value by Event

EVENT NUMBER	WAGER	TOTAL INVESTED	GROSS WIN	NET WIN
1	$30	$30	$45	$15
2	$60	$90	$180	$90
3	$100	$190	$300	$110
4	$150	$340	$450	$110
5	$200	$540	$600	$60
6	$300	$840	$900	$60
7	$450	$1,290	$1,350	$60
8	$750	$2,040	$2,250	$210
9	$1,150	$3,190	$3,450	$260
10	$1,650	$4,840	$4,950	$110

You will notice a recurring pattern of win amounts. We begin with the base 3 unit bet ($15 on each, for a total of $30), and if we win immediately we will gain a $15 profit. We bet the same again, and if this hits again, we still win that $15. However, if we lose, then the next bet is as indicated—which is $60. If we win, then we have made a $90 profit, and we go back again to the base $30 wager. If we lose, then the next wager is $100, and if we hit on this, then our profit is $110. The pattern of wins, therefore, starts with the very aggressive jump in the first four wagering differentials, tapers off slightly on the next three events, jumps aggressively again for the next two events, and tapers off proportionally on the next event. Extrapolating this sequence (which you can do for yourself), you should maintain this same pattern, relative to the wagers and total amounts. This method was structured in this manner because the vast majority of events will be among the first four or so sequences. If we get into a protracted series of losses, and are still losing after event 4, then we cut back a little and save some of our exposure, to see if this is one of those highly anomalous protracted series of consecutive losers. By the end of event 7, we are pretty sure that this is one such situation, and so we get very aggressive and push the wagers for a large profit if we hit at this point. We give this two shots, in events 8 and 9. If we are still losing, now we know that this will most likely be a negative session. Depending on the amount of our session bankroll, and the relative table limits, we either continue with the sequence farther, into the next several events (in wagering parity, of course), or take our losses and quit. Of course, if we hit a winner before we hit the table ceiling, or before we exhaust the allocated session bankroll, then we have recovered, and have defeated this highly unusual anomaly.

By the time we get to events 7, 8, and 9, we should be pretty sure that this may in fact turn out to be one of those negative expectation sessions, where we will lose either all or part of our allocated session bankroll. That is a determination you will have to make for yourself, because such decisions cannot be forecast, being dependent on whatever amount of money and chip unit value you have chosen to allocate, as well as the table limits. If we continue with the amounts in these examples, then we would have a minimum session bankroll of $5,000 ($15,000 total for correct bankroll), and a table limit of $10,000. By event 10 we would have lost $4,840 from our $5,000 minimum session bankroll. It is at this point that you should decide for yourself if this session should be extended into a double session. Since you have a total accessible bankroll of $15,000 (as recommended), you could extend this series further. I would recommend that if you run into this long a losing streak, and have depleted your $5,000 minimum session bankroll, consider this a loser, take your loss, and quit. This is the safer option. The more aggressive option is, of course, to continue the session into the rolled double, add the second $5,000 into the total mix, and proceed with the prorated series of events. This will allow you about three to five extra events before you either run out of your bankroll entirely or hit the house betting ceiling. Either way, such sessions are losers, and these situations will eventually happen.

If you quit after the tenth event, with the loss of the $4,840, it will take you an average of about 62.86 winning spins to recover that money. Since most of the time your winning events will be within the first five on the scale shown earlier, your average win per spin will be about $77. You can, therefore, easily calculate how long it will take, on average, to recover from any losing streak. In the above example, take the $4,840 loss and divide it by the average win of $77, and this gives you the expected average 62.86 winning events you will have to realize to recover that loss. On a busy table, the spin of a Roulette wheel takes about five minutes. This can be longer or shorter, depending on the situation. If you are playing on one of those high-roller tables—which is quite likely given the kind of action you will be giving the casinos—you may be one-on-one with the croupier. In this case, the spins will probably take about three minutes each. Allowing for the greater, let us consider that it will take five minutes per spin. At that rate, you will have twelve spins per hour. Therefore, to recover the loss from a catastrophic protracted series loss such as when you end the session at the $4,840 loss limit, it will take you about 5.24 hours. Easily achievable in the same day.

I have spent a lot of time in this section discussing the potential catastrophic loss of the session bankroll, and how this will affect your play with this method. There is a point to all of this, and that is to satisfy mostly those who will critique the overall expectation, because they vest their perspectives on Roulette in the mathematical inevitability of the independence of each event with the constant house edge of 5.26% on American Roulette, or 2.7% on the single-zero wheel. While I agree that this is inescapable, when viewing the game from that perspective, it has little to do with this method or your expected average events or wins. It simply doesn't matter what the events are, how independent they are, or what the house edge is or how constant. We are playing a method designed for a financial benefit, in a very short-term slice of individual independent probability, over sessions extended into blocks, and continued. Each step in the wagering progression not only exploits the probabilities within the mathematical model, but also allows for the financial gains that statistical theories simply ignore. One of the reasons why Julian Braun was such a great innovator in Blackjack theory was that he considered at the very outset that the purpose of beating the game was to make money. The mathematical probabilities and theories came second, as beautiful as they were. The same principles apply here. At no time do I dispute the perspective of the mathematical expectations, theories, or probabilities, or the independence of random events, nor do I dispute the dependence of sequential events, such as the cards drawn from a deck of cards in Blackjack. Whether the events are independent or dependent makes no difference. What *does* make a difference is how the wagering is being treated and how well the methodology of the financial gain is being applied to the game in question. These aren't miracles, and they do not really fly in the face of mathematical theories or perceived realities. These methods do exploit the very situations that the math and the probabilities themselves assure—the eventual certainty that something will occur, based on the rules and parameters as defined. Here in these methods, I take into account both the negative and the positive fluctuations in probability theory. However, I also account for the fact that the vast majority of time the probability theory will fluctuate merely in minor increments, almost rhythmically so to speak, like the tides of an ocean. Yes, there will be times when the ocean will flood the beach, and there will be other times when the water will recede far back and dry out the beach, but most of the time the tides will come and go in pretty much the same patterns, deviating only slightly from the defined expectancies. I am well aware that pattern recognition in gambling games is merely the applied perception of the individual, but statistics allow for the occurrences of sequential events and that probability theory itself actually allows for the occurrence, and recurrence, of serial events, both pro and con. If we try to illustrate this algebraically, we can isolate individual independent events as follows: (a), (b), (c), where any (a) event in the sequence thus shown is a positive "tide," while any (b) event is the applied negative—the negative event, the "escaping tide"—with the (c) events being the occurrences of incalcitrant variables. So, we can have a recurring pattern of events as follows:

$$(a) + (a) - (b) + (a) - (b) - (b) - (b) + (c) + (a) - (b)$$

This is a string of ten events, corresponding to the earlier example of ten events. Here, however, we can easily see that we did not have a protracted series of losing events. This shows the standard "norm" of expected events forming a more balanced sequence than that shown in the earlier examples of vast anomalous streaks of consecutive losses. However, these methods also allow for the understanding of grouped events, and these are the perceptional patterns that we tend to recognize. For instance, in the above event string, we would easily recognize the pattern of two wins, followed by a loss, followed by a win, followed by a pattern of three losses in a row, followed by an incalcitrant random event, followed by a win followed by a loss. It is an easily understood basic pattern of Win-Loss, and can more readily be shown as follows—where W = win, L = loss, and X = incalcitrant variable:

$$W - W - L - W - L - L - L - X - W - L$$

The only reason I put in the variable is because all valid theories of math and probability should always include the unforeseen. In the case of Roulette, this could be as simple as (1) the ball bouncing off the wheel and to the floor, which, therefore, invalidates the event; (2) someone bumping the wheel, which would cause the floorman to invalidate that spin; (3) a customer throwing up on the table, which would also invalidate the spin (it happens); or (4) any number of other variables that can happen and would account for the interruption to the statistical probability of events and invalidate one or more of the events in our string. Now, we can apply the patterns to our sequence and therefore come up with the following plausible event formula for such event strings:

$$[a + a] - [b + a] - [b - b - b] + [c + a] - [b]$$

Applying numerical values, we can easily see that the numbers are as follows:

$$[a + a] \quad = \quad 2$$
$$- [b + a] \quad = \quad 0$$
$$- [b - b - b] = -3$$
$$+ [c + a] \quad = \quad 1$$
$$- [b] \quad\quad\; = -1$$

Therefore, our statistical sequential string, in numerical values is this: $2 - 0 - 3 + 1 - 1$.

This equals -1 overall. Applying the wagering to this formula, we can easily see that in the above string, we have expended financially as follows:

$[a + a]$	=	2	$30 profit
$- [b + a]$	=	0	$90 profit
$- [b - b - b]$	=	-3	$190 loss
$+ [c + a]$	=	1	$110 profit
$- [b]$	=	-1	$30 loss
Total			= $10 overall profit

Thus, even with a string like that, where we have more losers than winners (the −1 in the alphanumeric sequence), and we have had one of those occurrences of a variable, we will still have an end-result *financial* profit, namely a positive result even to something that is by all indications a very negative series of events. Viewed individually, as event by event, we can easily see how the fallacy of the probability theory often infects and influences perceptions among statisticians, particularly when applied to gambling games. Most of the time, the pure theory of probabilities simply fails in gambling games because it doesn't, and cannot, account for the human factors, the variables and, most important, the ability of the player to vary the wagers. By applying incremental and fractional differentials to wagering, we are able to take what otherwise would be a very negative statistical string, resulting in an overall loss value, but still resulting in the end-sequence positive profit value. That is the primary reason why these methods can, and do, work, even on negative expectation games like Roulette and even in situations of protracted series of losing events concurrently or sequentially. The end result will always be a profit—in *money.*

And that is the other problem with purely statistical analyses of gambling games: Where is the money? The money won or lost almost never follows the probability theories as expected, when considered from within such a conceptual model. Money won or lost cannot be quantified by the theories because it is not part of the theory, it is only the perceptual outcome of the application of that theory to the game at hand, and done so by human beings. Statistics don't care about money, because it doesn't mean anything to the mathematics. Money only means something to people, and as a result money falls into the category of perceptual variables. That is why we can do things that machines can't. It is possible that eventually we will have machines that can do everything that people can, but the programming of these machines will most likely have the same kinds of limitations as those implicit in these gambling games. The machine may be able to recognize the events, and understand the wagering progression, but even a really good robot will never have the ability to understand money or the joy and value of winning it.

We are a successful species, and the dominant species on our planet, because we can transcend our environment. Rather than being merely part of it, or a victim to it, we can reform it and formulate it to fit our goals, desires, and objectives. This makes us incredibly successful predators and also environmental parasites. It also allows us to reshape reality in the way we want it, and in the way we wish to understand it. Just because what we understand as mathematics says that 2 + 2 = 4 doesn't mean that it does. All it means is that we have come to an agreement that we will understand those constructs in that manner and thus build other understanding upon such foundations. It doesn't mean that these are actual foundations or that reality is actually anything like this. All it means is that we have agreed that we will understand precisely that, in that way. There is a whole lot more room in thought, and in gambling profits, than has ever before been realized. I know of no book that has taken the fallacies of applied theories to these points, to format a principle that can exploit them for financial profits in gambling games. Although I will agree that they aren't perfect, at least these methods are useful, able to make profits, and are interestingly new. At least I hope so, and yes, I do understand that I could be wrong—although the likelihood of that cannot be easily quantified.

Bankroll Requirements

I have already mentioned what I consider to be a workable bankroll for this method and indeed any of the other methods described in this book. The most useful gauge by which to determine at least the minimum bankroll is to have 1,000 times the amount of the minimum bet for any one session, and 10 times the minimum session amount as your working bankroll. For example, in this Roulette Strategy #2, our base bet is $5. Therefore, our session bankroll should be at least a minimum of $5,000, as shown earlier. For your total bankroll, you should have $15,000 per session (3 chips times 1,000 each, $15 equals $15,000), and a total bankroll of a minimum of $50,000, which is 10 sessions at $5,000 per session ($150,000 overall). That 10 sessions is the "block" I have spoken of frequently. Later you can extend this to another block, and so on and on, for as long as you want to play.

Although these may seem like large amounts of money to many people, the truth is that in gambling—and professional gambling in particular—these are small stakes. Professional poker players have no qualms about betting $100,000 in just one hand. Sometimes more. Many of these players regularly risk millions of dollars at the tables. Baccarat players can often wager in excess of $250,000 per hand. Many Blackjack players bet $1 million per hand, and even more bet $10,000, $50,000, or more per hand. The point is that in professional gambling money is the essential tool. It is like the hammer and saw for the carpenter—without these tools he can still do the job, but not nearly as well, as fast, or as profitably. The professional gambler, or the semi-pro, must have the bankroll or he can't do it. It's that simple.

If you are scared of these amounts, you aren't ready to play this method, these methods, or these games in this manner. There is no half way in this choice. You either decide to do it, or you don't. There's no shame in it. If you balk at these requirements for bankroll, don't be discouraged. There are many other methods of play that can be applied to lower financial requirements, and you can still play quite successfully. My other books tell you how. Here, however, we are focusing specifically on the professional approach, using strategies I have designed to maximize the winning potential. For this, you need these kinds of bankroll amounts.

So, to play Roulette Strategy #2, you will need at least $5,000 for each session, and at least $50,000 as your block bankroll. You should have $15,000 accessible per session in case you decide to extend any playing session beyond the ten-deep losing streak, as we have shown previously, provided that becomes necessary, is possible, and you choose to do so (which I do not recommend). Of course, you should have the full $150,000 available for your ten session block as well. While this may still sound aggressive, bear in mind that your bankroll is not at risk—it merely has to be there, available, so you can get to it when you need to. These methods are designed to always make a profit in the end, and they will, as long as you continue with the methods unabridged, unwaveringly, dedicated, and always perfectly in accordance with the rules and directions. In most situations, your session bankroll will never be depleted and will never be at risk. I illustrated those anomalous occurrences simply to prepare you for the fact that they can happen—at some point and not necessarily while you are playing—and to show you that the method is ready for them.

How Long to Play?

That depends on you, your abilities, your selection of game, bankroll, levels of play, speed of game, casino, and numerous other factors particular to you, the game, and the casino where you are. As a general gauge, however, play for 100 events, or until you have doubled your session bankroll, whichever comes first. For example, if you play Roulette Strategy #2, each spin will take about five minutes (less or more depending on the circumstances), and this means that 100 spins will take you about 8.33 hours. This is about the length of the average workday, and since you are working at this, it shouldn't be an issue. Of course, we need to take breaks, have lunch, take a walk to clear our heads, and so on, and that's all okay. In fact, you can easily break this session into two subsessions, each of fifty spins, which would be about 4.16 hours. If you tire easily, you can split this session into two days. It doesn't matter, as long as when you return you continue the session at the next bet level, remember where you are in your session, and don't use any of your playing bankroll, or accumulated wins, for other purchases or uses. One of the greatest problems a professional gambler has is the attrition of the playing bankroll due to its uses outside of its designated purpose. For example, you start your session with the $5,000 bankroll, tire after four hours, and decide to quit and continue the session later. While this is okay to do—although inadvisable—you will now have to remember where you are in your session progression and all of the other items you need to keep in check. Now, though, you decide to go have dinner, and your waiter won't accept your room charge. You use some of your bankroll money to pay for the dinner, drinks, tips, and so on, and then go to bed. Next morning you decide to continue the session, but you have forgotten that you dipped into your playing bankroll for that payment last night, and now when you finish your session suddenly you see you don't have the results you should have had. This is the worst thing you can do. It is a simple example, but this kind of bankroll misuse and attrition can sneak up on you so quickly and so innocuously that many times you won't even know you did it. Therefore, protect your playing bankroll like the gold it truly is. Never use it for anything else—until, that is, you decide to quit playing for good, and end your life as a professional or semi-professional gambler. Until then, keep your playing bankroll completely separate from anything else, and never use it for anything else, no matter how tempting.

Once you start dipping into your playing bankroll for any reason other than to play, you become like the carpenter who pawns his hammer and then doesn't have the tools to make the money to pay for the pawn ticket to get his hammer back. Keep your bankroll in an envelope, and mark it with the session number. Envelope #1 will be for Session #1, and when that session is over, that money goes back into that envelope. And so on. Each time you end a session, add up what's left. If you made a profit, return the original session amount back into the envelope, and place the profits aside into another envelope marked "Profits Session #1." If your session ended with a loss, write the date and loss amount on the Session #1 envelope. At the conclusion of your ten-session block, dip into your set-aside profits and replenish your bankroll in that envelope (and any others also so marked). Doing this will safeguard you against using your playing bankroll for other purposes, and from using your profits for reckless spending.

Of course, you will need to extract some of your profits for yourself, so use this formula: Divide your profits into thirds. The first third will be your "replenishment fund." This is the portion of the wins that you will use to supplement your session bankroll when a session results in a loss. The second third will be your "slush fund." This is an amount that you will bank in a separate account, to be used to supplement any catastrophic losses, such as when you wipe out several sessions (highly unlikely). This same "slush fund" is also used to accumulate playing profits so you can grow your action and increase your stakes as your money grows, if this is the appropriate course of action for your playing style and starting capitalization. The third portion of this division will be your "keep money." This is your money, your income. Bank it, use it, and pay taxes on it. Keep your accounts straight, and you will never be in trouble with your income, your playing bankroll, or the government. Do it right, keep it straight, and you can and will profit.

ROULETTE STRATEGY #3: QUARTERS

In the previous two methods, I made it a point to make sure you understand the difference between playing the board as opposed to playing the wheel. The numbers on the board are arranged sequentially, in numerical order, while the numbers on the wheel are not. When you place numbers on the board, which are there shown as being next to each other, for example, the numbers 1, 2 and 3, these numbers are not so arranged on the wheel itself. On the wheel, the number 1 is next to the 00, and the number 2 is next to the 0, and these are directly opposite each other. The number 3 is located between numbers 24 and 14, and is located four spaces to the left of the number 1. Similarly so for the other numbers on the board and the wheel. This is done for two reasons: one, having the layout showing the numbers sequentially makes it easier for players to make bets. Two— and this is the real reason—the "scrambled" arrangement of numbers along the wheel itself is done to further randomize the spins. Sometimes—not very often—the wheel becomes a little lopsided (often referred to as a "biased" wheel) and will favor a certain group of numbers. Casinos take many precautions on a daily basis to make certain that their Roulette wheels are not so biased. If it should happen, and you were able to spot this, and the numbers on the wheel and the board were all equally sequential, it would be very easy for you to make your bets and exploit this situation. But because the numbers on the wheel are scrambled, to make these bets would require you to reach all over the board and try to put your bets down in time before the ball drops. This is very hard to do.

While many various situations in traditional Roulette methods can often work, many are highly dependent on other factors, such as the casino failing to properly balance their wheels at the beginning of each shift, and so on. A huge sequence of events will have to go wrong before a situation such as that occurs, and when it does you still have to be there at the time, spot this, and take advantage of it—all under the real-world in-casino conditions—which are really hard to do well. Actually, both of the following two methods will have the problem of putting the bets down. These two methods are structured to overcome the randomization effect of the non-sequential number arrangement of the wheel and make it possible for us to exploit high-value bets in sequential groups. This is, therefore, playing the wheel, and not the board. We begin with a method called Playing Quarters (see Figure 4 on page 142).

This is one of the two methods, mentioned earlier, which are somewhat more difficult, but more profitable. Strategy #3 is the easier of the two versions. Here, you divide the wheel into four quarters. *Do not confuse this with the Quads method!*

Take the wheel layout and divide it into as equal increments as possible and then arrange the numbers sequentially. Here are the numbers, arranged sequentially for each quarter of the wheel:

Quarter #1:   1, 3, 5, 13, 15, 22, 24, 34, 36

Quarter #2:   8, 10, 12, 18, 19, 25, 27, 29, 31, 00

Quarter #3:   2, 4, 6, 14, 16, 21, 23, 33, 35

Quarter #4:   7, 9, 11, 17, 20, 26, 28, 30, 32, 0

Notice that Quarters #2 and #4 have ten numbers each, while Quarters #1 and #3 only have nine numbers each. This is because of the two extra house numbers, the "0" and "00," which must be included in the method to have a complete coverage of all available bets.

In this method, you will play any one of these quarters. You can also play two quarters, but that becomes unmanageable, the physical requirement of being able to reach all over the board and make your bets on the correct numbers, corresponding to the sequential order of the numbers as

		0	● 00	
1 to 18	**1st 12**	1	2	3
		4	5	6
EVEN		7	● 8	9
		●10	11	●12
RED	**2nd 12**	13	14	15
		16	17	●18
BLACK		●19	20	21
		22	23	24
ODD	**3rd 12**	●25	26	●27
		28	●29	30
19 to 36		●31	32	33
		34	35	36
		1st	**2nd**	**3rd**
			COLUMNS	

Figure 4. Roulette Strategy #3: Quarters

shown above, is very hard to do. For the Quarters Method, it is best if you play only one selected quarter. You could play two quarters with a partner, of course, but both of you would have to be very good, and you would have to be able to manage your bets as a single player, since you would be making a half-wheel bet using two players. This is possible, but is very hard to manage accurately. In Method #4, we will discuss a variation of Quarters, which are called Playing Thirds. This will be more difficult than playing Quarters, but is based around the same principle.

In both these methods—#3 and #4—bets are all straight-up, each winner paying 35:1. This is important, because both these methods were designed to exploit the higher-value bets. Of course, the higher the payoff, the bigger the risk. I have designed a method that allows for the higher risk and always produces good profits in the end, when played correctly. Playing correctly means that you don't make mistakes. Just one mistake in your betting progression, or the overlooked omission of a wager on a certain number, or at the specified time, and your overall profitability will be severely diminished. In my book on Video Poker, I show how the tiny alteration on payoff for just one coin in payback can result in a devastating swing in favor of the house and an insurmountable increase in house edge. When you play this method, or any of the methods in this book, remember that any mistake means you will have a big problem—often one you won't realize you made until after the series is over. While you can recover from it—and I actually allow for such situations in some of these methods that can be that flexible—it is better if you practice your skills and discipline and make certain you do not make any errors. It is not as hard as it may seem and once you get the hang of it, you will see that it can become second nature. It will be at that point in your expertise—with any of these methods—

that you will truly shine and be able to assure yourself of nice and steady profits.

For Roulette Strategy #3—as well as #4, which is next—the rules are simple. Select your quarter and then bet all numbers straight up for each spin. That's it. Well—almost. Now comes the hard part. To avoid the inevitable losing streaks, and still ensure a profit, we once again have to call upon our by now famous tiered wagering and fractional differential principles. These simply mean a betting progression strategy designed to make profits without exhausting our session bankroll and running up against the house table ceiling. While simple in concept, again it is difficult in realization. Each method, by its nature, must have its own methodology. In the case of this strategy, the Quarters, it is designed to fit this one method, and this one method only. Although the principles can be shared among many methods, and are in fact highly similar to Roulette Strategy #4 (next), they cannot be applied to anything other than the method for which they were designed. This is because the wagering strategies and fractional differentials are specific to this case, this method, this betting, and not any other. They work only for these Quarters, and even though they seem almost identical to that for the Thirds (below), they most definitely are not. Keep this in mind in case you ever get the itch to try and "mix 'n' match." It won't work, and you will hate yourself for even trying. Stick to that which is shown here, and you will be much happier. I have spent thousands of mind-boggling hours working this out and I am probably responsible for making Tylenol the foremost brand in headache pills (just kidding, of course).

For Roulette Strategy #3—Quarters—the following is the recommended table for wagering methodology. Each is based on the base wager of $1 per chip unit, with a spread of $10 over ten numbers, such as those in Quarter #2, which I will use here as the example guide. There are, of course, two Quarters that only have nine numbers, and if these are the ones you wish to play—since they are a little easier to manage—simply prorate that to these progressions and work out a new table for yourself, following the guidelines as shown here. I have chosen to use the ten-number Quarter #2 because it will be a better exercise for you to become familiar with progressing to the next level—Strategy #4, the Thirds, coming up next. That will be the most profitable method, but also the very hardest to play and to manage correctly and without mistake. We'll get to that in a little while. For now, here are the numbers I will be using as my example:

Quarter #2:   8, 10, 12, 18, 19, 25, 27, 29, 31, 00

There are ten numbers in this quarter. This method of betting makes it possible for you to isolate a full 25 percent of all of the available numbers on the wheel and force the bets to reflect the sequential arrangement of the numbers as they actually appear on the wheel. This is very useful especially in the rare situations when you spot a biased wheel or a tendency among the numbers to hit in a certain portion of the wheel. Even if this is not the case, and the wheel is completely random, making your bets in these groups assures you that anytime the ball drops within that area of the wheel, one of your numbers will be a winner. More specifically, the main advantage of this strategy is that you are forcing a 35:1 payoff by creating a situation in which you have a 1-in-4 chance of winning. So, while you are gaining a payoff of 35:1 each time you hit a winner, you are wagering in a manner that reduces your odds of winning from 38:1 against to only 4:1 against. Simply put, betting any number straight-up means you have a 1-in-38 chance of hitting a winner, but by betting all your ten numbers in that quarter as your single wager, you are still gaining the 35:1

payoffs plus you are also gaining a 1-in-4 chance of winning. You are simply cutting down the odds against you. Although it is mathematically true that any ten numbers would statistically prove to perform in the same manner, the reality is that it happens more frequently when you isolate a sequential quarter of the wheel. Although when considering this statistically, such appearances are indeed merely human perceptions, the fact that the real world is just that—real—and not a laboratory statistical analysis also means that nothing in the real world is ever so perfect as to completely, accurately, and consistently reflect the reality of the statistics. No matter how well balanced, no Roulette wheel is ever that perfect. Many have imperceptible wobbles and imperfections, often so tiny that they never even show up in the balancing of the units. Unless you put the spindle and bearing under a spectrometer, or perform a subatomic analysis of metallic cohesion, the very fact that the thing spins will always cause wear and tear. It's inevitable. There is also the human factor and the balls themselves, which are handled by humans. Fingers have dirt and skin oils. These get transferred to the ball and then to the wheel. In a few minutes the results of the spins can easily become far from totally random. While selecting these situations and picking the correct quarter is difficult, this method is designed to exploit the situation of quarter wagers so that you can modify your quarter selection for the next session on the same wheel if you spot something like this. Even if you don't you are still better off playing quarters in this manner, because it will assure you of knowing a win each time the ball lands anywhere in your selected quarters. Combined with the wagering strategy this will always produce a profit for you, and even more so if you happen also to become skilled at exploiting the errors in the wheels and human spins.

One more interesting thing to remember—you are getting a 35:1 payoff whenever you hit and are risking only $10 on your spread. So, you could easily go for three spins without ever increasing your wager and still have a profit if you hit on the third spin. But, that's just an aside. The real value is in the strategy as here designed. So, now, the wagering strategy chart:

Aggressive Table of Wagers: Win Value by Event
All amounts shown in dollars ($)

EVENT	WAGER	TOTAL	GROSS WIN	NET WIN	ADD	NEXT BET
1	10	10	35 + 1	25	1	20
2	20	30	70 + 2	30	1	30
3	30	60	105 + 3	45	1	40
4	40	100	140 + 4	40	1	50
5	50	150	175 + 5	25	5	100
6	100	250	350 + 10	100	5	150
7	150	400	525 + 15	125	5	200
8	200	600	700 + 20	100	5	250
9	250	850	875 + 25	25	10	350
10	350	1,200	1,225 + 35	25	15	500
11	500	1,700	1,750 + 50	50	25	750
12	750	1,450	2,625 + 75	1,175	25	1,000
13	1,000	2,450	3,500 + 100	1,050	25	1,250
14	1,250	3,700	4,375 + 125	675	25	1,500
15	1,500	5,200	5,250 + 150	50	end of session	

To read the chart, remember that each line is a separate event. You make your bet, add the bets together, and this becomes your total. If you win, that becomes the gross win (don't forget that the wager on the winning number stays and therefore is counted in the gross win). Deduct the cost of the wagers and action up to the point of the win, and this gives you the net win. If that event was the winning event, that concludes the information particular to that event number. When you quit after the winning event, add the last wager to the net total, shown as a "+" number above, and you will have that much more to take with you because that last item was a winning event and, therefore, that wager stayed on the table for you to pick up as you leave. Don't forget to do this!

If that event was a loss, we continue along the line of information. Now we have the recommended add-on, which is the relative fractional differential increase of wagers proportionate to the recommended procedure for gaining the maximum win value. This then gives us the next bet in the series. Therefore, the next event will begin with that wager. And so on. Each time the result is a win, we start all over again. It's that simple. There are only two options to quit: Either quit after a winning event, or quit after the fifteenth consecutive loss. Only these two events can ever end a session! Do not ever end a session earlier, or for any other reason!

You will notice that in this progression of bets, we have again taken an aggressive rhythm to the betting structure. The majority of winning events will happen in the six, seven, and eight range of events. Statistically, we should expect a winner about once in each four spins. However, since the real-world events have a nasty tendency to not reflect the theory perfectly all the time, most of the reality you will discover are sequences of wins after about six, seven, or eight consecutive losses. That's why these are the most aggressive wagering situations with the highest profits—the "meat" of the strategy, so to speak. Of course there will also be the converse times when you will have several wins in a row, or wins that follow more frequently than the statistical average of 1-in-4. There will be times when you win several events in a row, or win one and lose one, then win two and lose one, then lose three and win two, and so on. All of this is accounted for in the wagering method, and each winning event always produces a profit. I have also taken into account the standard anomaly of many more consecutive losing events than can statistically be expected. This method, per session, goes all the way up to fifteen losses in a row. Therefore, this method requires a session bankroll of $5,200. This will allow you to make the fifteenth wager, should you be facing such an enormous bad streak. If you do, bite the bullet and take your loss, always mindful of the fact that you will never really lose overall, just in this session, or in that block. As much as it will hurt to fail to hit so many times in a row, after having spent all that money, remember you are playing a method that will win this back for you, and then some. Smile politely to yourself as the dealer looks unhappy for having to take so many thousands of your dollars without a winner, and smile politely as the pit boss comps your room, food, beverage, shows, and invites you back at any time, completely free of charge—"on the house." Think of the value of all these perks, then think of the fact that this was a very unusual anomaly and that this method will win it all back for you, plus a profit.

You will also notice that we got really aggressive in our betting on events 12, 13, and 14. This is because at that point it would be senseless to try to extend the session. Huge consecutive losing streaks can and do happen, many times more than the fifteen for which we allowed in this method. Once we recognize that we are facing such a situation, it is foolish to stretch the wagering out and try to outlast the sequence. The best we can do is to make or break the session right then and there. If we have lost eleven in a row, knowing full well that we should win one of every four spins, we know that we are facing a huge negative aberration. We therefore have the chance to exploit the inevitable end to this aberration. Of course, we don't know just when this will happen, and because the wheel doesn't have a memory we don't know if it will be in the next three to four spins. But, we also know that, based on independent statistics, we should average one win in every four spins, and therefore here we have the ideal opportunity to exploit the singular independent event statistics to our favor. Thus, we bet up. If we hit the twelfth, thirteenth, or fourteenth spin, we have made our session. If we hit the fifteenth, we have recovered our session. If we are still a loser, we notch it up to the inevitable, accept the loss of our session bankroll, realize we did this correctly and that we can and *will* win it back, enjoy the commiseration of the dealers, and thank the pit boss for giving us $2,000 worth of free stuff, such as dinners, rooms, drinks, shows, gifts, and return complimentary room, food, and beverage ("RF&B full comps"). Plus, we know we can come back after dinner and win it back just as quickly.

If we do suffer such a loss, we will make it back through accumulated wins in other sessions. We realize that this was a very unusual situation, and if we didn't recover, we then have to face the total loss of that session's money. Most of the time we will have winners within the first eight events, so we will not have to face this situation. However, at least once in our lifetime we will face such a huge losing streak, and we'll have to deal with it. Assuming we were so unlucky as to hit this the first time we played, and have therefore not accumulated previous wins in our "slush fund" to cover such session losses, we will need to calculate how long it will take us, at our average win rate, to get that $5,200 back. Since most of the time our wins will be in the eight-event range, this provides us with the workable figure of an average per-spin win of $61.25. Since there are about twelve decisions per hour at a leisurely Roulette game, this means we can expect an average per-hour win of $735. Divide that into the session money we "lost," and we can easily see that it will take us merely 7.07 hours to make all of that back. It's a little faster than Method #2, but more exhausting, so we will probably break this session into two bits of about 3.5 hours each.

Remember: In the end, we will always win. It simply

doesn't matter what happens in each session, or on each event.

Bankroll Requirements

As I mentioned earlier, for this method you will need a minimum of $5,200 per session, so that you can make that fifteenth bet if you must. Though it is true that over the majority of your sessions you won't have to go anywhere nearly as deep as the fifteenth bet, there will be a time when you will. At least statistically you should expect to hit this wall at least once, and when you do, you are likely to have a losing session. If you hit this catastrophic losing session early on in your series, it will hurt a lot more than if you hit it later, because by that time you will have accumulated profits. Remember that no matter when this may happen, you will need to keep going. You will recover, and the profits will be there. It's merely a matter of persistence.

The formula of the minimum 1,000 times your minimum bet is a good "working frame," but you should also remember that here we are starting our wagers at $1 per spot. Although you can still start this method with the same 1,000 times formula, which will give you a $1,000 starting bankroll, you really should have the $5,200 very handy. When I first mentioned the 1,000 times the minimum chip unit as your session bankroll, you will recall that we were at that time discussing the $5 chips and chip spreads. Oftentimes your best application of the 1,000 times factor formula for the minimum session bankroll would be to first take into account the total spread of your wagers. For example, here we have a total spread of ten numbers. Therefore, at the starting chip value of $1 per spot, the formula yields the total required bankroll of $10,000. If you recall, that was the recommended amount when I first discussed this. I'm sure you can see by now that I am trying to provide you with a gauge so that you can easily make these decisions for yourself. As a general guide, these methods of calculating what you will need as your playing and session bankroll will give you a sense of security and longevity. The purpose of a large bankroll is *not* that it will always be used and always be spent. The purpose of your bankroll is to make certain you have the *adequate tools* of the trade to take advantage of the series and sequences of wagers that will happen and that are required to happen in order for you to *realize your profits*. Without these fluctuations, your profitability would be more steady, but bland. The beauty of these methods lies in the fact that they take the statistical anomalies into account and use them as the basis for the sequence profitability. It's kind of like having your cake and eating it too. While this may initially appear incongruous, it isn't necessarily so—it only appears this way because of the established conventions in which our thinking is mired. I do understand that this kind of "left field" thinking may give many readers some trouble, but the mental gymnastics really aren't that hard. Just remember to factor your bankroll to fit your level of financial comfort, and your skills.

ROULETTE STRATEGY #4: THIRDS

Again, this is playing the wheel and not the board. This is a variation on Method #3, whereby you divide the wheel into three thirds. Arranged sequentially, these thirds are as follows:

First Third: 6, 8, 10, 12, 16, 18, 19, 21, 25, 26, 27, 31, 33

Second Third: 2, 4, 7, 9, 11, 14, 23, 26, 28, 30, 35, 0

Third Third: 1, 3, 5, 13, 15, 17, 20, 22, 24, 32, 34, 36, 00

Notice that the Second Third has only twelve numbers, while the other two thirds have thirteen numbers each. This is because of the division into thirty-eight by thirds, leaving a fraction that is not possible to bet. Therefore, one of the Thirds has one less number. In this method, you can play any one of these Thirds. You can also play two Thirds, but that becomes unmanageable. Bets here are all straight-up, each winner paying 35:1 (see Figure 5, on the next page).

A direct extension of the Quarters Method, this method is much harder to play, mostly because of the requirement of having to manage thirteen numbers in a third (or twelve numbers if you pick the one section that must have that one-fewer number). The requirement for the management of the thirteen total numbers is actually the only thing that is different from the previous Quarters method; the playing principles are the same. The only other major—or significant—difference is in the area coverage. Earlier we divided the wheel into four equally sequential groups of numbers, thus allowing us to win anytime the ball drops anywhere in that designated area; however, here we are extending that to cover fully one-third of all the numbers. We are doing this sequentially as the numbers actually appear on the wheel, as opposed to how they appear on the layout. This will mean that we will have the great task (and trouble) of making bets all over the table layout to keep the sequential order of the numbers constant, as they actually are on the wheel. This is important, because what we are trying to do here is to pick a third of the wheel where we can exploit the frequency of landed numbers. This is the method best used to exploit anything like a biased wheel, for example, or even the simple occurrence of certain trends whereby the ball tends to land more often in a certain area of the wheel, whatever the reasons may be (or cause). Though it is not important that this be the case—because this method is designed to work even on a perfectly balanced and random

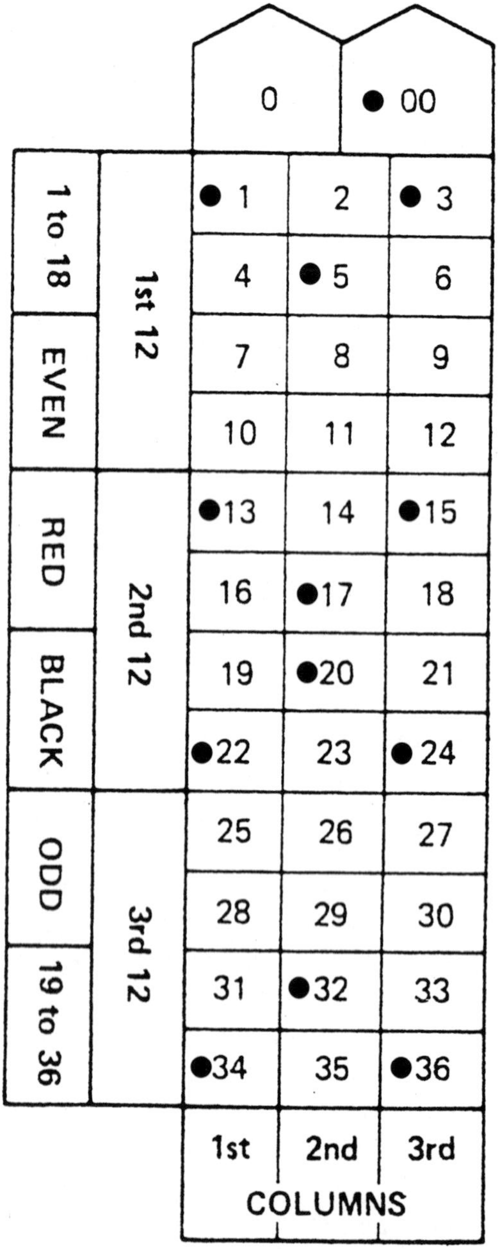

Figure 5. Roulette Strategy #4: Thirds

wheel—it is an ideal tool to use if you happen to be skilled enough, and observant enough, to spot such a situation or trend.

Basically, what we are trying to do here is to play a game in a way in which we have a 1-in-3 chance of getting a winner, but getting paid 35:1 for each win. So, while the odds are against us, this still means that we should statistically expect a winner once in every three spins. This is similar to that which we discussed in the Dozens. There, we were paid at merely 2:1 on our wins, but that was a much easier method to play and manage. Here, we are getting paid at 35:1 for each win, but this is a very much harder method to play and manage, not only because you will have to reach all over the layout in order to pace your bets—and do so before the ball drops, or the croupier announces "No more bets"—but also because you will have to keep track of all your bet amounts at the same time and then be able to have the correct denomination chips and amounts ready for all thirteen numbers (or the twelve if you play that one third with the twelve numbers). I do not wish to frighten you—on the contrary—that is a *part* of this method and part of your playing skill. It will be hard, but it will be rewarding. I have played this myself and found that one person has a hard time trying to make these bets in time, especially on a table with other players. I do not wish to dissuade you from this method, but in this kind of play either you will need to be very quick, and play on a table where you are the only player, or you will need to have a partner.

A partner is a blessing and a problem at the same time. Having a partner means that you can easily divide the thirteen numbers into two groups, one of seven numbers and the other of six. These can be selected so that one group is among the numbers to the top of the actual table layout, while the other is at the bottom. For example, let's say you will play this third, containing these numbers:

Third Third: 1, 3, 5, 13, 15, 17, 20, 22, 24, 32, 34, 36, 00

This sequence of numbers appears consecutively on the wheel itself, but is all over the board on the table layout. To make these bets yourself, you will be reaching all over the layout from one end to the other to make these bets, all the while having to do so in time before the next spin, as well as having the correct value bets ready, without mistakes. With a partner you can make this much easier by dividing these numbers between you. For example, one of you can position himself at the top of the table layout, near the wheel, and the other toward the middle of the table layout, or at the lower end, farther away from the wheel. That way, the first partner can play these numbers, which are all within easy reach:

00, 1, 3, 5, 13, and 15

This is a sequence of six numbers, all of which are close enough to each other on the table layout so that a player sitting near the top of the layout can easily reach them and make bets. Your partner will, therefore, sit toward the other end of the table (closer to the middle with this sequence), and play the following numbers:

17, 20, 22, 24, 32, 34, and 36

This is a sequence of seven numbers, and these are the other portion of that one-third that you are playing as a single block. This way, the two of you can easily manage to make the required betting spread before the next ball drops. The player with the fewer numbers (the six) can be charged with managing the bets, while the other will be charged only with making sure his numbers are covered correctly and in time. The first player (the one who makes fewer bets but keeps track of the sequence amounts) will make the first bet in the next series. His partner will then follow. Even if the partner is not skilled in the actual calculations of the required next bet, all he has to do is follow the amounts as placed by the first partner. For example, if the next bet in the series calls for a bet of $10 on each number, the main partner starts off by placing the first bet. His partner simply needs to see what that amount is and then place the same amounts on the numbers assigned to him. And so on. It is a very manageable means of playing this very complex method.

The problem is, of course, both in the selection of your partner and in your ability to maintain the proper sequence of bets. Of course other situations are likewise important, such as the tracking of the total amounts expended and the sharing of the playing proceeds (such as when your partner's numbers are hitting and you need him to shovel you some chips), as well as the general cooperative nature of this method. Plus, of course, the split of the proceeds, and so on, which you will need to arrange for yourselves prior to playing. The best means of approaching such partnerships for this method is for both partners to be thoroughly familiar with this method and equally skilled so that the partnership positions can be interchangeable, and one partner can correct the other in case there is a mistake made in the wagering sequence. These, and other such considerations, are all part of the professional approach to this kind of gambling. It is work, but your exposure to the game is for profit, not for fun.

Let us now postulate that you have made your selection and covered the bases, you have read the previous description of the Quarters, and you are now able to extrapolate that to those parts that apply in this method of Thirds, so you are ready to play. Here, therefore, is the wagering chart, structured similarly to that appearing for the Quarters. By following this chart you will assure yourselves of the most profitable sequence with the least risk exposure.

Aggressive Table of Wagers: Win Value by Event
All amounts shown in dollars ($)

EVENT	WAGER	TOTAL	GROSS WIN	NET WIN	ADD	NEXT BET
1	13	13	35 + 1	22	2	39
2	39	53	105 + 3	52	2	65
3	65	118	175 + 5	57	5	130
4	130	248	350 + 10	102	5	195
5	195	443	525 + 15	82	10	325
6	325	768	875 + 25	107	25	650
7	650	1,418	1,750 + 50	332	25	975
8	975	2,393	2,625 + 75	232	50	1,625
9	1,625	4,018	4,375 + 125	357	end of session	

At this point, we have exhausted our sequence. Although we could easily extend it into further events, this would be counterproductive. With our base $5,000 bankroll per session, the tenth event would requite more than $6,000 as a total wager spread, and this would place us into a fast-spiraling expenditure. Of course, if you have the bankroll to match, and are playing in a casino whose table spread is, say, $25,000, you can continue this sequence for as long as you determine for yourself. This version is, however, best managed as shown. It exposes you to wins and limits your exposure to excessive losses. Any session loss of these nine events that results in the loss of the $4,018 last wager does two good things (among the bad, of course): First, we didn't lose the entire session bankroll of the $5,000 we have with us. Second, we managed our session loss to the lowest amount, thus making is much easier to recover the losses in subsequent winning sessions. Therefore, by not losing more we made it easier to make faster profits in other sessions. Let me again remind you that no single session is ever the determining factor in the overall profitability of any of these methods. Even though it is inevitable that such losing sessions will happen—at some point in your playing career—this doesn't mean that they will happen always, immediately, often, or that they are to be singularly considered as the end-all decision. As I have shown in all the previous situations, I am here outlining the worst-case scenario, a situation in which you will extend your wagering structure past the point of being able to make the next wager and, therefore, suffer a session loss. This doesn't mean that each such session will be in this category. Remember that in Thirds, you will statistically hit a winner once in every three spins. Therefore, even allowing for the inevitable statistical streaks one way or the other, at worst you will most often be in the middle of the above shown scale, with wagers hitting after four to seven sequences. At worst, your general exposure will be at around the $1,418 mark, and on average somewhere less than that before hitting the inevitable winner. On average, your exposure will be about $202.57, with an average per-spin profit of around $107.71. This is indeed very workable. Assuming you can make the proper bets (or in conjunction with a partner), the vast majority of the time you will never face the complete loss of your session stake. On those occasions that you do have a losing session, if we take into account the average level of win per spin, it will take you an average of 37.30 spins to recover that previous session loss. This is about 3.11 hours of play, about one-third of your working day.

All of this is designed to demonstrate that even under the most severely adverse situations, the end results are always profitable. Most people have problems understanding sequences in wagering because they get so caught up in the actual singular event itself. Each losing spin produces desperation and disappointment. A series of consecutive losses produces anger, often to the point of recklessness, abandonment, or fury. Then, a losing session in its entirety can easily set these emotionally unstable people into a frenzy of accusations, self-reproach, and unmanageable anger. None of this is permissible if you really wish to gamble professionally or at least semiprofessionally. In gambling for money, as opposed to primarily for fun, there can't be any emotional attachment, either to the events themselves or to the money. The money is merely the "tool of the trade." The events are merely a series of situations that are being worked with the tools. For example, if you wanted to make a baseball bat, and brought home a piece of raw lumber, put it on your lathe, turned it once, and it didn't immediately become a Louisville Slugger, perfect with all the printing as well, would you get angry at the wood? Of course not. Well, why do people get angry at the first losing spin of the Roulette wheel? Or the first hand in Blackjack? Or the first gambling event of any game? Just as you realize it takes time and skill to make the lathe produce the desired bat, the same applies to gambling. Your skills + your knowledge + your tools of the trade (the money) + patience + persistence = profits. Just because you go 1 spin, 10 spins, or 100 spins without a winner, you shouldn't get angry at the events themselves, just as you wouldn't get angry at that piece of wood because it didn't turn into a complete bat after a few turns of the lathe.

This is the greatest problem that most people face when they gamble, especially when they try to gamble professionally or semiprofessionally. They get so intensely focused on the individual events that they completely lose sight of the big picture. Every professional gambler who is worth his mantle—regardless of what methods, system, or strategy he uses—will tell you that the *process* is the determining factor, because it is the process that is the job you have chosen to work at for your livelihood. Therefore, if you are seriously contemplating playing any of these methods I have shown in this book, or whatever methods of gambling strategy you decide to use, you must eliminate from your person all emotion, all focus on single events, and all attachment to your tools. The casino will now be your workshop and each game you play will be the wood you use to shape into the desired result. The "wood" are the games, and the desired result is the end profit. As long as you continue to work the wood, and use your tools wisely, you will always produce the "bat" in the end, the profit in our case. There are only two ways you can fail:

1. You quit before turning the profit.
2. You just aren't good enough to play this way.

If you fail because of the first item, you started either undercapitalized, or without the required conviction, knowledge, discipline, and commitment. If you fail because of the second item, you did so because you couldn't learn well enough and couldn't apply your skills, such as they were, to the actions required. Either way, unless you are prepared to substantially alter your life, and most important your perceptions on life and the realities of actual events, you won't be able to play casino games this way. Not many people can, and that's why casinos can continue to exist even with professional gamblers winning millions each year. Casinos win *billions* from players who *think* they can gamble, but can't do it for real, and, as a result, lose. Plus, of course, there are the tens of millions of tourists and casual gamblers who just want to have fun, and that's perfectly okay. If that's how you wish to play, I suggest you read the rest of my books, because they will show you how to have a great time and to win money even without making gambling your life's choice of work. But, if you are serious about making money from gambling, throw out everything you are, everything you learned, and start over. In addition, make sure you have the personality, temperament, skills, knowledge, money, security, and all the rest of the requirements to be able to actually do it. It's hard. Believe me, I know this well. Though even some professionals will get really lucky quickly, the majority will have to work long and hard to make headway. At first, this will be in small pieces, and your ability to keep these pieces together, and make them grow, will be just as important as your discipline in managing the rest of your life. Most of us who play professionally, or semiprofessionally, or who used to be professional gamblers, have to work at it. We are mostly not among the favored few who get really lucky all the time. We make our luck through diligence, persistence, and hard work. The people who see us cashing in $5,000 for the day, or whatever the amount may be, think it's a lucky hit. They don't see the sixteen hours it took, or the ten years of study and learning and practicing and observing and trying and improving and working it took to be able to exploit the right situations and circumstances. They congratulate us, and we smile politely, saying things like: "Oh boy, did I get lucky!" And so everybody is happy, these people think how nice we were, and off they go into their deluded little world thinking that they too can get so lucky sometime. And so they will, eventually, even with blind luck. But for us, this was the result of hard work. And that's what makes the difference—we *know* that it was hard work. And for that we are proud, but quiet.

The most successful professional gamblers are those nobody knows anything about. They don't say "I'm a professional gambler." On the contrary, when playing among people, they mostly say things like "How lucky I got," or some other innocuous expression like this, designed to defuse the envy and continue with the game. These others just don't know, and won't know, and that's precisely what the professional wants—to skip the issue, skirt the discussion, make himself appear as much as possible as just a poor slob, the perennial loser who just got lucky. Once you reach this point, you too can chuckle to yourself as you see others make fools of themselves making idiotic decisions and comments, all the while you know what they will never know, or mostly not ever be able to comprehend. It can be a powerful motivator.

Bankroll Requirements

As mentioned previously, we mostly have established the $5,000 per session as the mainstay of a gambling bankroll for these series of Roulette methods. This session bankroll is a pretty good one to always keep with you. In some methods, such as Blackjack, the $5,000 bankroll is actually a whole block of sessions. The formula of 1,000 times the base bet, or base bet spread, can also be used by you to determine what your personal bankroll should be. More is better, but that doesn't mean you will always spend it or use it. Having it available is far more important than actually spending it, because if you are spending it that can only mean one of two things: One, you are in a protracted series of losses, such as those catastrophic sequences I have shown here for these methods, that will happen eventually. Two, you have gotten reckless and have overextended yourself beyond the disciplined boundaries of your own circumstances. With the first, you can't help it. It will happen, so deal with it. Limit the session losses to the bring-in bankroll for that session, as suggested by me, or whatever that amount may be as adapted by yourself for yourself. Then move on. Remember that it doesn't matter. It's an event and it will be overcome. Of course, if you are facing number two in this example, then you have lost it. You are gone, done, dead meat, you have become reckless with your money and lost all semblance of professionalism. If this is the situation you are in, end immediately. Leave. Go home. Stay away from the casino for at least a week. Recoup, and recover your senses, discipline, and clarity of mind. If you can't do that, no amount of suggestions, recommendations, or advice I can give you—or anyone can give you—will help you. If that happens, realize you aren't cut out for this kind of life. Nothing to be ashamed of. It's a reality for 99 percent of all people who think they can gamble, or who think they can gamble professionally or semiprofessionally. This life has a very high washout rate, and there's no shame to it. I myself am no longer a pure professional. I "washed out" because of age, health, lack of endurance, basically having become "tired" after twenty years. There's no shame to that either. I now play semiprofessionally, and that suits me just fine. Also, as an author of gambling books, I share my acquired knowledge, which has become my main focus. Focusing is also very important, because you must have this singular focus, that passion to win to drive you to these levels of gambling and to those successes.

It's very possible, and many people do this every day. But be realistic, and realize that you are much more likely to fail than to succeed. The failures will mostly be the result of your own circumstances, rather than of the games or the methods and strategies used. If you fail, remember to first look deep in yourself. Chances are you will find that the failure had a lot more to do with your own self, and your own life, than it did with the methods you used. Blaming the wood, or the tools, is easy. Realizing that the blame actually rests with the craftsman is a lot harder, but more rewarding. Only then will you be able to grow, learn, improve, and progress. And that will enrich your life, whether or not you make it as a gambling pro.

Strategy for Blackjack

INTRODUCTION

Blackjack, known as "21," is the most popular casino table game played today. Each casino has many tables playing different kinds of Blackjack games and with different rules. Any casino over 35,000 square feet will have at least ten or so Blackjack tables, with most major casinos offering more than sixty tables. It's a hugely popular game, regrettably most often played badly by "casual" gamblers. Since Edward O. Thorpe's breakthrough book, *Beat the Dealer* in the early 1960s, hundreds of books have been written about this game, and an equal number of strategies have been propagated. Chief among such strategies have been the card-counting programs. These actually do work—or did, that is, until the casinos began to change the rules of the game to a point where even an expert card counter can have problems. There are several main problems with card counting:

1. *Card counting is extremely difficult to learn and put into practice.* It requires enormous mental skills and

mathematical acumen, particularly advanced counts with a true-running count, combined with Basic Strategy modifications and a side-count of Aces and 5s. It can be overwhelming and is a hard job. It's work, and very hard work at that, full of risks and pitfalls.

2. *Standard card-counting strategies often require huge bankrolls, and equally huge risks and per-bet amounts.* Even an "expert" card counter can at best eke out something like a 1.6 percent edge against the house, which means that to win $1,600 he has to risk $100,000! If you have $100,000, you can put that to much better use than playing Blackjack that way.

3. *Rules change.* Casinos constantly change rules of the game to combat card counting. It's not illegal, but casinos really frown upon it and can be very nasty to you if they suspect that you are counting cards. These rule changes may be subtle, such as requiring dealers to "Hit soft 17," a small rule change virtually always ignored by casual players, but one which increases the house edge by several percentage points. Other subtle rule changes are the cut-point in the deck, called "deck penetration." Most casinos which play two decks, for example, will cut off one full deck, and therefore you are playing with only half the cards! Yet, most people just don't get this, and keep on giving the house their money. For shoe games, six decks are often eight decks in some casinos, and some of these casinos also cut at 50 percent, instead of less than 25 percent as they should on shoe games. Hundreds of other little rule changes, all designed to defeat the card counter and get as much money from the "casual" gamblers as possible. Single-deck games are no better, because no casino will ever allow you to play that game to its optimum player advantage. They will deal only one hand to a table,

and then shuffle. They will only deal one or two hands to you if you're heads-up. They will cut the deck at 50 percent. And so on.

4. *Casinos have the right to bar patrons.* Remember that casinos are private clubs, and because of that they can, and will, refuse service to anyone they choose, for any reason, and can do so without justification. Your "rights" are suspended when you walk into a casino—you only have the rights that the casinos determine, and your right to be present on their premises can be revoked at any time without prior notice, or reasons given. That's why card counters often have to resort to exorbitant disguises, many of which no longer work because of the increased use of face-recognition technology. With my strategy as presented here, you won't have to worry about that.

5. *Different games have different rules in the same casino.* If you take the time to investigate this, you will find that many casinos have a variety of Blackjack games that have different rules. This is designed to exploit the unwary player and further combat the card counters. It is remarkable how different Blackjack games can truly be, not only between casinos, but between tables in the same casino!

These, and other similar problems, have reduced the "time honored" Blackjack strategies, and companion "systems," to virtual obscurity and inapplicability. Only Basic Strategy remains as a useful player tool, because by playing Basic Strategy alone (even when played perfectly) the house can still make its average of 0.5 percent per player, per table. Basic Strategy players who only play that way are no significant risk to the casinos.

The successful "strategy player," therefore, has to have something new. Not Basic Strategy alone, and not the card-counting strategies, but something entirely new and different.

That is what you have here, in this chapter on Blackjack Strategy.

This strategy has been developed over many years, and with a substantial amount of "insider's" knowledge. It is the *only one* that can actually give you an end-result profit, and do so without any of the encumbrances listed above. It is remarkably simple, but its simplicity belies the complexities that went into creating it, proving it, testing it, and playing it. This was not done overnight—it was done by tedious years of playing, testing, refining, and modifying.

This strategy is based on applying Basic Strategy—preferably my MBS (Modified Basic Strategy)—as modified in the rules, and playing the game in sequences within sequences, and with a specifically designed progression of bets.

The block is a sequence of ten sessions, each session divided into one event of about 100 hands, which will equate to about 1.45 to 2 hours of play at a casino Blackjack table. Each individual session is not considered singly, but as part of the overall ten-session plan. And, in turn, the ten sessions are part of a plan of twenty sessions, which, in turn, are part of a forty-session plan, and so on. The strategy is open-ended, *and* you can continue or stop at any time. However, once you begin the first session, you *must* complete the ten-sessions block. Otherwise the strategy will fail.

Betting progressions and amounts of individual bets are dependent on results in each hand played. This will be shown in the strategy rules, which follow.

Of all Blackjack hands dealt, 80 percent will fall into the category of a WIN followed by a LOSS, or a LOSS followed by a WIN. This is the core of the strategy, but it isn't all of it.

Of the remaining 20 percent, individual hand results will be several wins in a row followed by a loss, or several losses in a row followed by a win. It is at these points where your betting progressions and strategy rules make the greatest impact.

No *one* hand will ever be a determining result. It doesn't matter—to the overall plan—whether you win or lose any individual hand. In addition, it doesn't matter—to the overall plan—whether or not any one session is a winning one or a losing one. In the end, after your entire sequence of sessions is played, the end result will *average* to the case examples shown following the presentation of Strategy Rules, below. You will win an *average* of $1,620 for each *completed* sequence, regardless of what happens to the individual hands and to individual sessions (based on the bets and bankroll as stated here).

This strategy is based on playing a six-deck shoe game, where you can double-down on any two matching first cards, split, and resplit and double-down on splits and resplits. Most Las Vegas casinos will offer these rules on shoe games. You can also play this strategy on eight-deck shoes and even in casinos that don't offer all of the preferred rules, but in these cases your overall average win expectancy will be lower.

Your base-starting bet amount is $5 per hand. You build from there, as shown in the Strategy Rules. Your required bankroll is $5,000. This is divided into ten sessions, each with a $500 buy-in. Yes, you can play at lower levels, but you will have to modify the strategy accordingly. It is not advisable to do so. This amount of starting bankroll is necessary to allow you to reach the full potential of the strategy.

Divide your bankroll into ten envelopes, marked "Session #1 = $500," "Session #2 = $500," and so on. This will allow you to track where you are and how you are doing, and is also an easy way to tally up at the end. Carry these envelopes with you, hidden, and take out each stake for each session prior to arriving at the table.

When you begin, take out envelope #1, remove the $500 stake (out of sight of casino employees, such as in the restroom), then select your table and buy-in for the entire $500. You are now ready to begin.

Following each session, change the chips you have left into cash, place this money back into the envelope, and put this envelope away somewhere, separate from your remaining envelopes.

When you have completed all ten-session block for that sequence, take out all the envelopes and count up. Mark the contents of each envelope as either a *winning session* by that dollar amount over and above the original stake for that envelope, or a *losing* session. Then add up your envelopes. Wins + wins - losses. This will equal your end result for that completed ten-session stretch. If you have allocated more than ten sessions, in equal blocks of ten sessions each (by increasing your base stake amount), then follow this process for that number of sessions.

A word of caution! Once you begin the *first session,* you must be prepared to *complete the whole ten-session block.* This can be done in about twenty hours. You can split this into two to three days, but don't split it into several weeks, or months, between sessions. This could result in your corrupting your "remembrances" of what happened and where and how.

The most powerful situation with this strategy is that at no time will any one hand or session matter. You can lose that hand, and even that session, and still come out a winner in the end—*if* you play the strategy correctly. Consequently, it really doesn't matter how you play the hand, what cards are dealt to you, or what the result of that hand is. But Basic Strategy play will enhance your results, and particularly so my MBS, so play that way. This will also help "hide" your identity as a strategy player.

Always remember that your individual session bankroll

is never at risk. It doesn't matter if you lose part of it, or all of it, in any *one* session, because in the end, overall, this is insignificant. You will have more *financial* winners than losers.

Stick to the 100-hands maximum. Don't play fewer than 99, and don't play more than 110. Casinos usually deal about 60 hands per hour. On a busy table, this can be slowed down to about 50 hands per hour, sometimes fewer if there are slow players, shift changes, payouts, or chip runs. This means that your 100 hands will take about 1.45 to 2 hours, depending on these circumstances. You can also keep count of the hands either mentally, by using chip positions on the table to remind you of the number of hands played, or by keeping a simple counting device in your pocket and clicking it as each hand is played (not recommended because it's too cumbersome, but may be of help to those players who can't keep several decisions in their minds at the same time).

Always know where you are in your betting progression, and have your next *two* bets ready to go, depending on what the outcome of the hand is to be. Remember, most of the time a WIN will be followed by a LOSS, so have that next bet ready. Likewise, a LOSS will be followed by a WIN, so have that bet ready as well. For the rest, be prepared to make these bets instantly, without any decision-making processes at the table. Don't fumble your chips. Don't show the next two bets ready as neat stacks in front of you. Disguise them in your chip pile, but know what they are and be able to get your hands on them immediately upon the conclusion of each hand played.

Always take advantage of each double-down and split and resplit opportunity. However, *do not* count these "extra" wins as part of your betting progression. *Only the bet in the box* is what determines your next sequence of bets, win or lose on that hand. Any win on a double-down and/or split and/or resplit is a *bonus* to your bankroll, but *must not* be counted as part of the *next bet sequence.*

Never take insurance against a dealer's Ace-up. Let the bet be decided as it will. It doesn't matter to the overall strategy.

Double-down on any first two cards that total 11, even against a dealer's Ace-up.

Double-down on any first two cards that total 10, *except* against a dealer's Ace-up—in that case HIT instead. Other rules now follow.

RULES

1. After each loss, expect a win, so double your last bet amount.

2. After each win, expect a loss, so *bet half the previous bet amount, or the table minimum,* and start over with Rule #1. That new amount—if larger than the table minimum—will now become your *new* starting unit value.

   - If you lose after a loss, start over per Rule #1—which means to expect a win and therefore double the bet. If you lose again, then expect a win, so double that bet. If you lose again, expect a win, so double that bet. After you have so doubled the bet three times, then stay at that third amount until a win, and then follow the rules from Rule #2.

3. If you win after a win, let it ride.

   - If you win again, take back the original bet amount and let the rest ride.

   - If you win again, take back the win, let the rest ride, and so on for any *consecutive wins.*

4. When you finally lose after a series of consecutive wins, expect a win, so double your previous bet and proceed with Rule #1 and so on from there.

5. Do *not* make more than three consecutive doublings of your bet. *Stay* with the third-double bet amount until you get a loss, then proceed with Rule #1 and so on from there. (Remember that if you have suffered a loss at any time during this sequence, Rule #4 applies.)

6. Quit any session after either:
   - You have made a 100 percent profit over your session stake (regardless of whether you had hit your 100 hands).
   - You have reached approximately 100 hands played (about 1.45 to 2 hours of play).
   - You have lost and cannot make the next bet in your sequence progression.

7. When you win the first bet after sitting down to play your first hand, treat this as in Rule #3. If you lose the first bet after sitting down to play your first hand, treat this as in Rule #1, and so on.

8. Play Basic Strategy—preferably my MBS—with the following modifications:
   - Never hit your hard-12 or hard-13 against dealer's up card of 2, 3, 4, 5, or 6. Hit these hands only against everything else.
   - Don't hit soft-18.
   - Double-down on any first two cards that total 11, even against a dealer's Ace-up.
   - Double-down on any first two cards that total 10, *except* against a dealer's Ace-up (in which case hit the hand instead).

- Double-down on all *soft* hands of 13, 14, 15, 16, and 17 against the dealer's up cards of 3, 4, 5, or 6.

9. Always take double-down and split and resplit opportunities as dictated by Basic Strategy (or my MBS), and allowed by house rules, except as modified in Rule #8.

10. Never count any double-down or split wins/losses in your general strategy progression of bets. It is *always the first bet in the box* that determines where you are in a betting progression and what your next bet ought to be.

11. Never take insurance, and *never* ask for "even money" when you have a Blackjack and the dealer is showing Ace-up.

12. Play only six-deck shoe games where "Dealer must STAND on ALL 17," and where you can double-down after splits and resplits (You can play eight-deck shoes, but bear in mind what was said earlier).

That's it.

What follows are several charts showing some case examples, as compiled from my play.

TEST CASE ANALYSIS

Here is an example of a twenty-session block, shown with actual graph analysis of each individual session from session #11 through #20. (Sessions #1 through #10 were statistically identical.)

Player Statistics per Session
Session #11

Bankroll ($)	Current	165
	Initial	500
	Highest	860
	Lowest	115
Hands	Played	101
	Won	46
	Lost	45
Blackjacks Received		7
Longest Win Streak		5
Longest Loss Streak		11
Total Amount Wagered ($)		2,410
Return on Wagers		−14%
Number of Dealer Blackjacks		4

Overall session status = loss.

In this session, note that although we won more hands than we lost, we did lose overall for the session because we suffered an eleven-deep losing streak. Such a long losing streak of consecutive hands lost is a substantial aberration and is accounted for in the overall strategy. Here, in this *individual* session, at the point of the long losing streak we were at the $40 per bet amount, and at $800 in total session capital. That eleven-deep long losing streak had a substantial negative impact over this one session, but the point to always remember is that this one session is not the deciding factor in the overall strategy. Even here, after such a long losing streak, we did not get wiped out. Also, six of the losses in that long losing streak were either double-down or split situations. Had this not been the case, we would have had much more of our bankroll left at the end of this session. This is also accounted for in the overall strategy, as you can see from what follows.

Session #12

Bankroll ($)	Current	653
	Initial	500
	Highest	733
	Lowest	380
Hands	Played	101
	Won	43
	Lost	48
Blackjacks Received		3
Longest Win Streak		4
Longest Loss Streak		5
Total Amount Wagered ($)		2,255
Return on Wagers		7%
Number of Dealer Blackjacks		5

Overall session status = win.

In this session we had an overall win, despite having lost more hands than we won. It is worthy to point out that in this strategy, we can lose more hands than we win and still come out profitably at the end.

Session #13

Bankroll ($)	Current	730
	Initial	500
	Highest	915
	Lowest	480
Hands	Played	108
	Won	42
	Lost	53
Blackjacks Received		5
Longest Win Streak		5
Longest Loss Streak		5
Total Amount Wagered ($)		2,615
Return on Wagers		9%
Number of Dealer Blackjacks		3

Overall session status = win.

Here note that the overall session was a win and that we achieved that win even though we lost eleven more hands than we won! And we still made a profit at the end.

Session #14

Bankroll ($)	Current	275
	Initial	500
	Highest	585
	Lowest	125
Hands	Played	107
	Won	43
	Lost	57
Blackjacks Received		2
Longest Win Streak		8
Longest Loss Streak		8
Total Amount Wagered ($)		2,510
Return on Wagers		–9%
Number of Dealer Blackjacks		9

Overall session status = loss.

Here notice three items:

1. We lost fourteen more hands than we won.
2. Dealer had nine Blackjacks.
3. We suffered an eight-deep losing streak.

All of these instances are aberrations in the overall context of the strategy. Under these conditions, it is impossible to win the session, *but we only lost less than half our stake—* even in these terrible cases.

Session #15

Bankroll ($)	Current	433
	Initial	500
	Highest	713
	Lowest	318
Hands	Played	100
	Won	36
	Lost	56
Blackjacks Received		5
Longest Win Streak		4
Longest Loss Streak		6
Total Amount Wagered ($)		2,975
Return on Wagers		–2%
Number of Dealer Blackjacks		4

Overall session status = loss.

Here notice two items:

1. We lost twenty more hands than we won!
2. We had a six-deep losing streak at the $120 per bet level.

And yet we only lost $67 overall!!

Session #16

Bankroll ($)	Current	850
	Initial	500
	Highest	850
	Lowest	380
Hands	Played	103
	Won	46
	Lost	48
Blackjacks Received		2
Longest Win Streak		6
Longest Loss Streak		5
Total Amount Wagered ($)		2,085
Return on Wagers		17%
Number of Dealer Blackjacks		3

Overall session status = win.

Again we lost more hands than we won, *but we still made a profit!*

The *average* "magic number" is 7—we can, *on average,* lose seven more hands than we win and still make a profit at the end of any one individual session.

Session #17

Bankroll ($)	Current	550
	Initial	500
	Highest	688
	Lowest	363
Hands	Played	100
	Won	42
	Lost	45
Blackjacks Received		9
Longest Win Streak		4
Longest Loss Streak		5
Total Amount Wagered ($)		1,985
Return on Wagers		3%
Number of Dealer Blackjacks		9

Overall session status = win.

This session is a statistical dead-heat. The session didn't swing one way or the other to any significant percentage. Again, we lost more hands than we won, but we still made a profit at the end. Also, despite nine dealer Blackjacks, we made a statistical profit of 3 percent.

Session #18

Bankroll ($)	Current	1,010
	Initial	500
	Highest	1,010
	Lowest	473
Hands	Played	99
	Won	50
	Lost	44
Blackjacks Received		6
Longest Win Streak		7
Longest Loss Streak		4
Total Amount Wagered ($)		1,990
Return on Wagers		26%
Number of Dealer Blackjacks		7

Overall session status = win.

We ended this session after ninety-nine hands when we reached the 100 percent profit margin over and above our initial session starting stake.

Notice that we only won six more hands than we lost, but also notice how much more profit we made in comparison with similar contrary events in negative situations. That's one of the many great features of the strategy; winning sessions are so much more profitable than comparative situations in losing sessions.

Session #19

Bankroll ($)	Current	578
	Initial	500
	Highest	698
	Lowest	323
Hands	Played	101
	Won	40
	Lost	51
Blackjacks Received		3
Longest Win Streak		6
Longest Loss Streak		9
Total Amount Wagered ($)		2,230
Return on Wagers		4%
Number of Dealer Blackjacks		6

Overall session status = win.

Here notice that we again lost eleven more hands than we won, and we had a nine-deep losing streak at the $40 per bet level, plus the dealer had nine Blackjacks, and yet *we still made an overall profit!*

Session #20

Bankroll ($)	Current	573
	Initial	500
	Highest	598
	Lowest	343
Hands	Played	104
	Won	44
	Lost	50
Blackjacks Received		2
Longest Win Streak		5
Longest Loss Streak		5
Total Amount Wagered ($)		2,350
Return on Wagers		3%
Number of Dealer Blackjacks		6

Overall session status = win.

Again we lost more hands than we won, but *we still made a profit!*

Final Analysis
Sessions #11 through #20

10-session total stake	=	$5,000
Total winning sessions	=	7 (same as in #1 through #10)
Total losing sessions	=	3 (same as in #1 through #10)
Total net win over 10 sessions	=	$817

Total net win is calculated by adding winning sessions and subtracting losing sessions to arrive at net result. Net result is over and above the starting ten-session stake.

Win/Loss by Session

SESSION #	$ WIN	$ LOSS
11	0	335
12	153	0
13	230	0
14	0	225
15	0	67
16	350	0
17	50	0
18	510	0
19	78	0
20	73	0

Average win per session = $81.70 (based on 10 total sessions)
Average win per hand = $ 8.17 (based on the average 100 hands per session)

These statistics, and averages, are independent of your per-session stake. Notice that *at no time* is your individual per-session stake *ever at risk*. Simply put, the money with which you buy-in for any individual session simply doesn't figure in the overall plan of the strategy.

Final Analysis Over 20 Sessions

Total net win = $2,457.00

Average win per session = $122.85

Average win per hand = $12.29

Average win per hour = $61.43 (based on each session lasting 2 hours)

Average win over multiple session blocks = $1,620.00.*

*Multiple session blocks mean combined 10-session events in blocks of 10 total multi-session events, which equals 100 total session blocks.

Final Note

If you have read my Blackjack book, the first thing you will notice with this strategy is that the rules here are just a tad different from those shown in [the simplified version of this method] that earlier book. In that book I recommend increases of one-third, and decreases of two-thirds. Here, I recommend increases by double—100 percent more—and decreases by *half* the previous bet amount, or back to the starting base minimum unit (whatever that starting chip unit value may be for you; here in my examples, this was $5). The simplified version of this method offered in my book *Powerful Profits from Blackjack* was intentionally streamlined to make it more accessible to the general casual player. It allows casual players with limited bankrolls and limited time at the game to play for better profits than otherwise, and is also the ideal alternative to such headbreaking systems as card counting, which require a whole lot of brain work and can't always be done well even under ideal conditions.

In this book, this strategy is far more detailed and far more aggressive. This version of the strategy is implicitly reliant on your desire to play Blackjack for profit, and thereby professionally or at least semiprofessionally. This method is formatted to exploit the sequences of sessions, fully mindful that you are playing it with the proper and complete knowledge of the game, as well as the wagering methodology outlined here. In addition, you are playing within the rules of this method and never make mistakes (at least not very often). By having this kind of dedication, you have separated yourself from the "general public," and are therefore sufficiently equipped to play this way, with this method. Although this method is more complicated than the shortened version, it is not that hard to play once you have fully grasped how it works. This will take some practice so that you get the idea of the betting progressions and how to manipulate your bets. This method is designed to be aggressive when increasing the wagers and very aggressive in the reduction of wagers. For example, if you are at the level of the $40 bet, and in accordance with the rules your next wager should be increased, in this method you will go immediately to the $80 bet level. When your strategy rules call for a wager reduction, you immediately go back to half the starting chip unit minimum amount (or the table minimum, which in my examples was $5, but that amount can be whatever you select, as long as you have the required session bankroll based on it). So, in accordance with Rule #1, you would bet $20 on the next event. If the strategy then called for that to be increased, you would double it, and therefore your next wager will be $40. And so on. This way you will always be growing your wagers when winning, and always lowering your wagers to the bare minimum when you are losing. Therefore, you will win more when winning, and lose less when losing. This is perhaps the greatest value of this method because it forces you to increase your wagers when you are winning, and conversely forces you to dramatically reduce your wagers when you are losing. The value of your end-result profits will come from extended streaks of consecutive wins, many of which will occur in the range of two to seven in a row. During these, any double-down and/or split that also wins is added profit. Conversely, you will likewise experience sequences of like losses in a row, equally averaging two to seven or so in a row. In the win streak, you are betting more, while in the losing streak this method forces you to quickly reduce your bets all the way to the minimum, thus saving your previously accumulated profits. For example, if you are at the $120 per bet level, and you experience a four-deep winning streak, you will win as follows: $120 for that first win. Then, expecting a loss, you will bet the minimum in accordance with Rule #2—a bet of $60. Now you win again—your second consecutive win—and so you apply Rule #3 and let the bet ride. Therefore, your next wager will be $60. Now you win for the third consecutive time, and you apply Rule #3 (first bullet entry), take the win, and let the previous bet ride. So, your next bet is still that $60, but you have already made a profit. Now you win for the fourth consecutive time and apply Rule #3 (second bullet entry)—you take the win and let the rest ride, intending to keep doing so from this point on as long as you are winning consecutively. However, that was your fourth win in a row, and now you suffer the loss of that $60 on the fifth hand. So, you apply Rule #4, and double the bet, expecting a win after a loss, so your next wager will be $120, and then proceed with that as if that was your starting wager per Rule #1. If you lose again, as a consecutive loss, apply Rule #2 (first bullet entry) and keep doubling for three consecutive losses, and stay at that level until a win or until the situations as indicated occur.

All that you have read thus far, and the analysis examples as listed, demonstrates that the Blackjack Strategy does perform as designed. How this will work for you when you play it is determined by how well you will learn to play it and how few errors you make during the course of events, as well as in how many session events and session blocks you participate. I again caution you to first master the strategy, as well as the game itself. *Practice.* Know what you're doing at every step of the way so you don't have to think about what you'll be doing when you're in the actual playing situation. Once you have mastered this, all your play will be automatic, and you will never have to make any decisions. It will all work like a well-oiled machine, and that is the beauty of this strategy. Once you have experienced it in this manner, having mastered it and the game, and all the practical principles required of your self-discipline and strategy-and-game knowledge, then you will be able to play it without having to give any individual event any thought. It will simply be obvious to you, and you will perform the functions automatically. You will always know that no matter what happens, your individual per-session stake is never at risk, and that what happened to the hands of games in any one session simply does not matter to the overall end result.

ADDENDUM TO BLACKJACK STRATEGY

During a recent book signing event for my book *Powerful Profits from Blackjack*, I had an interesting discussion with one of the participants. This man—let's call him Brad—was asking me questions about the strategy I presented in that book—an abridged version of the advanced strategy that is fully presented in this book.

In my *Blackjack* book I outlined a method of playing that I have developed over many years and many millions of hands played. These methods are even more fully detailed here in this book. At the time I wrote my *Blackjack* book, my intent and purpose was to make Blackjack clear and simple to understand; to show the methods that were used in the past as successful strategies; to show why such strategies and methods can no longer be used as effectively in the modern twenty-first-century casino; and to offer a streamlined version of my Blackjack Strategy in a simplified manner so that anyone reading that book could use it as a simple alternative to the rigor of learning to count cards. That version of this Blackjack Strategy is self-contained and can be used successfully if its users actually read that whole book, and then are able to play it correctly, as directed.

I made sure that readers clearly understand that the strategy shown in my *Blackjack* book is a *simple* version of a more complex and more professional approach to Blackjack, and that for the full and complete understanding of how that works, readers should refer to *this* strategy book. I also made certain that readers of the *Blackjack* book are perfectly informed that the strategy is a "simple" strategy, and that its more complex cousin is much more fully described in my strategy book.

I was greatly surprised by the discussion that took place in that bookstore. As I began to discuss Blackjack in general with Brad, it became apparent that not only did he fail to read the book, but also that he had preconceived notions of what a Blackjack strategy should be and how it should be stated and enumerated. It soon became clear that his entire understanding of Blackjack was mired in the narrow scope of purely theoretical mathematics and furthermore firmly grounded in the dogmatic, zealous, and worshipful belief that math and statistics are the complete and only possible explanations of Blackjack events, and therefore are the only methods applicable to any strategy. He missed the point of the *Blackjack* book entirely.

Brad was completely immersed in the dogma of old thinking, so much so that he not only did not read the whole book, he didn't even read the whole chapter! He simply fixated on two pages, and only on two points within those pages, and obviously considered that to be the "strategy."

I make a point in all my books that the ultimate test of any strategy I showcase is *your ability to so play it.* Nothing I put forth is any kind of a "system" that "guarantees" you a win "if you do this." These are the kinds of bogus systems you get in direct mail offers. I state often that all strategies are *directly dependent* on *your abilities* to play them and to play them correctly under the most favorable conditions you can find. They are based on skills, not on a flimsical once-in-a-while hit-and-run.

I am adding this addendum to this chapter in order to show how important it is for all readers to read my book thoroughly before you attempt to play the strategies in the actual casino environment. You must practice, and then practice some more, and only *then* try it out in the casino. And then, make sure you are doing it correctly. If you miss out on the success you thought you would have, question yourself. Most of the time if you fail to gain the results that I know are possible, it will be because you didn't do something that was required or didn't do it correctly. Playing skill-based strategies, as offered from my unique perspective on casino games, is not a process of learning only the few numbered points that summarize that strategy. It is a *process* of the *entirety* of your knowledge, experience, practice, understanding, skill, dedication, abilities, bankroll, and all of those other necessary items. The strategy itself is only the foundation upon which you must build the house of your gaming success. How well you build that house is up to you, and no one can tell in advance just how well you can do it. Or can't. That also seemed to totally escape Brad.

Once again: *These strategies, and those I showcase in my other books, are not to be played singly, alone, from their points only, or without the understanding of everything that was written in those books and about them as a totality. They are skill-based and completely reliant on your abilities to play them.*

Nothing in any of these strategies is described as a "sure-fire win every time system." They are *methods*, not *systems*. There is a big difference, which I also made abundantly clear. You won't win every time, as I say in all my books. Being able to make money playing these strategies will require dedication to the stated sequences and the understanding of concepts that encapsulate many others. It also requires you to free yourself from dogmas acquired from reliance on too much old information, such as that made for games and their rules that no longer exist in the twenty-first-century casinos.

Brad didn't want to be bothered with the methods in their entirety, and he was hell-bent on approaching everything from his own highly prejudicial and dogmatic perspective. He was the perfect example of the man in the box who was convinced that the sun appears blue and would never agree with anyone who comes in from the outside and states that the sun appears yellow. Nor would he ever consider that he is even inside a box or understand that there actually *is* a box he exists inside of, and that the reality is greater than merely the sum-total of what he happens to think.

The first item to which Brad pointed in my *Blackjack* book was the basis of the strategy, as follows:

- Eighty percent of the time, Blackjack hands will fall into the pattern of a win followed by a loss, followed by a win, followed by a loss, and so on—a kind of W-L-W-L-W-L scenario.
- Of the remaining 20 percent, individual hand results will be several wins in a row followed by a loss, or several losses in a row followed by a win.

Brad's challenge to me was based on what he called "the law of independent events." "How can this be?" he asked. "Each hand is an independent event." First, Blackjack is *not* an independent game, it is a *dependent* game, just like live poker. What hand you get is directly dependent on the cards that were dealt before. That is the basis for *all* strategies in Blackjack, including those based purely in the mathematics of the game, as well as those time-honored card-counting strategies. Brad failed to understand even the most fundamental points of his own question. So, the first answer is: Events in Blackjack are *dependent* events, *not* independent events. Although I tried to explain this, Brad seemed to focus on the statement: "80 percent of the time, Blackjack hands will fall into the pattern of a win followed by a loss, followed by a win, followed by a loss, and so on—a kind of W-L-W-L-W-L scenario." He took out a coin, flipped it, and asked, "What are the odds of the next event being heads or tails? 50-50, right?" he also answered.

Two problems here. First, the Blackjack statement refers to "patterns of groups," not to individual flips. Also, flips and hands of Blackjack are not comparable, because Blackjack events are dependent, while flips of a coin are independent events. Nevertheless, even if we consider this purely from Brad's skewed perspective, and we acknowledge for the sake of this example that Blackjack events could be, or perhaps are, independent events, the example of the flip of the coin actually proves the validity of the assumption of groups as event patterns. If you flip a coin 9 million times, you will discover that about 80 percent of the time the coin lands in a pattern that can be identified as a head followed by a tail followed by a head followed by a tail, and so on—a sort of H-T-H-T-H-T scenario. Sounds familiar? Well, it will also turn out that of the remaining 20 percent of the coin flips about 10.048 percent of the time the coin will land on consecutive tails—for any sequence from two-in-a-row to as many in a row as is statistically feasible—and about 9.952 percent of the time there will be a similar sequence of events where a pattern of consecutive heads will occur. The reason why these aren't equal is the second part of the coin-flip example problem, as Brad presented it to me in a challenge to the strategy I showed in my *Blackjack* book.

Even though cards as dealt out in Blackjack can form

equivalent patterns, coin flips do not equate in occurrences of heads versus tails. This is the second part of Brad's fallacy. U.S. coins do not fall 50-50 when flipped millions of times in a statistical test. Flipping a coin as an indicator of independent events or as an example of "the law of independent events" is okay, as far as this goes. It *is* true that the coin has no memory of how it fell in previous tries, but it is *not* correct to suggest that the person who flipped the coin has no memory of the sequence of two events or the understanding that a group of two events can be viewed as a group of two, and that that group can then be used as a single event in comparison with others.

Thinking of Blackjack strategies as only single events akin to a flip of a coin would defeat even the most stringently mathematical card-counting strategies, because they *all* assume the player's ability to sequence events and make assumptions and decisions accordingly. Even pure mathematics, as understood by mathematical "laws," allows for the occurrence of linear events forming a sequence within nature, as well as within one's cognitive abilities to comprehend and make use of such occurrences. It is the "human ability to make use" of such events and occurrences that makes any kind of a strategy possible, whether in gambling, surveying, the stock market, political predicting, or anything people do.

The flipping of a coin is not a 50-50 proposition for even any single event. If we use the U.S. quarter for example, it happens to be a mathematical fact that the "tails" side will land "up" more often than the "heads" side—this is because the head side of that specific U.S. coin contains slightly more metal for the raised head image, and as a result is a little more heavy. It is enough to make tails appear more often to several tenths of a percentage point higher than heads, while, of course, conversely, heads lands heads down equally more often.

The point is that the basis for the challenge Brad used was flawed and faulty from the beginning. He completely misunderstood the very principles of the strategy, which were firmly founded in the correct use of the very "laws" of mathematics, probability, and statistics he used. There is nothing in any *applied* mathematical theory, however pure, that disallows as part of its core premise the occurrence of more than one event. Applied mathematics and applied theory are only as good and only as useful as people can make them—which is the *application* part of this process. And that, dear reader, is the very foundation of my Blackjack Strategy as presented in my *Blackjack* book, and as shown in more enumerated detail in this book. It is the *application of the process by you*—the player—that is the defining and deciding factor, and not the numbers and points that enumerate the theory of the strategy. This also entirely escaped Brad.

So that I make this as clear as possible, here are some other details from that discussion:

- First, I say clearly that the strategy is based on a *series of sessions*, and not on a one-time event. Such sessions are in themselves composed of at least 100 events each, with 1,000 such events contributing to a session. Each such block of sessions is the single event, thereafter to be viewed and understood as such, with another such block completed thereafter forming the group #2 block, then considered singly, and so on.
- I clearly state in the book *Powerful Profits from Blackjack* that "I will simplify this methodology for this example. The actual structure of the entire process is somewhat more complex and considerably more involved. For those of you who wish to know the entire process in all of its detail, and therefore are

willing to invest some additional learning time to master this, I refer you to my book on *Winning Strategies.*"

- I also say, again in no uncertain terms, that "To accomplish this, you must use a tiered structure with a fractional differential. Increasing your bets by whole units will not work."

Any person playing only one day, for perhaps only a few hours or so, cannot view the success or failure of their results as being anything other than merely the first portion of a protracted series of events, *all* of which need be completed before the strategy can yield a workable result.

I also say clearly that my perspective on Blackjack is not to be understood from within the standard perspective of mathematically derived strategies or such understanding of singular events. Persons mired in the "old thinking" of only looking at Blackjack events as a "flip of a coin" will fail to understand the very foundations of "group events theory," even though such are more than adequately enumerated in much of academic thinking. Basing one's understanding of the validity of any strategy also requires that one free oneself from the prejudices of one's own perspectives, and seek to understand what is actually written and offered, rather than to dismiss it without first gaining the basis upon which it was founded.

Brad also asked me, "Have you ever shown this to a mathematician?" The answer is, "Yes, I have." The late Lenny Frome first pointed this out to me when I was asking him questions about anomalous occurrences within Blackjack events I was working on at the time, when the results I was getting didn't seem to be workable or profitable when understood from within the "law of independent events" model (we talked about this more in terms of probabilities, but that is close to what I think was Brad's question). I offered Lenny the basis for what later became my strategy for Blackjack, which is fully enumerated in this book. To be sure, Lenny and I had some interesting arguments. It was he, however, who first let me in on the basis of viewing what can be individually considered as independent events in the format of groups, then using the groups as the single events that form other great groups, and so on. Learning to understand the mathematics of combined event theory from within the format of an applied "law of independent events" model—for us more of a situation of probabilities of protracted group events—allowed for the understanding of how seemingly anomalous events can actually still be truly independent, yet can also be used in a workable format when applied to a limited-time sequence exposure. Therefore, even if quantified from within the mathematical model as "truly independent," this nevertheless provided a "workability framework" for the creation of a strategy that allowed for the insertion of the human element of pattern recognition, allowing for the implementation of a workable strategy for applying this to a series of Blackjack events. The objective for this application was not the validation of any mathematical theory, but rather the exploitation of financial profits over the protracted series of combined events among such applied groups. Sadly, Lenny and I never pursued this further. I lost interest for a period of time due to other personal situations, although I did continue to play Blackjack in the casinos as well as continuing my computer tests. Over the years I evolved this understanding to what I have now presented as my Blackjack Strategy, based solely on *my own* abilities to so quantify, analyze, and present this method.

There is also a much more fundamental difference between how I view these strategies and how pure mathematicians, like Brad, see them. This is more in the field of a philosophical difference of opinion, difficult to explain to mathematicians. Math persons look at events such as those we are discussing here as being independent. As proof, they cite natural law, or mathematical law. Unfortunately, this presupposes that there is any such thing, or that what is so understood—by human beings—as being able to be *numerically* understood may in fact be something wholly different. Understanding events from within the "quantification" model is okay as long as they can be so quantified, and as long as everybody agrees to so view them. Nevertheless, they do not reflect reality, because that perspective of what reality might be is only vested in that one and very specific assumption that mathematics is somehow a window to what is really happening. Suffice it to say that this is an academic dispute between physicists and mathematicians, and philosophers and metaphysicians. While mathematicians absolutely believe firmly in the dogma of "mathematical reality," philosophers tend to point out that this is only *their opinion,* because there is nothing in what they claim that can prove or disprove anything, and to make that attempt presupposes that we can understand and apply something that we don't even understand in the first place. Confused? I spent nine years in college arguing precisely these points.

To a theorist, there are human perceptions and the human being's ability to take actions, with such actions often not easily quantifiable, or understood only from the basis of mathematics. Mathematics is a useful guideline to the understanding of gambling games and strategies, but it is not the "holy grail" or the only tool to be so applied. There are other such "tools," and one of them is the ability to view events without encumbrance of "established" perspectives.

The strategy I listed in my *Powerful Profits from Blackjack* book is a version of the greater effort and is designed to provide players with an alternative to the grind of counting cards, even if such a player is able to master those methods and still can find a game where he or she is allowed to use them. If Brad had read the book thoroughly and actually learned to understand what was being offered, and then did as instructed, he would know (before ever beginning that one day, or one hour, at the casino) that this strategy is not the tell-all or end-all. If this method is played correctly—with full understanding of what I said in the *entire* book and not just that one page with the few points—it provides a workable alternative to the requirement of counting cards. This strategy is designed solely and only to help a player navigate the game of Blackjack as it is now played; it is offered as a means to a greater end, while making it possible for the player to play Blackjack immediately and for more fun than if he played without knowledge or any kind of plan or strategy. That is all it was designed to do.

If you use a hammer once, and you hit your thumb instead of the nail, it's easy to blame the hammer and to seek to challenge the theory of the use of a hammer when trying to hit a nail. Applying the same analogy to the Blackjack Strategy in my *Blackjack* book, trying it once and failing is akin to blaming the hammer for failing to hit the nail.

If learned properly, if everything written in the book is understood as it should be, it provides the results it was designed to achieve. If, however, it is instead pulled out singly and looked at only from that one item and so challenged from only that one perspective and in regard to only that one event, such is akin to trying to build a house while wearing a blindfold and never having read the blueprints nor understood the preferred use of the hammer.

Brad just didn't want to invest the time to read the whole book, looked at one or two pages, and thought this was all that there was to it. But *all* that is written in the book needs to be read and understood, and practiced and learned, before you can hope to begin to play. Everything I have written presupposes that you read it *all* and did not just focus on a few items on two pages or so, thinking you're then ready to play the strategy. I wrote the book *Powerful Profits from Blackjack* to provide the basis for the learning, expertise, and understanding of the game and to make the readers able to *play* the game well, and perhaps even with the strategy I outlined. The same applies to this book. Do not make the mistake Brad made. Read it *all,* and try to understand what it *actually* says, instead of what you *think* it says. Free your mind from the pollution and dogmas of old thinking, and explore the possibilities inherent in a new ability to comprehend events and situations as they are usefully applied, and not merely theorized. The success is not in the strategy itself, it is in the player using it.

If you still don't get it, well it's okay. Some of us just aren't cut out for playing gambling games in the real casino in these ways. If you are one, at least you now know something that will be useful to you, even if you can't do it exactly that way. At the very least, I hope this addendum has been entertaining and informative, and has provided you with a window into another way of thinking.

And now, on to the next chapter.

Strategy for Craps

INTRODUCTION

Oh what a wonderful game Craps is! Next to Blackjack and Baccarat, Craps is the only other main casino table game that offers some of the best odds to the players. Some games can offer as little as 0.02 percent house edge on the pass line bet with 100 times odds, and come and place bets with full odds. This makes Craps among the best games for the player.

This game is fast and furious. You can win, and lose, a lot of money very quickly, if, that is, you play Craps the way that most players do, by relying purely on some of the tried-and-established principles of Craps play. It's noisy and crowded and can be intimidating. Don't worry, since in this Craps Strategy you will learn how to play Craps without intimidation and for profits, regardless of what happens and what the other players, or shooters, do or don't do. You won't have to make complicated bets, and you won't have to be concerned with anything else. Your strategy play will allow you to enjoy the game knowing that while all the other players are excited over silly things, you will always be in profit at the end result of your combined sessions play.

As with all my strategies, I assume that you already know the game, bets, odds, and how to make and place bets and odds. This strategy is *not* intended to teach you the game, but is designed to maximize the profits for players who have already mastered Craps. If you need a refresher course in Craps play, I recommend my book *Powerful Profits from Craps.*

One of the benefits of this Craps Strategy is that even if you do not know *all* there is to know about Craps, you can still play the game by learning this strategy and applying it. To do this, all you will need to learn about Craps is how to make and place these bets and odds, and how to maintain and manage your strategy and bets as you play.

There are *two* Craps strategies in this chapter.

- Craps Strategy #1 is based on pass line bets and place bets.
- Craps Strategy #2 is based on playing the hardways with a side bet on the pass line.

Both can be played simultaneously, although I would advise against it, unless you are playing a buddy method with another player. This is split-strategy play, whereby one plays Strategy #1 and the other Strategy #2, having combined your bankroll and wins together. This can be tricky, since you will both need to be on the same page at the same time and know exactly what is going on with each other's play, bets, progressions, and bankroll status. It is simpler, therefore, for you to play *either* one or the other of the two strategies. You can alternate your sessions between the two, but it is best if you simply play one or the other consistently for your entire block of selected sessions.

If you are a good manager of your money, however, and have good knowledge of Craps and can maintain consistent mental acumen for your play, you can play both strategies at the same time. This will not be easy, but it is possible. To do this, you will need to treat the two strategies as independent events and manage your money and bets accordingly. In addition, you must combine the methods of play and delicately alter the strategies accordingly. This will become possible for you once you have mastered the strategies themselves. I caution you, however, that *any mistake* at any time during play will result in a defeat of the strategy itself and therefore diminish your success. Even just one mistake at any time will be catastrophic. Further, if you are playing both strategies at the same time, such a mistake in any one of them will corrupt the other. It is mentally extremely challenging to play both at the same time, so I will again advise you not to do this until you have thoroughly understood and mastered each of the two strategies here presented, and done so in actual in-casino play for significantly proficient time periods

Although the strategies you are about to learn appear inherently simple, they are very thoroughly designed. Their simplicity belies the details that went into creating them, and the overall mathematics which allow them to be so profitable—when played correctly and consistently, without mistakes.

Finally, you must play these strategies *mechanically,* without emotion, and without alteration *no matter what goes on* around the game and table itself. These strategies are designed to hide your identity as a strategy player, so don't get distracted or discouraged by individual events. Remember that individual events do *not* matter to your strategy play—what *does* matter is your overall end result, which will be achieved if you do what you must in accordance with the strategy instructions.

CRAPS STRATEGY #1

This strategy is based on the following principles:

- A betting progression of an *increase* by 1 chip unit each time a *loss* occurs.
- Betting the pass line bet with a starting bet of 1 chip unit on the come out roll, and with *double odds* after a new point is established, and then *placing* the 5, 6, 8, and 9.
- The major action and betting progressions take place on the 5, 6, 8, and 9.
- The pass line bet, and odds, are used only as insurance against losses on the 5, 6, 8, and 9, and as a bonus payoff if the point is made, or a winner if a 7 or 11 is rolled on the come out.

Rules

1. Each come out roll, bet 1 chip unit on the pass line.
2. When the point is established, bet double odds behind the pass line bet.
3. After the point is established and you have made your double odds bet—place the 5, 6, 8, and 9 for the incremental equivalent of 1 chip units each, times the requisite increments for correct-odds payout.
4. If the point is either of the numbers 5, 6, 8, or 9, place the other three, since one of these four key numbers is now covered by the pass line bet and odds that will win if the point is made.
5. Each time any placed number *wins,* take that win and let the original bet ride.
6. Each time any placed number *loses*—which happens only if the shooter does not make the point—then bet

2 chip units on *all* the place numbers next time (after the next new point is established, prior to which you make your 1 chip unit pass line bet).

Always make sure that each chip unit is correctly configured for the best odds. For example, your single chip units for the 5 and the 9 should be $5, while for the 6 and the 8 the single chip unit must be $6; therefore, when betting double, as indicated in this clause, your bets will now be $10 for the 5 and 9, and $12 for the 6 and 8, and so on for each such increase, always in correct increments.

7. If you *lose* your place number bets again, in consecutive losses, which can happen only if the shooter fails to make the point in consecutive rolls, increase your place bets by 3 chip units next time, and so on for any *consecutive* losses.

Keys to Remember

- Treat the 5, 6, 8, and 9 as a *single* unit.
- Only the 4 and 10 can be a point without one of your place numbers being the point.
- The initial 1 chip unit bet on the pass line must be at least $5.
- The initial 1 unit bets on the 6 and 8 must be either $3 or $6 or $12 or $24 to allow for payment of correct odds (and incrementally increased in units of a minimum of $3 or $6 thereafter).
- The initial 1 unit bets on the 5 and 9 must be at least $5 (but can be $2 if 6 and 8 have a $3 bet as a unit, provided the casino you are at allows for less than $5 per single bet).
- It is *not* recommended that you play this method with

bets of less than $6 each on the 6 and the 8, or less than $5 each on the 5 and the 9. Your minimum starting requirements should be at least the $6 and the $5, each bet viewed as 1 unit. The recommended starting point is twice that, or $12 minimum on the 6 and 8, and $10 minimum on the 5 and 9, with a $5 pass line bet and $10 odds (double odds each time).

Bankroll

Minimum $800. Recommend $1,000 to $1,500.

Test Case Analysis

Figure 6 represents one of the thousands of test cases that were incorporated into the process of creating this strategy.

Each roll is identified by an alphabet letter, and all the sequences here shown constitute one test and session. Each lettered roll is a come out roll, followed by the results. Each sequence ends with a crap out. If the point is made, the sequence continues. Each entire session can only end with a crap out. The asterisk (*) signifies the *point*.

Analysis of Bets

Starting bets are at $5 for the pass line before the come out roll, with $10 odds after the point is established, then $5 each on the 5 and 9 and $6 each on the 6 and 8, progressing to $10 each on the 5 and 9 after a total loss and $12 each on the 6 and 8 after a total loss, and incrementally thereafter in equal units. Below is the analysis of the sequences, with the "W" meaning a WIN of that amount, and the "L" meaning a LOSS of that amount.

CRAPS STRATEGY #1: CHART

ROLL	RESULTS OF ROLL	NOTES
A	7 7 7 6* 8 11 8 7	ends with crap out
B	4* 8 10 4	point wins, pass line wins, place bets stay in action for next come out but are called OFF
C	10* 6 11 5 10	point wins, Place bets called "working" as soon as the new point is established
D	8 7	ends with crap out, this ends the entire sequence which began with piont 4 in Roll B
E	5* 8 5	point wins
F	11 11 6* 6	point wins
G	3 7 7 10* 9 7	crap out; ends sequence begun with point 5 in Roll E
H	6* 3 9 6	point wins
I	9* 9	point wins
J	6* 2 6	point wins
K	9* 7	crap out; ends sequence begun with the FIRST point 6, in Roll H
L	7 4* 8 4	point wins
M	9* 8 5 7	crap out; ends sequence begun with Roll L (from now on, you should know how this works)
N	4* 9 4	point wins
O	4* 5 12 8 9 6 11 10 8 6 10 9 12 10 10 9 6 10 7	crap out
P	4* 6 5 4	point wins
Q	4* 10 6 5 8 11 3 7	crap out
R	10* 7	crap out
S	4* 6 10 6 10 8 7	crap out
T	10* 8 9 7	crap out; ENDS TEST CASE. End can ONLY happen on crap out.

Figure 6. Sequence of Rows

SEQUENCE	RESULTS				NOTES
1	W5	W5	W5	W7	end resulted in a total loss of all numbers and line
	For ENTIRE sequence: Losers = $32; Winners = $22				
2	W14	W37			point wins, sequence continues
3	W14	W14	W38		point wins, sequence continues
4	L	L	L		all bets lose, ends sequences
	For ENTIRE sequence: Losers = $34; winners = $117				
5	W7	W34			point wins
6	W5	W5	W34		point wins
7	L5	W5	W5	W7	then all lose, ending sequences
	For ENTIRE sequence: Losers = $11; Winners = $97				

Progressive Total for ALL sequences: Losers = $77; Winners = $236

Figure 6. *(cont.)* Craps Strategy #1: Table of Events and Analysis

CRAPS STRATEGY #2: HARD WAYS

This strategy is based on the following principles:

- Starting bet of $5 on the pass line, no odds.
- Starting bet of $5 on each of the four hard ways: 4, 6, 8, and 10.
- Incremental increases on the hard ways by $1 each time a loss occurs on any one, or such an increase on all if a total loss occurs (which can happen only on crap out).

Rules

1. Always make a $5 starting bet on the pass line, no odds, on the come out roll.
2. After the point is established, make $5 bets on all the hard ways.
3. From then on, each time any hard ways bet loses, press *that bet* by $1 for the next sequence, and so on.
4. If all the hard ways bets lose (on crap out), press all hard ways bets by $1 next time the new point is established.

For example: If the bets on 4 and 6 were at $6 each, and the 10 was at $9 and the 8 was at $5, press them all by $1 next time, so that now you have $7 each on the 4 and 6, and $10 on the 10 and $6 on the 8. And so on. This can get tricky, but that's where your mental skills come into play. You can help yourself do this by using the rail to prepare your next sequence of bets for all the bets, using single chips as dividers for your next bet amounts. In many casinos you can actually use pencil and paper to help your tracking of bets, but that tends to give you away as someone playing a strategy or trying to play one. As long as you are losing, the casinos won't care, but once you start winning, they will keep a close eye on you, as will the surveillance cameras. Your face will then be captured by the face-recognition software and your image will be instantly posted to every casino as a strategy player. It is better to gain your expertise by memorizing your betting progressions and practicing at home or at a casino with very low stakes where you can pro-rate your methodology to those wagers. Then you can go and do this "for real"—so to speak—and you won't be tracked and won't need to write things down to know your next series of bets.

5. Each time any hard ways bet *wins,* take the win and let the previous bet ride.
6. *Only increase your bets after a loss !!*

Keys to Remember

- Any sequence begins with a come out roll and ends with a crap out.
- If the point *is* made, the sequence continues because hard ways do *not* automatically lose in this case; they should be simply called off for the next come out roll, and then called working for the continuation of that sequence roll.

Bankroll

Minimum $1,000. Recommend $2,500.

Test Case Analysis

Figures 7 and 8 (pages 112 and 113) represent one of the thousands of test cases that were incorporated into the process of creating this strategy.

Each roll is identified by an alphabet letter, and all the sequences here shown constitute one test and session. Each lettered roll is a come out roll, followed by the results. Each sequence ends with a crap out. If the point is made, the sequence continues. Each entire session can only end with a crap out. The asterisk (*) signifies the *point.*

The letter (e) after any hard-way number signifies that this number was rolled easy, meaning a loss of that hardways bet, signifying that an incremental increase was called for.

The letter (h) after any hard-way number signifies that this number was rolled the hard way, meaning that a win was made and the bet stays in action as is.

Figure 7. Craps Strategy #2: Table of events

ROLL	RESULTS OF ROLL																NOTES
A	8*	7															crap out
B	3	4*	6e	5	5	9	7										crap out
C	6*	8e	7														crap out
D	6*	10h	7														crap out
E	9*	11	6e	5	5	3	6h	11	10e	2	4e	8e	4e	5	9		point wins
F	7	9*	4e	4e	6e	12	2	7									crap out
G	10*	5	6h	5	4h	3	8h	4e	5	9	6h	5	7				crap out
H	8*	9	2	8e													point wins
I	7	4*	7														crap out
J	8*	8h															point wins
K	2	7	7	5*	11	3	11	9	11	6e	10h	11	9	6e	3	7	crap out
L	4*	8e	7														crap out
M	11	12	6*	7													crap out
N	4*	7															crap out
O	3	8*	9	10h	10e	8e											point wins
P	6*	9	2	9	12	6e											point wins
Q	7	9*	6e	11	8e	3	10e	10h	10e	9							point wins
R	7	8*	3	7													crap out
S	9*	5	8e	3	4e	5	5	4e	4h	8e	11	4h	7				crap out
T	2	10*	9	2	7												crap out
U	3	11	9*	4h	4e	9											point wins
V	7	6*	5	4e	6h	5	10h	2	6e								point wins
W	7	5*	5														point wins
X	7	7	10*	5	2	5	10h										point wins
Y	5*	7															crap out
Z	5*	7															crap out
AA	7	3	7	8*	9	9	3	5	9	12	11	8e					point wins
BB	10*	7															crap out
CC	2	7	9*	8e	8e	7											crap out
DD	7	11	10*	7													crap out—here we end the test

Figure 8. Analysis of Bets

ROLL	PROGRESSION OF BETS 4	6	8	10	SEQUENCE LOSS	SEQUENCE WIN	
A	5	5	5	5	25	0	Loss of all bets on crap out
B	6	7	6	6	35	0	ditto
C	7	8	8	7	35	0	ditto
D	8	9	9	8	34	56	win on hard 10
E	11	11	11	10	0	99	win on hard 6 and win on point, therefore no loss
F	14	13	12	11	50	0	win $5 on come out 7, but loss of $5 on crap out, so no win
G	16	14	13	12	60	481	wins on hard 6, hard 4, hard 8, and hard 6 made this profit
H	17	15	14	13	0	5	pass line winner
I	18	16	15	14	68	0	pass line win but then crap out = no win
J	19	17	16	15	0	144	the 8 was the point and it won
K	19	19	17	15	70	105	crap 2 plus two win 7's plus crap out = wash - no win on pass line bet
L	20	20	19	16	80	0	
M	21	21	20	17	84	0	FROM NOW ON THE REST OF THE ANALYSIS SHOULD BE OBVIOUS
N	22	22	21	18	88	0	
O	23	23	23	20	0	140	
P	24	25	24	21	0	5	
Q	25	28	26	24	0	168	
R	26	29	27	25	107	0	
S	29	30	30	26	120	406	
T	30	31	31	27	129	0	
U	31	32	32	28	0	217	
V	32	32	32	29	0	491	
W	32	32	32	29	0	5	
X	32	32	32	29	0	218	Hard 10 was the point, line wins, plus two 7's wins on come out
Y	32	32	32	29	130	0	
Z	33	33	33	30	134	0	
AA	34	34	34	30	0	5	
BB	34	34	35	30	138	0	
CC	35	35	37	31	143	0	
DD	38	36	38	32	142	5	Here we end sequences and test session

TOTAL LOSS FOR ENTIRE SESSION $1,672.00
TOTAL WIN FOR ENTIRE SESSION $2,550.00
FINAL RESULT = PROFIT OF   **$878.00**

NOTE: We had 19 losing events and 16 winning events, meaning more losing events than winning ones, yet we still made an overall profit in the end. That is the point of this method. Each sequence is an independent event unto itself. At the end of the string of sequences, the sequence block, add up the wins and subtract the losses. This gives you the final net profit.

Strategy for Reel Slots

INTRODUCTION

The general history of *Reel* Slot Machines (referred to simply as Slots from now on) is rich and very interesting. Slots have been around for more than 100 years, and many of the historical machines can be found in museums, particularly in Las Vegas. They were called "one-armed bandits," and rightfully so in those olden days. Old-time Slots were clumsy things with mechanical reels that would clang loudly as they were spinning. They were "set" by means of lead weights, similar to the balancing weights your auto mechanic puts on your car tires to balance them. This made the Slots prone to tampering, and as a result they were hugely unreliable. In fact, they were so bad that the "mobsters" favored them as a means of making huge illicit profits, and hence the term "one-armed bandits" (because those old monsters really did rob you).

Technology, and law enforcement of illegal gaming operations, gradually helped make the Slot Machine a more acceptable form of gambling entertainment. However, they were still deemed to be "entertainment" or "diversions,"

214

and no "serious" gambler would ever be caught playing them. This mentality persisted throughout the 1950s, '60s, '70s, and '80s.

And then came the revolution.

The revolution had to do with computer technology and the invention of Video Poker. The very simplicity of the Video Poker Machine turned huge numbers of gamblers into Video Machine—and hence Slot Machine—enthusiasts. This phenomenon grew and grew, and continued with advancing and improving technology. Today, Slots are terrific machines, all of which are computerized, regardless of whether they appear to have "reels," or appear as "video" displays. This makes them far more accurate and predictable. This also means that their "alterations" cannot be as easily made and, in fact, cannot be so done under law unless the casino, or manufacturer, or both, first obtain legal permission and licensing to do so, in which case it really becomes a different machine altogether.

These advances in Slot Machine technologies and innovations have given birth to a revival of the Slot Machine industry, to a point where some of the best casino games now available are—lo and behold—Slots! As a direct result, virtually all casino visitors now play Slots at one time or another during their visit. The fact that most Slots now pay back upwards of 94 percent (and much more in many casinos) also makes then an overall good bet.

Nevertheless, Slots are still machines, preset to "hold" a certain percentage for the house, and are random, and as a result can still be difficult to beat. Difficult, but not impossible. The main problem with any kind of a Slot Machine strategy is the fact that Reel Slots are all negative expectation games. Simply put, this means that the machines will always hold a specified percentage of all the money played in them for the house. So, if the machine's program is set to pay back 98 percent, this also means that this machine is set to "hold" 2 percent for the house. This way the casino is always assured of a profit. The second problem with Slot Machine strategies is that each spin is an independent event, as opposed to a dependent event. Just like Roulette, or Craps, Slots are games where the previous event has no bearing on future events, each being independent of any other. This is different from games like Blackjack, for example, in which your odds of winning (or losing) are directly dependent on which cards have been dealt out in each round of dealing and in subsequent rounds of dealing. This is because Blackjack uses a finite arrangement of cards, those that were so created after the shuffle, cut, and burn. This is also why Blackjack can be beaten for consistent player profits, with proper play.

In this section we are discussing Reel Slots, as opposed to Video Slots or Video Poker. Video Slots and Video Poker will be treated separately, although the principles of play outlined here for traditional Reel Slots can be adapted to *Video Reel Slots* as well. The normal Reel Slots are those machines that have the traditional look, with a handle and a window and reels that spin. Although all of these machines are now controlled by computers, and in reality are no different from any video reel machine in their computerized nature, there are still some features that allow these machines to be played differently from the video reel machines. Of course, Video Poker is completely different. Some Video Poker Machines have programs that allow them to be played to over 100 percent payback, and this makes these Video Poker Machines a positive expectation game. As a consequence, these machines can also be played consistently for profit (see my book, *Powerful Profits from Video Poker,* for more details).

Reel slots are not usually programmed with over 100 percent payback, except for a specific occasion—some kind of a casino promotion, or perhaps tournament machines.

The majority of traditional Reel Slots can be found everywhere—there are thousands of them in every casino. Most Las Vegas casinos will have at least 1,000 Slots, and many will have over 4,000 (depending on the size of the casino, of course). Generally, the average is somewhere between 1,200 and 3,000 Slots per casino. This is a lot of machines. About half of these will be Reel Slots, which are still among the most popular forms of gambling entertainment available. Although Video Slots are now gaining ground, Reel Slots will always be a staple of the casino floor, if not because of their traditional appeal, at least simply due to variety. Though they are still all computerized, just like the Video Slots, their look and feel is different enough to attract millions of players annually. Their programming and payoffs are also different.

While most of the Video Slots have become popular because of the many lines that can be played, and the many tiered bonuses that can be accomplished, the Reel Slots have remained popular largely due to their simplicity. Most are three-reel machines, which makes it easy for any player to understand how to play; they can easily see if they won anything, and what that was. Much of the problem players have with Video Slots is the seeming complexity of the various symbols and pays. Many players simply don't know what wins and how, which makes it difficult for them to become excited at the prospect of shooting for the Jackpot. This is not so among the traditional style Reel Slots. There you can usually see quite easily what the pays are, and how to achieve them. Mostly, if you line up the required symbols across the payline in the window, you win that amount. If you don't, you lose. It's that simple, and it is this apparent simplicity that makes these machines so attractive to so many players. It is not my intention to describe the complexities of Reel Slots in this book no matter how simple they may appear, and no matter how simple their playing may seem. For this information, I refer you to my book *Powerful Profits from Slots.*

Here, we are concerned with strategies that can be used to win on Slots more regularly than would be possible by pure chance alone. While negative expectation games cannot be mathematically beaten in the long run by using traditional playing strategies, it is nevertheless possible to exploit some of the quirks in the machines. After all, no computer program is always perfect, and no machine is truly random. Also, regardless of the preprogrammed house edge, all Slots have to pay out something, even the Jackpots. Otherwise no one would ever play them; they would just gather dust. Therefore, casinos have their machines set to pay back the vast majority of the money invested and are happy to keep only a small portion because they know that their machines will make this all the time, 24/7/365. Making a little bit all the time is better than making a huge chunk but getting no action.

Most casino Reel Slots are set to pay back between 92 percent and 98 percent for the $1 and $5 reel machines, as well as the high-roller Slots of $10, $25, $100, and $500 versions. Some casinos also have banks of $1 or $5 Reel Slots with payback percentages of 99 percent, but those are rare. Most of the casinos in Las Vegas have their Reel Slots set to pay back between 94.7 percent and 98 percent, for the $1 and $5 machines. Machines in other gaming centers are traditionally set at a lower payback percentage. To find out what this may be, write to the Gaming Control Board or regulatory agency in your state and request a copy of the casino's Slot payback statement. This will show you the entire average payback for all the Slots in all those denominations among all the casinos in your state.

Quarter and nickel Reel Slots are traditionally the worst-paying machines on the casino floor. Their payback ranges from the regulatory minimum of 75 percent up to about 88 percent. Generally speaking, avoid all quarter and nickel Reel Slots altogether. In fact, don't ever play them when trying to use this method, even though it is possible. I strongly advise you to keep your play to the $1 and $5 machines. If you can afford to play higher, by all means do so, as long as you can prorate the bankroll requirements to those levels. Also make sure the casino has all of their high-roller Slots set at the better payback percentage. Ask your Slot host and he will find out—particularly if *you* are a high roller and they want to keep your patronage.

For the rest of us, we can easily confine our play to the $1 and $5 Reel Slots, which are plentiful in all casinos everywhere. Sometimes we may also wish to venture higher, into the $10 and $25 machines, but this we can easily do after we have accumulated more money from our play on the lower-denomination machines.

There are now so many varieties of Slot Machines that to discuss any one group individually is all but impossible. It is not the purpose of this book to teach you how to play Slots, nor to teach you which machines are the best ones for your gaming dollar or how to find them. As with all my methods, Slots Strategy also assumes you already know how to play Slot Machines, how to understand which are the better ones, and how to exploit all the various nuances of Slot Machine play.

When playing this Slots Strategy in the actual casino, you will need to do some odd-looking and odd-sounding things. Don't be bothered by this, and don't be afraid of looking like you don't know what you're doing. That's all part of the strategy and is designed to hide your identity as a strategy player. Also, don't be bothered if any casino employee looks at you strangely or tries to offer you some "better" advice—they may mean well, but they don't know, so smile, be polite, and continue to play the way this strategy is designed. If you do this correctly, you will never be in danger of being "discovered" as a strategy player. In fact, casinos are far more worried about "strategy play" at the table games than at Slots, because they still hold the general industry opinion that Slots can't be beaten, and as a result no gambler can profit from their play on a consistent basis. This delusion on behalf of the casino industry and their on-the-floor employees is one of the primary factors that allow this strategy to work so well.

WHAT NOT TO DO

1. Don't play nickel or quarter Reel Slots! Ever! (Video slots in the nickel versions, where you play forty-five coins or ninety coins or more, are okay, but you will have to prorate your strategy and bankroll accordingly, since these machines are really $2.25 and $4.50 machines, and *not* "nickels" in the traditional sense.)
2. Don't play during traditionally "busy" times, such as lunchtime, mid-afternoons, dinnertime, after dinnertime, or over weekends and holidays (if possible). During these times the selection of Slots will be limited, the casino too busy, and generally your strategy play can be severely hampered and limited due to these and other factors.
3. Don't play undercapitalized. (See Bankroll requirements, below.) It is *essential* to the success of this strategy that you have the required bankroll to sustain play.
4. Don't play "gimmick" Reel Slots, such as Reel Slots that offer various "hidden" or "mystery" bonuses. These are *not* the good Slots and generally are notoriously bad payers.
5. Don't play any kind of "progressives." This strategy

is designed for the *standard* kinds of Reel Slots. Progressives, of whatever kind, are a different breed of machine and are *not* a good investment for strategy play.

6. Don't play Slots with more than three reels.
7. Don't play Slots that take more than three coins as maximum coins in. (This requirement is different for Video Slots.)
8. Do *not* use the bill acceptors (validators) on the machines (unless the machine no longer accepts coins, which will increasingly be the case with many machines—in that case, you will have to use the credit meter and currency acceptor, but keep track of the number of spins relative to the credits used from the original buy-in, as dictated by the remainder of this method and its play rules).

WHAT YOU SHOULD DO

1. Play *only* $1, $5, $10, and $25 Reel Slots.
2. Preferably, play only two-coin-maximum machines; however, for the purposes of this strategy, you can also play three-coin-maximum machines (this is a derivative suggestion which is a departure from the "standard" gaming advice for Slots).
3. Play at "graveyard hours" if at all possible. This will offer you the best choices and the best shot at employing the strategy to its full potential. This is not a hard requirement, but it will serve you well if you can handle the hours.
4. *Always* join the Slot Club and *always* play with your Slot Club card. This will allow you to accumulate "comps" and points redeemable for a variety of gifts, merchandise, and added cash, all of which consti-

tute the additional bonuses you'll earn with this strategy, and these, cumulatively, account for *substantial profits*.

5. Preferably, play machines that are advertised as paying a specified flat percentage, such as 94.7 percent payback, or 98 percent payback, and *not* the kinds advertised as paying "up to. . . ."

Machines that are shown paying these percentages with the words "up to" in front of the displayed percentage of payback do not mean that all such machines will pay that payback. Such paybacks with the words "up to . . ." mean that the *average* between all such machines is the stated percentage, but that doesn't mean that the majority of these machines will so pay. But—machines that say, categorically: "98 percent payback," or similarly, are all set to that payback percentage. If you can, seek them out. In the $1, $5, $10, and $25 denominations, you shouldn't have any difficulties locating them.

6. Play *only* with coins or tokens. This will allow you to better manage your money and the strategy (unless the machine is a coin-free game, or a multiwager multiline Video Reel Slot Machine, in which case refer to my earlier comments).

7. Divide your play into sessions, and always buy in for your entire bankroll for each session.

8. Generally, try to seek out machines which have all, or most, of the following features:
   • Double or triple symbols that also substitute for all other symbols.
   • Bonus symbols that are wild and also substitute for all other symbols.
   • Bonus and/or double/triple symbols that also pay "scatters."

9. Play consistently and without diversions. Be dedicated. You are not there to be entertained; you are there to win money. Remember that.
10. For multisession play, adapt the Blackjack Strategy requirements.

Rules

1. Divide your entire bankroll into sessions, each with a specific amount *per session*. Adapt the session splits from the Blackjack strategy.
2. Buy in for your entire *session* stake in coins or tokens.
3. Select the best possible machine (see previous information).
4. Always play maximum coins.
5. Insert your tokens or coins for *each* pull.
6. Use the credit meter on the machine to *keep track of how much you have won*. Do *not* play off your accumulated credits!!
7. After you have played all the coins or tokens from your entire session bankroll, see what you have left on the credit meter. Then, as follows:
   - If you have doubled your starting session bankroll, quit and end this session.
   - If you have more than 75 percent over and above your starting bankroll, but less than 100 percent profit, quit this session.
   - If you have less than 75 percent over and above your starting bankroll, but more than 50 percent over your starting session amount, cash out and play that same machine again following the principles from Rule #5 and so on.
   - If you have less than 50 percent over and above

your starting session bankroll, quit and start a new session on another machine.

- If you have exactly the same amount as your session bankroll—even money—quit this session and start a new one on another machine.
- If at the end of each session you have less than your starting session stake, quit and start a new session on another machine.

8. *Never* play the same kind of machine in any *consecutive* sessions unless as indicated in Rule #7. Variety is the key.

9. Play for 10 sessions at a time. These are block sessions—see the Blackjack Strategy for additional session-split information that is adaptable.

10. Use your Slot Club card to gain additional benefits from your play.

11. *Never* recirculate your money from any one session (except as allowed for in Rule #7).

12. At the end of your ten-session block, add your wins, subtract your losses, and arrive at the end result. If you have played correctly, and on the suggested kinds of machines, you should have an end-of-sequence profit of about 10 percent over and above your entire bankroll (often more), all sessions combined. Plus you will have accumulated Slot Club points for added value.

Bankroll

- For $1 machines, overall, you should have a stake of $10,000, to be divided into ten-session blocks of $1,000 each, each block then divided into ten sessions, each with $100 per session.
- For $1 machines that take two coins as maximum,

you will need a *minimum* of $1,000, divided into ten sessions of $100 each session.

- For $1 machines that take three coins as maximum, you will need a minimum of $2,000, divided into ten sessions of $200 each session.
- For $5 machines that take two coins as maximum, you will need a minimum of $5,000, divided into ten sessions of $500 each session.
- For $5 machines that take three coins as maximum, you will need a minimum of $10,000, divided into ten sessions of $1,000 each session.
- For $10 and $25 machines, you will need a bankroll incrementally higher, as based on the above formula. This also applies to any play that you may have on machines in higher denominations, such as $100 or $500 Slots, if you can handle that kind of action.

It is *essential* that you have these bankroll requirements. Otherwise, you cannot play the strategy to its full potential. Also, don't make mistakes. This will seriously diminish your profit potential. Similarly, don't use your gaming money for anything else. Use other money for tips, drinks, dinners, shows, general expenses, and so on. Your gaming money must be *only* for gaming—otherwise you may forget what you spent and think your sessions didn't produce as good a result as they really did had you not spent that money on other things.

If you think that these bankroll amounts are too high, I highly recommend that you first save up and play this strategy once you have accumulated the required bankroll. Otherwise you will be playing undercapitalized, the *primary mistake* the majority of Slot players make. This strategy will work *only* if played perfectly correctly at all times, without mistakes and, principally, *with* the required bankroll amounts.

You can further enhance this strategy by increasing the amount of your bankroll and adding more session blocks. If you can, create two 10-session blocks and combine them. And so on. The more session blocks you can play, the better the strategy will work. This will be possible even if you don't have the higher starting bankroll amounts for multi-session blocks, because if you play correctly, eventually you will accumulate enough profits to allow you to then parlay the profits into additional session blocks. It will become self-propagating, but you must make the conscious decision not to reinvest your end-result profits into either any single session or into other kinds of gaming, but save it as additions to your continued progress. Once you are able to reach 100 sessions—in 10 blocks of 10 sessions—then you are on automatic and will make very large profits over time.

A NOTE FOR LOW ROLLERS

I have often discussed this strategy during my speaking engagements, and it has come to my attention that some people do not understand the bankroll requirements. When I mention the bankroll requirements, this is intended to demonstrate the *optimum* means of applying this strategy to its *best and fullest potential*. As I have said many times: If you can't afford to play at these stakes, save up and play when you have the required bankroll. This seems to escape some readers.

To those of you who say "I only play nickel and quarter Slots," I again remind you of the folly of your Slot play. When referring to Reel Slots, for which this strategy is intended, the nickel and quarter machines are the absolute *worst* kinds available. If you say you don't have the money to play this strategy at the bankroll requirements I mention, and then say that you "only play nickel and quarter slots," you leave me dumbfounded. How much do you gamble on these machines? $50? $100? $200? How can you then say you don't have "enough" to play this strategy in the amounts and on the machines I have indicated? If you can afford to spend $1 on gaming, you have enough to save up until you can play this strategy the way it should be played. No excuses.

However, if you still insist on spending your money on the nickel and quarter Reel Slots, it is possible to apply this strategy to those machines as well. It won't be as successful as in the higher denominations that I recommend, but it is possible. To do this, all you need is some simple mathematics. Fractionalize. My bankroll requirements are listed in the previous pages, as based on the kinds of machines I recommend. Take the $1 machines' bankroll and divide it accordingly to the kind of quarter machines you wish to play.

If you play two quarters at a time, the bankroll requirement will be one-fourth of the total two-coin $1 machine requirement ($2 equals four times 50 cents, therefore a play on a quarter machine that takes two quarters per pull will be one-fourth of the $1 machine maximum coin play budget requirement). This means you will need a bankroll of at least $250. And similarly for machines that take 75 cents per pull, and nickel Slots which take two or three nickels per pull. You'll just have to calculate this for yourselves. Again, I caution you: This is *not* the best way to play this strategy.

Strategy for Pai Gow Poker

INTRODUCTION

As with all the *Winning Strategies for Casino Games,* I assume that you already know how to play Pai Gow Poker [PGP] and are intimately familiar with playing conditions, terms, setting of hands, common decisions regarding hands, hand values, and betting. If you don't understand something in this chapter, or don't think you know PGP well enough, study the game first. Once you know the game you will quickly realize how powerful, and powerfully simple, this Pai Gow Poker Strategy really is. If you already know the game well, this chapter will make abundant sense. As with all the strategies in this book, I again caution you that you must play the strategy accurately and in accordance with the guidelines, bankroll, full knowledge of the game, and without mistakes.

I first learned to play PGP many years ago, at a time when not many Americans played the game. As a result, I used to be the only non-Asian at the gaming table. The benefit of this was that I learned several words in Chinese.

PGP is a derivative of Dominos, played with cards instead of tablets. It is an easier game to learn than dominos—at least so it was for me. I quickly found out that the rules of the game are pretty favorable to the player—as well as the house in some instances—but that in the end PGP is not nearly as volatile as Let It Ride or Caribbean Stud. About 80 percent of the hands are a push. This means that only 20 percent of the time the hands will be decided as either a winner for you or a winner for the house. To develop a successful strategy, therefore, one has to concentrate on what to do in the majority of instances—in this case the no-decision push hands. But more on that later.

One of the key PGP factors is that while the house has to play all hands *exactly the same way all the time,* you, the player, have the choice of being able to set your hand however you want. This comes into good effect in marginal decision hands, such as low pair-pair, or in hands where you have three (or more) possibilities, such as either a very high high hand (a flush, for example) but a very low second highest hand (9-8, for example) while also having the possibility of busting your high hand and going with two small pair-pair instead. This is intended as an example, and not as a suggestion of how to set your hands, but there are many such instances in the game where the player's decisions in how the hands are set can work in the player's favor, particularly if the house always plays the same way for all hands (which they almost always do in all major U.S. casinos).

What this means, as an another example, is that if the house always has to play high hand back no matter what the second highest hand may be, you can save yourself a lot of losses by shopping for the push, and, in many instances, likewise shop for—and get—a winner. Such situations come into play particularly in cases where the house *must* play pair-pair in two-pair situations of at least one pair being 7s or higher, as well as in situations where low pair-pair must be played with Ace up as second highest hand, or the highest card(s) up with small pair-pair as two-pair for high hand (and similarly). This allows you to have a much higher degree of control over your play than in many other table games, and for these reasons PGP is a very good game.

WHAT TO LOOK FOR

Before you sit down to PGP, check out the house rules at the casino where you plan to play, as well as the actual rules at the table where you intend to play. Similarly to Blackjack, many casinos have different playing rules for PGP, and in some casinos, such rules can vary even between different tables offered in the same casino. Don't be shy; ask. All dealers must tell you, and if their explanations aren't to your liking, request a brochure with the house rules, or request to speak with the supervisor, or whomever you must speak to in order to determine the rules. Then, once you have determined that these rules indeed *are* the favorable ones, come back later—on a different shift, or a different table with the same rules, or wait until you get a new dealer. This will help protect your identity as a strategy player, particularly if you first had to raise a little hell in order to get the answers you need. Look for games where the house rules demand that dealers *always* must play small pair-pair (7s or less) as pair-pair in back, with no-pair second up front. Also rules where dealers must always split high high hands into two-pair (one back and one up front if there is such a pair-pair possibility also in their set of cards) even in the event that they have a much higher high hand, but one which would result in a very low second highest hand. These two sets of house rules are most crucial for your play, for reasons as stated above.

PGP Strategy Rules

As you will shortly see, these PGP Strategy Rules that I have developed are very simple. However, their simplicity belies the complexities that went into creating them. They are extremely effective in the long-term application of the multi-session play strategy (refer to Blackjack for the example of what this means).

1. Start with a $25 base wager bet.
2. If you lose the *first* hand, bet $50 on the next hand.
3. Each *push* add $50 to your next bet.
4. When you get one win, take the amount of that win and let the previous bet ride.
5. If you win again after a win, add $50 to your previous bet amount.
6. If you win again, after a win, and for all subsequent *consecutive* wins, add $50 each time, and so on for as long as you have consecutive wins. If you have a push in this sequence, apply Rule #3. Continue this until you get a loss.
7. Whenever you lose, bet *half of the previous bet* on the next hand (in whole $5 chip unit increments). Continue to so reduce your base wager bets for each consecutive loss until you reach your original base wager bet of $25, at which point you apply Rule #1. If at any time your losing streak is interrupted by a push, apply Rule #3. If your losing streak is interrupted by a win, apply Rule #4. And so on.
8. Quit only if:
   - You have doubled your starting session bankroll amount.
   - You have played about 100 hands (around 2.5 to 3 hours of play).

- You can't make the next bet in the sequence.
- Your next bet would have to be *over* the table limit.
- You have played 3 hours.

At any of these above circumstances, end that session and begin a new one after accounting and a break.

Bankroll

You must have a large bankroll in PGP to sustain the strategy and maximize its profit-making potential. Yes, you can play this strategy at lower wagers, but you will not realize nearly as much profit as you will by playing at the levels that are part of this strategy. You will also need to adapt the strategy accordingly if you are betting lower amounts than indicated, and this could cause you to make mathematical and accounting errors. I therefore recommend that you play the strategy as shown, for which you will need a starting base session bankroll of $5,000. You will actually not need to spend it, and in fact it will never be at risk; however, it is necessary for two reasons:

1. $5,000 is usually the table maximum betting limit at a $25 table (sometimes $10,000, but mostly the $5,000).
2. You may run into the anomalies where you must be able to make the next bet in the sequences, and this means you must have the requisite bankroll in order to allow the strategy to gain you a winning session (and overall winning sessions cumulative profit).

Neither of the above means you will be betting $5,000 on any one hand. This simply won't happen, but your bets can run into *several hundreds of dollars* at some points, and *that's precisely where you want to be*—because by that time you are in the principal position of maximizing your strategy profits. The strategy will not make you a large profit at only $25 base bet, and in fact the strategy will fail if you do not adhere to the rules and play flat bets only. That's not the purpose of the strategy, because flat-betting is financial suicide in any gambling game. Do not try the PGP strategy until you can afford the bankroll requirements. You could fractionalize and set your own strategy limits—but if you do this, you face the danger of compromising the strategy.

Strategy for Let It Ride

INTRODUCTION

Let It Ride [LIR] was developed to market the shuffling machine. There's a whole story behind this game, but that's not the subject of this book. There are now two basic versions of this game:

1. A game *without* the "red spot" as an optional side bet for bonuses.
2. A game *with* the optional side bet which plays for *all the bonuses.*

The *second* version of this game is now played in most of the major casinos. Some of the other versions of LIR are played in some tribal gaming casinos and on riverboats, but this is dependent on the various gaming rules and regulations, and licensing agreements, for the specific states or locations where the game is offered. Mostly you will encounter version two of LIR, and therefore all further discussion will be confined to this particular game. As with all my strategies, I assume you already know how to play the game, how to make the bets, and what all the side bets mean. This Let It Ride Strategy is not intended as a guide to teach you the game.

ABOUT LIR

LIR is in reality a Slot Machine played on a table with cards. It is a notoriously streaky game and extremely hard to beat. The reasons for this are obvious, since players have no choices in how they play the hands. Each decision on each hand played is an independent event, and players live or die by the hands they are given. The fact that the dealer's two cards are common for all players has little effect on this and is beneficial only when the dealer's two cards constitute a paying pair. It is *not* a good game for your gaming dollar. Its house hold is about 3.2 percent, and this makes the game almost as bad as some low-paying slots.

LIR being what it is, there are simply very few methods that a player can use to allow for consistent strategy play. Unlike Blackjack, Craps, or Roulette, strategies for LIR are not as useful in the short term, largely due to the enormity of the house edge and the volatility of the game. This is derived to an even larger extent not just from the rules of the game, but primarily due to the shuffling machines employed in dealing it. This fact so alters any perceivable beneficial trends in favor of the player that I do not recommend playing this game as a profession. You will be far more successful employing my strategies for Blackjack, Craps, and Roulette, and even Slots. Nevertheless, there is a way to make your profits better from LIR. The *only* way to beat this game, or to at least reduce the house edge to a livable level, is to apply the decisions and betting strategies I will list here.

This Let It Ride Strategy consists primarily of a set of rules for the player and rules for betting. Applying the following factors will enable you to perform to a far higher degree of success than you would otherwise. However, I again caution you that LIR is *not* my recommended game for consistent professional strategy play. It should only be a diversion, not a profession.

Strategy Rules

1. Make the required bets in equal amounts.
2. Always bet the optional side bet (the bonuses are a significant factor in profitability).
3. Naturally, if you have a pat hand from your first three cards, stand.
4. If two of your initial three cards are 10s or higher, regardless of whether they make a pair, stay for the first turn and see what the dealer's first card is.
5. If you improve your hand to a pat hand, stand.
6. If you do not improve your hand to a pat hand, but have a draw to a flush or an open-ended straight, stand.
7. If you do not improve to a pat hand and do not have a draw to a flush or open-ended straight, take down your middle bet, then stand.
8. If, among your first three cards, you have only one high card (10s or higher), take down your first bet. If you do not improve your hand on the first turn, take down your second bet, then stand.
9. If, among your first three cards, you have any non-paying pair, stand for the first turn. If you improve your hand after the first turn, stand. If you do *not* improve your hand after the first turn, take down your second bet and then stand. (Of course if you have a paying pair from the start, you have a pat hand, and Rule #3 applies.)

10. If you improve your hand on the turn, then, naturally, stand. If you do *not* improve that hand, take down your middle bet and then stand.
11. Play only in position number one! This position, and *only* this position, will always get the *same set of cards*—the first three cards of the deal.

Every other position on the table will have their sequences of cards dealt altered as players come in and out of the game. This will mean that if you are sitting anywhere else on the table, other than the number one position, your sequence of cards will be altered if a player in front of you in the dealing sequence either leaves or comes in to the game. So, if you were getting a good run of cards, and a player sits in front of you, that player will now be getting the cards you would have received. Therefore, only the number one position at the table can be factored in this strategy play.

12. If you lose ten *consecutive* hands, end the session and leave. Start another session later or elsewhere. This is an indication of a negative aberration, and you shouldn't stay there playing into it. (At a $5 base wager bet, the maximum loss over ten hands will be between $50 and $100 on average, allowing for some hands where more than one spot is in action.)

These rules of play will assure you of maximizing your wins while limiting your losses. The rules apply equally well to any betting amount. The above assumes that you already know how to play the standard hands, such as a draw to a flush, full house, and so forth.

Betting Progression

To beat LIR, or to at least diminish the huge house edge, you will need to employ a betting progression. Remember, when you factor in the cost of the side bet, in LIR you will statistically lose about 22 percent of the time. In reality, the cards in the short terms are likely to "run" in significantly large swings from positive to negative, thus losses can be lengthy; likewise a sequence of winners can also be lengthy. In the end, statistically, the game will average to its overall withholding percentage. Therefore, it is advisable not to bet into *losing* sequences and instead maximize into *winning* ones. To do this, you will not only need the required bankroll (listed below), but also patience. You will also require a keen eye for spotting which sequence of trends you happen to be in.

1. For each win where you have won all three bets, increase your base wager by 1 chip unit.
2. For each win where you have won two of your base bets, increase your base wager by 2 chip units.
3. For each win where you have won one of your base bets, increase your base wager by 3 chip units.
4. For any *consecutive* wins, increase your base wager by half of the previous base wager bet from the *second* win on, and so forth (in whole chip amounts).
5. For any loss *after a win,* reduce your next wager by half the previous base wager bet.
6. For any loss *after a loss,* go back to your initial starting base wager bet, and begin from Rule #1 and so on.
7. If you win a hand that pays a bonus, place that bonus amount on the side. Do *not* include your bonus wins as part of your operating bankroll. These wins will fuel your end-result profitability.

8. Quit after you have doubled the amount of your starting bankroll for that session, or if you have lost ten consecutive hands, or if you cannot make the next bet in your sequence.

In this way of playing, you will assure yourself of maximizing your wins, and minimizing your losses.

Bankroll

For a $5 base bet ($15 at $5 on each of the 3 spots + $1 for the bonus = $16 total), you will need a minimum of $500 to sustain the game and give yourself the best chance possible to maximize the strategy. In fact, I highly recommend at least $1,000—and better still $1,500—to do the best possible job of playing. You won't lose this in any session, but you do need it in order to win. And if you don't have this bankroll, you won't win consistently because you will likely not be able to make the required sequences of bets to make the strategy work in the long term.

Strategy for Progressive Caribbean Stud

INTRODUCTION

Progressive Caribbean Stud [CS] has been played on cruise ships and in the Caribbean for quite some time, but it was not nearly as popular as it now is. The difference was the addition of the "progressive" feature, which made the game a huge hit with gamblers in the mainstream casinos. Some of the Jackpots are more than $500,000, and the intermediate payoffs are also fairly large. The attraction of this game, of course, is the big Jackpot. Many casinos now also offer larger bonuses, and it is these extra bonuses that players find to their liking for continuity of play. Virtually every major casino in the United States now offers CS with the bonuses and progressive features. (Some of the other versions of CS are played in tribal gaming casinos and riverboats.) Mostly, you will encounter the standard bonus plus Jackpot progressive CS, and therefore all further discussion will be confined to this particular game.

As with all my strategies, I assume you already know how to play the game, how to make the bets, and what all the side bets mean. This Progressive Caribbean Stud Strategy is not intended as a guide to teach you the game.

CS, similarly to Let It Ride [LIR], is in reality a Slot Machine played on a table with cards. Like LIR, it is also a notoriously streaky game and extremely hard to beat. Again, players have no choices in how they play the hands. Each decision on each hand played is an independent event, and players live or die by the hand they are given. The fact that the dealer must first qualify in order to play a hand, and then play the hand against the players, makes the game a difficult animal. About 70 percent of the time the dealer will not qualify, or will have a better hand, and all these factors combined make CS not only a slow game, but one that can be costly. At $5–$10 ante minimum, with the double-bet requirement, plus the $1 side bet for the bonuses and the progressive, you will be spending, at the low limits, $16 each time you play a hand. It is *not* a good game for your gaming dollar. Its average house hold is about 5 percent for the base game and about 28 percent for the bonus, and this makes the game just as bad as LIR. CS being what it is, there are simply very few methods that a player can use to allow for consistent strategy play. The *only* way to beat this game, or to at least reduce the house edge to a tolerable level, is to apply the decisions and betting strategy that I will list here. Unlike Blackjack, Craps, or Roulette, strategies for CS are not as useful in the short term, largely due to the enormity of the house edge and the volatility of the game. This is derived to an even larger extent not just from the rules of the game, but primarily due to the shuffling machines that are also employed in dealing it, just as in LIR. This fact so alters any perceivable beneficial trends in favor of the player that I do not recommend playing this game as a profession. Once again, you will be far more successful employing my strategies for Blackjack, Craps, and Roulette, and even Slots.

Nevertheless there still is a way to make your profits better from CS. My Progressive Caribbean Stud Strategy consists primarily of a set of rules for the player and rules for betting. Applying these factors, as described next, will enable you to perform to a far higher degree of success than you would otherwise. However, CS is not my recommended game for consistent professional strategy play. And that's why it should only be a diversion, not a profession.

Strategy Rules

1. Always make the $1 side bet for the bonuses and the progressive. Without this side bet in action, CS will eat you up and you will never get the kinds of payoffs you need to sustain any semblance of consistent winning strategy play.
2. Start with the minimum ante bet (usually $5 in most casinos, but now increasingly more common is $10; some casinos allow a $3 game, but stay away from those . . . you simply cannot make any significant money at those games).
3. Do *not* stay in the hand with only A-K, even if you have a Q or J as the kicker.
4. Always stay in the hand if you have any pair or better.
5. If you hit a bonus pay, put that bonus win aside. This is what will constitute your end-result added profitability.
6. Only play with your set starting bankroll for that session (see below for bankroll amounts).
7. Adapt the principles of the Blackjack Strategy sessions breakdown.

8. Play only until you have:
   • Doubled your starting bankroll for that session.
   • Lost 70 percent of your starting bankroll for that session.
   • Reached about 100 hands played per session (about three hours of play).
   • Hit a major bonus and/or mini-Jackpot and/or the Jackpot.
   • Lost 10 hands in a row ($160 at the $16 per bet minimum level, higher if playing larger stakes).

9. Play only in casinos, and on games where the 4-of-a-kind bonus pays at least $500 or more (some casinos pay only $100 for this).

10. Play only on games where the Jackpot amount is over $180,000. This will assure you of a good mini-Jackpot bonus of 10 percent if you hit the straight flush; this is hard to get, but it is even more painful if you do hit this and the 10 percent will get you only a few thousand dollars (or merely a few hundred), instead of the significant wins you would get on games where the Jackpot amount is the recommended higher amount.

11. Play *only* in position number one! This position, and *only* this position, will always get the *same set of cards*—the first set of cards of the deal.

Just as in LIR, for CS every other position on the table will have their sequences of cards dealt altered as players come in and out of the game. This will mean that if you are sitting anywhere else on the table, other than the number one position, your sequence of cards will be altered if a player in front of you in the dealing sequence either leaves or comes in to the game. So, if you were getting a good run of cards, and a player sits in front of you, that player will now be getting the cards you would have received. Therefore, only the number one position at the table can be factored in this strategy play.

These rules of play will assure you of maximizing your wins while limiting your losses. The rules apply equally well to any betting amount. The above assumes that you already know how to play the game and standard hands.

Betting Progression

To beat CS, or to at least diminish the huge house edge, you must employ a betting progression. Remember, in CS you will statistically lose about 20 percent of the time. It will seem like 80 percent of the time, because with most hands either the dealer does not qualify—in which case you win your ante but not your bet—or the dealer will qualify but have a better hand than you. And don't think that winning the ante is good, because you are in reality only getting $4 back for your $5 ante (if you are betting at the $5 minimum level, higher otherwise), because of your $1 side bet, which you don't win along with the ante for hands where the dealer does not qualify. Overall, the cards in the short term are likely to "run" in significantly large swings from positive to negative; thus losses can be lengthy, and likewise a sequence of winners can also be lengthy. In the end, statistically, the game will average to its overall withholding percentage. Therefore, it is advisable not to bet into *losing* sequences and instead to maximize into *winning* ones. To do this, you will not only need the required bankroll (listed below), but also patience. You will also require a keen eye for spotting which sequence of trends you happen to be in.

1. For one win increase your *next bet* by 3 chip units (includes ante).
2. For a win after a win, take the win and let the previous bet ride as it was.
3. For a win after the *second* win in a row, increase your base wager by 2 chip units.
4. For any *consecutive* wins, increase your base wager by *half of the previous base wager bet* from the third win on, and so forth (in whole chip amounts).
5. For any loss *after a win,* reduce your next wager by half the *previous* base wager bet.
6. For any loss *after a loss,* go back to your initial starting base wager bet, and begin from Rule #1 and so on.
7. If you win a hand that pays a bonus, place that bonus amount on the side. Do *not* include your bonus wins as part of your operating bankroll. These wins will fuel your end-result profitability.

In this way of playing, you will assure yourself of maximizing your wins and minimizing your losses.

Bankroll

For a $5 base bet ($5 ante + $10 bet + $1 for the bonus = $16 total), you will need a minimum of $500 to sustain the game and give yourself the best chance possible to maximize the system. In fact, I recommend at least $1,000 to do the best possible job of playing. You won't lose this in every session, but you do need it in order to win. And if you don't have this bankroll, you won't win consistently because you will likely not be able to make the required sequences of bets to make the method work in the long term.

Strategy for Video Poker and Video Reel Slots

I now wish to offer a strategy previously called "The Flaw," designed a few years ago for the newest crops of Video Slots and Video Poker Machines, including multigame machines. This strategy was originally developed by Tom Caldwell, writing as Terry Callahan, who offered it for limited release in the 1990s as part of our partnership at the time. Although I have since revised these principles of playing, and adapted them to more accurately reflect the modern casino games, the original concept is Tom's, and I wish to acknowledge his contribution to this strategy.

I briefly mentioned this flaw in my book *Powerful Profits from Video Poker,* where it was directed toward the winning hands made from holdings of a lone Ace. The strategy presented here is a derivative and can also apply to video machines. Casinos all over the world have machines with this flaw. They know it exists, but because most players do not know about it, the casinos would rather not have to fix it. Plus, it is expensive to correct, so, for the time being, it remains as part of most of the video machines now in casinos. Learning how to spot it and how to maximize your winnings are easy. There are no hard charts to memorize. A simple principle of playing is all you need to learn, and this will allow you to quickly find out if the machine you are playing has the flaw and how to exploit it to your maximum benefit. If you play smart, you will be aware that you have information that will increase your play time and your payout frequencies and give you a much better chance at winning the top Jackpot—and many, many pays in between.

In the information that follows, I refer to "winning" and "losing" cycles. In all instances, I mean winning and losing cycles for *you,* the player, and *not* the casino, and not necessarily the machine. Although the original intent of this method was based largely on Video Poker Games, because there are so many of them available, this strategy can also work for Video Slot Machine games, and even for a combination of Video Poker and Video Slot Machine games, as long as these are part of the same multigame machine. For example, many multigame machines have ten or more games, five of which will be Video Poker games, the other five various kinds of Video Slots. You can use this strategy to play all these games intermixed, or you can play it only on the Video Poker games or only on the Video Slot games. However, the best advantage to you is to play the Video Poker games as a unit or the Video Slot games as a unit. Once you start playing this strategy, you will quickly be able to understand the subtle differences that give you advantages. You will then be able to decide for yourself how you apply it to your particular gaming choices and play accordingly. As you become better, you will be able to modify the playing principles and continually adapt and enhance your play. This way, this method will grow with you as a player, and will continually be adaptable to your gaming, and to whatever other electronic games come onto the casino floor in the future.

The following guidlines offer general information about Video Poker and derivative games important to your winning.

Know the Game You Are Playing

With this method you will need to have a basic understanding of the five games (or more on many machines) that you will be using to implement this method of winning. Since games available in all multigame machines have different payoffs and different playing strategies, you should brush up on correct playing strategies for each of the games you will be playing, and are likely to encounter, in a multigame machine. If this is an issue for you, you should first read my other books if you're not sure what cards to hold or throw away in all circumstances, or which machines to choose and why. I will, therefore, now continue with my explanation of this method assuming you already know the best "hold" and "discard" strategies in a given situation. Although this method does not require that you have perfect play on all hands—because it gives you an advantage other players do not have regardless of your personal game acumen at the various games you will encounter—if you also know the perfect-play principles for Video Poker games, and Video Poker game derivatives, you will enhance the strategy and give yourself the opportunity for even bigger wins more frequently.

Pay Attention

Since you will be playing up to five games or more when implementing this strategy, it is important to keep track of which game you are currently playing and hold and discard the appropriate cards for that game. This is not difficult, and it will get even easier, in short order, as you play each of the games.

Discard Your Hunches

Play all games to your advantage. This means, first and foremost, that you must play the maximum coins on every hand you play. If a short bankroll is your situation, or you don't feel like playing maximum coins because you may not get as much play, I do not suggest you try this method until you can give yourself all the advantages. One of the many ways casino players become losers is by not playing the games to their optimum advantages—such as not playing maximum coins on all games, all hands, all the time. Worse still, some players do not bring an adequate bankroll to allow them to play the best possible way and play to that optimum advantage as a result. If you think you don't have enough money, don't play this strategy until you save up enough to make it work for you. Don't compromise! Ever! If you don't know what a good bankroll is, here are some tips:

Bankroll. With this strategy, you will be playing about five to ten games virtually simultaneously, switching back and forth as per instructions. To do this, your starting bankroll must be enough to let you begin the process and continue it throughout your session. On a quarter machine, $400 should be your minimum starting bankroll. On $1 machines, $1,000 must be your minimum starting bankroll. It may sound like a lot, but it isn't. You must remember that to get any machine started, fuel must be used. This bankroll is your fuel to get the method started. Once you get it going, it will support itself 70 percent of the time, and give you major wins 20 percent of the time. Yes, 10 percent of the time you will lose. That is inevitable in any gambling game. But—your losses will be limited only to your starting bankroll, while your wins accumulate. Casinos do not play hunches. They know their "methods" will win money for them. You'd be smart to take this attitude as well, while maintaining an understanding that winning at gambling for the average, casual gambler is akin to a miracle. You do not want to be the average, casual gambler. You want to win money.

Video Poker Pay Cycles

If you have played Video Poker or any of the derivative games, such as Deuces Wild, Joker Poker, or Double Bonus Poker, you have probably experienced periods of long losing cycles. Conversely, you may have experienced a cycle where payouts were coming like crazy. Understanding this, and being smart enough to capitalize on these win cycles and minimizing your losses during the losing cycles, is the key in utilizing this strategy to your advantage.

Only the Multigame Machines

Multigame machines only allow this strategy to be used to your advantage. To capitalize on it, you must be able to "leave a losing cycle and enter a winning cycle." Multigame machines only allow you to do this. Having five games or more to select from allows you to leave a "cold" or losing cycle on a given game and enter a "hot" or winning cycle on any one of the other games.

Drop Personal Preferences

Most Video Poker players have a personal "preference" for one or more games offered. I like Deuces Wild more than Joker Poker for example. If you want to win, discard your personal preferences and play the game that is currently in a winning cycle! The machine will "tell" you if you will just pay attention to what is happening in these cycles! Here are some key tips:

Losing Cycles. Knowing when a "losing" cycle is operating is key to your success, because you and only you can make the decision to leave the game during such perceived cycles. And, since the machine you are now playing has several other games that can be selected to play, why not do so? Here are some more hints:

If a machine has five different games, chances are that all five games will not be in a "losing" cycle all at the same time. However, the game being played that is currently in a losing cycle may severely diminish or even evaporate your gambling capital. Using all five games is to your advantage, whether you personally prefer a certain game or not. If you want to win at these machines, leave your personal preferences aside until you have won some of the casino's money to play with! Then, if you choose, play your particular favorite game, with the satisfaction that you are now "ahead."

Winning Cycles. All electronic casino gambling games eventually "cycle" to a series of events that appear to be a "winning cycle." I say "appear" because these are *perceptions* that we recognize, although to the machine this is nothing more than various numerical events without correlation to any other. However, since no random number generator (RNG) can ever be perfect, these machines can, and do, experience what we can identify as "pay cycles." For example, if the game you are playing is "showing" a lot of two-pair hands but paying you even money for these, you are experiencing a "losing" cycle, not a winning cycle. Here's why . . .

That game is paying off at *far less* than the odds of that event occurring. So, breaking even in these situations cannot be considered winning. Breaking even on a series of hands or an entire session is *not the goal*. Yes, these cycles are better than the long series of no wins at all, but not much. You must be aware that a win of "double" your investment (or more) on more occasions than "losing" events constitutes a winning cycle. The hands that you want and need to maintain your gambling stake are those that pay you at least twice your per-hand investment. Since these winning hands will not appear as frequently as losing ones, over the long haul, you must take charge and not allow yourself to be duped by "almost wins" or even-money payoffs that might entice you to try just one more time.

No science can tell you when a cycle will change for the better. However, I can tell you that if the next hand to be dealt out is a winning hand (assuming you play it correctly), that hand will come out the next time that game is played, whether you temporarily left that particular game or not. So, by leaving a losing cycle—whether it be a short losing cycle or a very long losing cycle—you have made the correct decision, because your chances of finding one of the other games "ready" to go into a winning cycle is better than trying to ride out a losing cycle. Finding the game or games that are in a winning cycle as soon as you can, with the fewest losing hands in between, is the goal here. I'll give you the rules for making these important decisions a little later.

Strategy Advantage

Most casual gamblers have a finite budget. Las Vegas statistics indicate that the average casino Slot player will spend around $550 in the casino. Casual gamblers have a tendency to play several different machines, hoping to "luck across" a machine that will pay them a decent win, rather than seriously playing one machine sufficiently to cycle it to its winning, if not Jackpot, cycle. The casinos love these players because they know that they are relying only on luck. And casinos pay off "pure luck" at far less than true odds. You are smarter than the average. You know that accumulation of coins or credits means you can play more hands—giving you more chances at hitting the top and secondary Jackpots. In many cases, by using this information to your best advantage, you can double the amount of hands you can play. That just increased your chances of hitting the top Jackpot by 100 percent. That's a hefty advantage!

Gambling Budget

Your gambling budget determines your level of play, your decisions, and your win potential. Understanding cycles, as described earlier, is the foundation on which you will begin to make your decisions. Along with that knowledge comes another factor that you must abide by: your level of play. By this I mean: How much are you willing to risk to hit the Jackpot? Remember, your goal is to win more than you lose. The following example applies to 25-cent five-coin-maximum multigame machines.

If the top Jackpot is $1,000, one-third = $333. If you are willing to risk between $300 and $350 to win $1,000, you are one-third more likely to actually use the machine's inherent programming to your advantage than almost all other players. This alone does not guarantee you will win. But now your chances of winning exceed the purely random programming.

Your Win Potential

Buy in for as much as you can afford to lose in one session. If your entire budget for a session in a casino is $100, the nickel multigames will give you the highest win potential. With a $250 to $350 budget you have a reasonably good amount to play 25-cent five-coin-maximum games. If your budget is $1,000 to $3,000, a dollar game offers you good potential. And, of course, if you score a big win you can always move up—with the satisfaction that you are now playing with the casino's money! Also, I suggest using credits rather than cashing out coins. This is the direct opposite advice to the Reel Slots Strategy, but in this case it is essential, particularly if you play the nickel Video Slots that take forty-five coins or ninety coins per pull, in which case the use of the bill acceptors and credit meters is absolutely imperative. Your credit meter is easier to read than guessing how many coins you may have accumulated in the tray. Further, you are not done playing until you have given this strategy its chance to work for you. This may be one hand or a thousand hands. In any case there is no advantage to cashing out until you are finished with your session—or you are getting paid by hand from a nice casino employee!

Know When to Change Games

I recommend this formula: If you lose five hands in a row or a total of 25 credits before hitting a win of at least 25 credits, change games (for Video Poker). Follow this rule with any other game on your machine until the same set of circumstances occurs. If you lose 25 credits before hitting a win of at least 25 credits, change games again, going to any other game available to you on that machine—other than the ones you have already tried. Continue this "hunt" until you recognize a game that is in a winning cycle. This is not hard to do. Note the number of credits on your credit meter when changing games. For Video Reel Slots, apply the five-count formula to whatever credits are required to play maximum coins for that one pull. For example: If you are playing a nickel Video reel machine where you must play forty-five coins as maximum wager (always play max coins), then the five-count rule would mean a swing of 225 credits. So, while for the five-coin max Video Poker games the five-count rule equals 25 credits, for the forty-five-coin nickel Video reel Slots this same five-count equals 225 credits. Therefore, whenever you play such a Video reel Slot machine and you lose 225 credits before receiving a pay of at least 225 credits, then it is time to change games, as called for in this strategy. This can be applied to any mix of games, be it Video Poker, Video reel Slots, or Video Poker and Video reel Slots combined, as long as they are in the same multigame machine. Also, if this is a multi-denominational machine, you should always play the Video Poker games at a minimum of 25-cent credits—$1.25 per hand—but then if you are called to switch to a Video reel game, you may want to switch to the nickel denomination and play at forty-five nickels (or simply stay at the 25-cent credit value, but play only 9 credits for the nine lines, which equals the same $2.25 wager per pull as with forty-five coins in nickels). There are many such modifications, and individual decisions, that you will need to make as you play this strategy, always mindful that the key is the Five-Count Rule—regardless of whatever denomination or number of credits is involved.

Managing Your Credits

Say your credit meter reads 240. If you reach 215 credits before hitting a payoff of 25 credits or more, change games.
Sometimes you will have to change games frequently.
Sometimes you will enter a cycle where you will be accu-
mulating credits. Say you started a game with 240 credits
and you hit a winning hand paying 125 credits. Now you
have 365 credits. Stay with that particular game until it
deals you five consecutive losing hands or your net loss is
25 credits, regardless of how long or how many hands you
are able to play. (In this case your credit meter would be at
340 when you leave the game to go back on the "hunt".) Go
to any other game from your machine's game menu and follow the five-count-swing rule. Occasionally you will have
to cycle through all the available games until your "hunt"
locates a "hot" game.

Which Multigame Machines Are Better Than Others?

There are four basic programs (dictated by the computer
chip inside the game) that "tell" the game how much to pay
for a given winning hand. By increasing your play time, as I
have suggested above, the better the game becomes for the
player. Look at the payoff schedule for each game in the machine's menu. Note which games pay what amount. If you
can find a machine that pays more for a given winning hand
than other machines, play the one that pays more. Keep in
mind that playing five games, or more, you may have to sac-
rifice some best-paying hands on some games in order to get
a couple of games with better-paying programs. Regardless
of which multigame machine you finally select to play, follow this method—it will increase your wins, regardless of
the base program of the games.

Using This Strategy with Non-Video-Poker-Based Multigame Machines

In the past four years or so, many new casino games have been introduced. These new games are often incorporated into a multigame machine. The principles of this strategy apply with these games as well, as long as there are five or more different games available to you on a given machine. Many of these newer multigame machines accept more than five coins as maximum per "pull". For each increase in coins, you must increase your budget. A "nickel" machine that accepts ninety coins as maximum is in reality a $4.50 machine. A typical and reasonable buy-in for a $4.50 per-pull machine would be $1,200 or more! If at least one of the top two Jackpots on these machines is not at minimum $5,000, they are not a good bet—the ratio of win potential to investment is not large enough. Don't be fooled by a $4.50 machine disguised as a nickel machine. Remember, playing maximum coins is the cardinal rule for winning the big pay-offs—but only on machines that do not "hide" the actual coin-in-maximum-play requirements, like many of these "nickel" machines do.

The Net Result

By following this strategy and by correct play on each of the games you will be playing, you will hit more winning hands, sooner extending your budget instead of depleting it by trying to ride out a losing cycle. More winning hands means more hands you can play and that means more chances at hitting the Jackpot.

Partnership Play

No method is foolproof. Sometimes you just cannot seem to get it together, and the cycles of all the games on a machine seem to be forever stuck in "take." A way to diminish this horror scenario is to share wins and losses with a friend. By having two players playing two different machines, the chances for both of you to be depleted of your buy-ins are lessened. One or the other will probably have a nice pay along the way, fueling the less-fortunate partner's play. The buy-in amounts for both partners need to be within the range of the win potential as outlined above. If you choose this added benefit, be sure to set the rules straight and agree on the terms of your wins and losses before beginning your partnership.

When to Play

If you have the option of being able to play early in the morning—in the "wee hours"—this can be a further advantage to you. Here's why: Machines that have recently been played extensively (say over a weekend) but have not yet cycled to a Jackpot, or a major secondary win, have a higher win expectation. Progressive machines tell you whether they have been hit recently by the amount on the meter. But this is not so with the non-progressives, and therefore you cannot tell—just by looking at them—whether or not they have paid out recently. That's why implementing the five-count is important. This count will allow you to gauge how your machine, and the game you are on, is performing. If all the games in your "hunt" result in your losing 25 credits in a sequence before hitting a pay of at least 25 credits (or whatever the total credit amount may be depending on your game as per the five-count), then this entire machine is "off"—has been hit recently, or is in the "take" cycle. Move to another of its kind, and start over. Your total loss on all five games—in this example—is only 125 coins, and this is better than losing your entire bankroll trying to push the machine.

Remember that the top Jackpots on Video Poker machines hit on an average frequency of about 41,000 hands played (for the *exact* numbers, please refer to my *Video Poker* book). Since you don't know how many hands have been played on the games you are on prior to your arrival, applying the five-count is by far your best strategy. It tells you how the game is performing, and will save you from long losing streaks. I have seen, and hit, machines that hit top Jackpots within minutes of each other, but I also know of machines that go "way too long" between hits. The point here is to be aware of all the factors that determine your winning success and prevent you from being just another "casual" gambler, a person who is merely "fodder" for the casino!

Your Win Goal

This you must decide for yourself. You can use the following suggestion: By doubling the amount of a session budget, even without hitting a top Jackpot, this can be considered a good day and the seed capital for another gambling session at another time—and quite possibly at a higher game level. Whatever your goal for a gambling session may be, play well, play smart, and use *all* the information you can access!

Well, that's it. My partner and I used this method of play successfully for quite some time. Its only problem is that it can get very tiring and often quite boring. It is not fun to play this way. For this reason, I have not played it for several years now. Additionally, the numerous innovations in Video Poker and Video Slot Machines and their programs render this method of play simply too volatile. I now prefer to use the Video Poker methods of play I have described in my book *Powerful Profits from Video Poker,* and those for Slots that I described in my book *Powerful Profits from Slots,* as well as the Slots Strategy shown earlier in this book. I do not intend to discourage you from playing this strategy, but I do wish to mention that it was originally designed for multigame platforms with computer programs that were much more primitive than those now used. Although the five-count and 25-credit rules are still a good gauge—or their multi-denominational equivalents—it is perhaps better, and much more fun, to play these machines with the methods I described earlier and elsewhere.

Postscript

Each time I complete one of my books, I find myself wondering if I have said everything that could be said within the boundaries of what each book is about. It is a very difficult task to consider the content and the objective, and to fit it all neatly into the required number of pages and words. My main concern is always the same: Did I explain what I am writing about in a way that will be useful for the beginner, while also contributing something to the expert?

I was recently playing in my favorite Poker game, at a small off-Strip casino in Las Vegas called Arizona Charlie's. Everyone there has known me for a long time, and I them. I often go there to relax and to lose myself among people who won't bother me if I wish to be alone, or who will join me in a friendly game or conversation when I wish to socialize. I like that place and the people who work and play there. During a recent game several of us were discussing my books. I was mentioning that each book in my series is on a different game, some have various strategies, and all are designed to be balanced between information for the beginner and in-

261

teresting hints for the advanced players. I was asked "What is new? Aren't casino games just the same? What could you possibly write that would fill a book?" I tried to explain how fluid the casino games really are, how they change almost daily, and how the games we first learned to play may look similar these days, but are much different. I also mentioned how different everything can be from casino to casino, and from one gaming region to the other. It turned into a very interesting discussion.

There are really two sides to that discussion. There are those books that tell the story of the casino games and their playing strategies from the "established" perspective. This is usually the mathematical model of expected frequencies and probabilities. Most books about casino games and gambling are in this mode. Then there are a few brave souls who venture and delve deeper into the issues as they apply to the casino games, the casino lifestyle, and the money. After all, playing casino games should fall into two main categories: having fun and making money. Neither needs to exclude the other. Unfortunately, many books about casino games insists that to make money you can't have fun. I still think it is possible to have fun even when playing as stringently as I have recommended in this book. Some authors write that having fun in the casino precludes the winning of money, other than the strokes of pure luck that often grace our way. I stress the value of gambling as a form of adult *entertainment,* not necessarily a job. It isn't easy to straddle this fence.

The ultimate outcome of that conversation—which sparked this postscript—was the fact that I identified my books as belonging in both camps: entertainment and profit. I don't think that having fun at gambling necessarily precludes the winning of steady profits. At the same time I also don't think that playing professionally, or at least semiprofessionally, precludes having fun at your job. I think the balance that can be struck is the one I have established in all my books, including this one, although here I have taken rather a more severe approach to gambling. I wanted to show you that becoming a professional gambler is not easy, that it most definitely is not that "James Bond" world, and that to do it well will require a lot of study, practice, dedication, and very hard work. I may have been too hard on you, dear reader, but that was by design. Yes, you can—and you will—have fun playing these strategies as a means of making a profit from professional play, but I wanted to make sure that the "having of fun" doesn't get in the way of "first learning the job."

Finally, I have here offered something new. I have gone out on a limb, so to speak, and presented—for the whole world to see—strategies that I have developed. I have played them many, many times, and have never found a circumstance where they did not work as shown. That's all I can do, or say, about them. This doesn't mean that they can't be improved. If there is something here that isn't working, find it and tell me. I'll apply it, and fix the problem—*if* there is one. However, you will have to convince me that such a situation exists! To do that, you will need to accomplish the same set of circumstances, and the same time line, to come up with results that can be comparable. I played nearly 10 million events over twenty years to validate these strategies, so if you find something, make sure you have at least a reasonable sampling that can be compared with what was done here. As I have said many times, I don't mind correcting myself if I can be proven wrong, but so far, that hasn't happened.

How many books and their authors can you name who took an adventurous new approach to casino games and their strategies? I can name four: Thorp, Braun, Uston, and Wong, over the past forty years. I am by no means in their "class." My book is a "working man's book", a player's guide to the games. I speak to single players, for each of your own personal situations. I took a chance writing this book, and I hope it will be worthwhile. Enjoy it. It is a "human" book, made from my own trials and tribulations. The age of individual innovation is fast disappearing. Soon, only the giants will not fear to tread. . . .

Acknowledgments

Many people have contributed in some way to this book and have influenced my life. I dedicate this book to my dear mother, because her life has been of such profound meaning, and of such complexity, that her story is a book in itself. She is by far the most deserving person to whom I can offer my thanks.

I also wish to thank my literary agents, Greg Dinkin and Frank Scatoni. Greg is an accomplished author in his own right and Frank a widely respected book editor. Through their agency, Venture Literary, they recognized the value of what I had to offer as an author of books on casino games and gaming. Without their efforts, this book, and the others in this series, would never have come to exist.

My thanks also to Bruce Bender, the managing director of Citadel and Lyle Stuart Books at the Kensington publishing group, who have published this book and this series. Bruce recognized that this book and this series offer valuable insight into the casino games as they really are, and that this book will enable almost all players to finally realize a happy and profitable casino experience. I thank the staff of Kensington for their help in this process—in particular, I wish to single out a lady who has become my friend—my editor, Ann LaFarge.

I also wish to thank my colleagues and staff at the *Midwest Gaming and Travel* magazine, particularly Cathy

Jaeger and Beth. Since 1984 I have published a continuous column on casino gaming in various publications, and for most of these years Cathy has been my editor and friend.

And now I am fortunate to also bring you a list of my friends, and others, who have helped me, and influenced my life in many ways.

I extend my gratitude and thanks to my longtime friend Tom Caldwell for the many things he has done to help me enrich my life. I have had many discussions with Tom about Blackjack, and my thoughts about the game have become more mature because of these discussions. I also send my thanks to Norreta, Sean, and Brent—for reasons they all know.

To the management, staff, and employees of Arizona Charlie's Hotel and Casino, in Las Vegas, in particular those in the poker room, and to all my other friends and associates in the gaming business—from owners, managers, senior executives, hosts, and supervisors—you all know who you are, and I thank you.

My friends in Australia: Neil and his family; Lilli and little MRM (Mark); Ormond College; University of Melbourne; the Governor of Victoria and my former master, Sir Davis McCaughey. Also his Proctorial Eminence R. A. Dwyer, Esq.; the Alumni Association of the University of Wollongong, NSW, Department of Philosophy; and Professor Chipman.

My grateful appreciation I also extend to Laurence E. Levit of Los Angeles—my steadfast friend, accountant, and adviser for two decades—whose faith in me and my work has never faltered. And also to Michael Harrison, attorney-at-law in Beverly Hills, California, whose expertise and help has always made my life more secure.

To Andrew Hooker and the "Cowboys" from Vietnam I also send my thanks. And to Edwin Slogar, a good friend.

And finally to all those whose paths have crossed with

mine, and who have for one reason or another stopped a while and visited. I may no longer remember your names, but I do remember what it meant to have these moments.

Thank you.

Index